ABOUT THE SERIES

Culture shock is a state of disorientation that can come over anyone who has been thrust into unknown surroundings, away from one's comfort zone. *CultureShock!* is a series of trusted and reputed guides which has, for decades, been helping expatriates and long-term visitors to cushion the impact of culture shock whenever they move to a new country.

Written by people who have lived in the country and experienced culture shock themselves, the authors share all the information necessary for anyone to cope with these feelings of disorientation more effectively. The guides are written in a style that is easy to read and covers a range of topics that will arm readers with enough advice, hints and tips to make their lives as normal as possible again.

Each book is structured in the same manner. It begins with the first impressions that visitors will have of that city or country. To understand a culture, one must first understand the people—where they came from, who they are, the values and traditions they live by, as well as their customs and etiquette. This is covered in the first half of the book

Then on with the practical aspects—how to settle in with the greatest of ease. Authors walk readers through how to find accommodation, get the utilities and telecommunications up and running, enrol the children in school and keep in the pink of health. But that's not all. Once the essentials are out of the way, venture out and try the food, enjoy more of the culture and travel to other areas. Then be immersed in the language of the country before discovering more about the business side of things.

To round off, snippets of basic information are offered before readers are 'tested' on customs and etiquette of the country. Useful words and phrases, a comprehensive resource guide and list of books for further research are also included for easy reference.

CONTENTS

FOREWORD

It was in 1968 that I first set foot on British soil, on one of those charter packages that cost a fraction of what they would today but at considerable cost to plane comfort. I think I was already enamoured of all things English, as, since a tender age, I had been drenched with the history of the British Empire and the Commonwealth, Keats, Wordsworth and Shakespeare. And it didn't end in school. Playing the board game 'Monopoly', I was buying and selling Park Lane and Mayfair properties long before I strolled along these swish avenues. My history, geography and literature teachers were Welsh, Scottish and Irish, and they brought to life what I learnt from books. The daily morning assemblies were raised voices in homage to the Men of Harlech, a Welsh rugby song transplanted to the empirical tropics. In this way Anglophilia had rubbed off on me at an early age.

When I actually set foot on British soil, it was with a feeling of curious excitement about seeing first hand the land I had read so much about; Monopoly come home. Primarily, it has been an extended sojourn; geography, literature and history come to life and an education process no less absorbing than one about any culture outside one's own. That four-week holiday merely skimmed the surface of 'touristy' Britain, but it was enough to intrigue me about the whole British psyche. National pride aside, I have always subscribed to an open mind about life beyond my doorstep.

The reasons why I have chosen to live and work in Britain since 1983 were as much providence as the logical result of being immersed in British mores for the better part of my school life. Having made the decision to come here, it would have been blinkered and negative not to assimilate, observe, learn and generally be at ease within an alien environment. Britain was, and still is, essentially alien but definitely not a constant source of discomfort. You come to grips with the problems, co-exist with them and it is only with the confidence that nothing can take away your cultural heritage can you be comfortable in a foreign land.

The old adage 'any place you hang your hat is home' applies only when you've got your head screwed on right. Like not harbouring feelings of inadequacy, inferiority and all the other -ities that cloud your sense of identity and belonging, wherever your hat stand. In the 22 years that I have actually thrust myself into the mainstream of British life, it has been a process rife with problems, complications, cross wires, joy and satisfaction. I had to rid myself of preconceived notions, prejudices and hang-ups to make the best of my chosen lot. I try as often as possible to mix with the British, cultivate their friendship and build up my store of knowledge to understand them better. I did not want to end up as a statistic in reports about social integration problems among émigrés. This still remains a sticky problem with many foreigners who have come to live in Britain by their own volition or for political reasons.

It is impossible to give a blanket statement about life in an adopted country because of the variables. In my protracted observations of the British, I have encountered many things that are at odds with my own philosophy but as much that I have embraced with enthusiasm. What's most comforting is their sense of fair play, integrity, humour, the sublime and the ridiculous. Fundamentally, it's the realisation that I am different from them rather than the other way round. I am the foreigner and most of the accommodation has to come from my quarter. The British are no different from any other race in basic terms—they just talk, live and pursue their ambitions in different ways. You either muddle through or glide with them.

I have had my nose to the British ground, my ears to British sounds and my eyes on British idiosyncrasies with the objective of understanding—not judging or changing—them. The best I hope to offer in return for getting under their skin is to let them under mine. In this light, I am better able to understand why British colonialists were the way they were, never giving up a slice of their 'British-ness' even in the depths of a Malayan rubber plantation. It is likewise for many immigrants here. Richer are those who assimilate without clouding their sense of identity.

I have learnt to be patient the British way and not get flustered because service people don't jump when I call. I have had to handle household chores with dignity and stop moaning about the dearth of cheap domestic labour. Most importantly, I have to think British to survive. It's got nothing to do with the loss of identity and everything to do with doing as the Romans do. It's the difference between uncomfortable existence and total peace of mind. I hope *CultureShock! Britain* will ease you into the country. If I have had to generalise in many instances, it's because there is no way to be specific; regard the information as a springboard towards your own astute analyses. While I have done a fair amount of research, much else is the result of personal experience gleaned from the unending journey of discovery.

MAP OF BRITAIN

ATLANTIC OCEAN

SCOTLAND

EDINBURGH

NORTH SEA

NORTH CHANNEL

NORTHERN
IRELAND

IRISH SEA

REPUBLIC
OF IRELAND

ENGLAND

WALES

ST GEORGE'S CHANNEL

CARDIFF

LONDON

ENGLISH CHANNEL

FRANCE

FIRST IMPRESSIONS

'I didn't wander lonely as a cloud for my first sight
of perky daffodils nodding their yellow heads in the
March sunshine. Wordsworth will understand why
I could already feel the spring in my step as in the air.'
—Terry's journal, March 1984

IT WAS EARLY SPRING WHEN I LANDED at Gatwick Airport, and unaccustomed as I was to temperate climes, it seemed like an arctic winter with a frosty nip in the air. It was deliciously different nonetheless, and I was literally jumping out of my skin with excitement. Imagine the anticipation of nearly three decades; of a world that had seeped into my soul since I was knee high to a grasshopper, and now in glorious reality. My four-week sojourn allowed enough insight into a lifestyle that had intrigued me for so long. It was an ardent passage of time unlike merely taking a holiday break. I saw, listened, absorbed and distilled much that this fascinating place offered.

The first perky daffodils and crocuses spoke a language I had hitherto not known; of the joy of the birth of spring, the seasonal changes of a temperate climate unbeknownst to me before. Indeed, my exposure to a different-hued people living in a former British colony was not entirely scanty. But here, even in a few short weeks, speaking to and interacting with English, Scottish, Welsh and a dozen or so types of people of Nordic and Celtic European ancestry was fascinating and enormously enriching.

Language aside, what I noticed most of all was the intrinsic politeness of people. When you have been used to the somewhat surly, unsmiling countenance of trades people that seem to be the hallmark of the Asian marketplace, this was a refreshing change. Queues were unending but the patience was palpable. Salutary 'thank you's and good mornings' were not in short supply.

The British Way to Queue

With typical Singaporean impatience, I once elbowed my way through a post office queue only to meet with the wrath of several people in the queue. Not so much chagrined as puzzled, it took me a few seconds to realise it just wasn't done. Today, even if I am one of two people in a bus queue, I obey this sacred rule. It's a good habit and one that is almost therapeutic!

What discomfiture I might have had about racism and attendant hostility dissipated quickly. I had known of the reserved nature of most British people, but soon learnt it was as much the fear of imposing on another's privacy as it was of guarding one's own. This is a characteristic that is often misinterpreted and I have had to shift many of my earlier preconceived notions about Britain and the British people.

No, the cold was not bone-chilling as some well-meaning but scare-mongering friends had told me, resulting in my investing in pairs of long johns and other assorted thermal wear that are now consigned to the bin. Yes, the people are slow to warm up to strangers but once thawed, are no different from Ah Beng, Khrisnan and Sven—in short, they are fully subscribed members of the human race but for the differences that come from living in a different climate and environment.

London, in which I spent more time than in any other British town or village, if something of a microcosm of Britain, was at the same time untypical of the rest of the country. I had nursed many romantic notions of English villages—years of reading Agatha Christie and Enid Blyton having set many a bucolic scene in my mind's

As a foreigner encountering Caucasians, especially anywhere in metropolitan London, one assumes they are English. The truth is in central London, a large percentage of people are anything but English; French Scandinavian, Middle-eastern et al and are themselves foreigners. So asking for directions will likely provoke a response in some foreign language and a negative shrug of the shoulders.

eye—and these were not entirely misplaced. I felt an instant love for thatched cottages, trellised roses sending forth their heady scents, cream teas and scones in rustic tea shops and the apple-cheeked innkeeper lady came to life in cheery mode.

I have had my nose to the British ground, my ears to British sounds and my soul tuned into British mores and idiosyncrasies with the objective of total assimilation. I utterly dismiss the silly notion that one is de-culturalised because of the adoption of a foreign country as one's home. I could no more become un-Chinese/un-Singaporean in the deepest sense than Joe Smith could become Lim Ah Huat for a geographical shift. And this is essentially what it is—a matter of geography.

When I first encountered the strangeness of some British mores—the endless queuing, tea, the obsession with the weather, cats, sausages, dogs, bacon et al—it took a while not to feel they were any different from what must have been my strangeness to my new British neighbours. What must have they been thinking when they had a whiff of my salted fish drying in the sun? Or of my wearing flip-flops in the midst of winter and grilling sambal *belachan*? It's all a matter of perspective.

Upon my first arrival in London some 40 years ago, hungry, I had stopped at a fruit stall in Victoria station. Unthinkingly, I plucked a grape from a bunch to test it for sweetness. It provoked an angry outburst from the stall holder who spat: "Oi, you do not do that." The fact is, in Britain, you do not touch anything, much less taste it, before buying. It is a sacrosanct code of trading.

It has been a continuous learning curve that I know will never end; a passage of tumultuous changes that have been sometimes strange, often baffling, but rarely unsettling or threatening. Moving to another town within the same country is unsettling, never mind moving to another country altogether. Armed with a sense of adventure, a good dose of rationality and the knowledge that people are essentially the same under different skins, you will find settling in Britain no more difficult than coming to grips with a television remote control. It's all about pressing the right buttons. And the big picture will be all too clear.

AN OVERVIEW

CHAPTER 2

'Think not of Britain as a country full of *ang mo*
(red haired) people. With 200 different nationalities
and as many quirky fashion ilks, hair can run the rainbow
gamut from punky neon green to the purple rinse of sweet
old ladies, and to none at all among skinheads. Nuff said.'
—Terry's journal, May 1984

WHEN YOU CONSIDER THAT most Australians and North Americans trace back their ancestry to the British Isles, it is not surprising that thousands of them come seeking their roots every year. The more prosaic come to find work or simply to assuage the inexplicable Anglophile need. But by contrast to its former colonies, the British Isles is a mere minnow to their whale. Some 60 million people are crammed into what is not altogether rolling downs and dappled woodlands.

The fact is many British children have never seen a cow or even a live chicken, having been born and brought up in urban concrete sprawls. Travel is relatively expensive, and many poor families would not think of spending their cash just to soak up a few hours of bucolic pleasure. The tourist brochures naturally sidestep the existence of these depressing urban pockets. Which visitor would find anything remotely romantic about a tenement block with scrubby, graffiti-laden walls, gloomy stairwells and sinister nooks? However, it is a priority that the government is working very hard at and much squalor has been alleviated in many places.

As a result, more and more of Britain's inner cities are being transformed to more salubrious levels with much government effort and property development schemes. These cities are not only more attractive as residential options but in many cases are positively bristling with newfound chic and sassy ambience that promises much business potential. One typical example is Newcastle-on-Tyne. I had first been to Newcastle-on-Tyne some 10 years ago and found it dismal and depressing. There was scarcely any ambience that cheered the spirit although it was a bright summer day. If I had been expecting a glorious ribbon of blue water, the Tyne River coursing through the city, I was to be disappointed.

Vehicular traffic and all that goes with it—pollution, lead contamination and plain hassle—are a part of Britain's transportation network which is constantly subject to environmentalist review. The green policy, fear of the hole in the ozone layer getting larger, acid rain, etc., all are issues very much under the skin and conscience of enlightened British. Of course there are also millions whose concerns end at their doorstep and who do not care about society at large.

As a newly arrived visitor, the option of whether to get involved with green issues or not is yours. But you will be hard put to ignore public outcry about the destruction of the earth, the disappearance of rain forests thousands of miles away, the plight of Third World communities and the hundred and one causes that prickle the conscience of millions of Britons. Probably you will notice quite soon after settling in that there is a marked contrast of humanity—the totally indifferent and insular and those passionately concerned about the most obscure problem somewhere thousands of miles away. For instance, in the aftermath of the recent Tsunami disaster, British people raised some £ 300 million in aid in a few weeks.

In a nutshell, the British Isles can offer you a completely fulfilling life, a choice of pastoral idyll or city razzmatazz; you can be quirky or serious, outrageous or plain lascivious. Almost everyone minds his own business, usually looking away when someone else is indulging in weird behaviour. But first a brief description of the country and a few statistics to ease you into what hopefully will be a stay of endless delights.

> When I visited Newcastle-on-Tyne a month ago, I was bowled over by the transformation of a city that a decade ago was really depressing. Today it is a chic, sophisticated place with handsome buildings, a place of bustling activity and loads of international eateries lining the riverbanks. It echoes the ambience of the Left Bank in Paris and this is saying a lot-with cafes, boutiques, tea shops and ethnic restaurants that beckon with delicious promise.

THE LAND

From north to south, Britain can be divided into the following regions: the Scottish Highlands, the Scottish Lowlands, the North, Wales, the Midlands, East Anglia, the West Country and the South-east. Each region is composed of several counties with major cities and towns which are in turn divided into boroughs and dotted liberally with villages. For instance, in London, Kensington, Camden, Chelsea, etc. are boroughs. The descriptions below do not refer to specific counties but rather point to a loose amalgam of areas and regions with similar geographical characteristics often reflected in their popular names, for example the Lake District or the Cotswolds, which may embrace counties as a whole or in part.

The Thames Valley

A historic link from London to Oxford, the Thames Valley embraces the royal county of Berkshire where stands Windsor Castle, the capital of London and its environs Hertfordshire and the Chilterns, Eton, Henley of the regatta and Sonning, regarded as the prettiest Tudor village of all. Oxford, in Oxfordshire, is not only an ancient university town, but a name given to many things from shoes to trousers. Not far is Blenheim Palace, birthplace of former Prime Minister Winston Churchill.

The Cotswolds

The Thames River takes its source in this region, in the village of Bell Weir Lock. This waterway gushes from a region known for its weathered honey-coloured stone used for building. The Cotswolds is rich with history from ancient Roman ruins in Cirencester to Shakespeare's birthplace in Stratford-upon-Avon. Once the wool centre, it is the foundation of much of Britain's post-industrial wealth. From here, England's major

As picture-postcard villages go, Bourton-on-the-Water is an absolutely charming visual that speaks volumes of the British love for country idyll. The place is studded with weathered, quaint and timbered houses, a babbling brook running across the centre, craft shops, pretty streets and nary a fast food place. It is a piece of pastoral perfection that one must not miss.

The Thames

waterway is a delightful cruise through history, hundreds of quaint villages, pastoral sights and handsome towns. Some of Britain's most idyllic villages are nestled within Warwickshire, Gloucestershire and Buckinghamshire, like the picture-postcard Bourton-on-the-Water.

Kent, East Sussex & West Sussex

These geological twin counties lie at England's most south-eastern tip. Blessed by Mother Nature, the region is a splendiferous orchard where one of the greatest joys of summer is to pick your own fruit. Eat as much as you like, free under the apple, pear, cherry or plum tree and pay for what you can cart away. The coast is very popular with holidaymakers, dotted as it is with the seaside resorts of Brighton, Eastbourne, Dover, Sandwich, Ramsgate and Margate. Much change has been going on for the past two decades and coastal cities like Brighton and Eastbourne have taken on a sleek 21st century veneer with ever-growing pockets of residential enclaves stuffed with condominiums and plush waterfront apartments, replete with anchored yachts and other pleasure boats. You are just as likely to come across a Thai restaurant in every one of these resort cities as you would a MacDonalds—such is the cosmopolitan ambience of these places.

Even on a cold blustery day, Brighton Pier has a holiday feeling with its candy floss and toffee apples stall.

East Anglia

A region of gentility and aristocratic heritage, East Anglia comprises Suffolk, Norfolk, Cambridgeshire and Essex in the rather isolated 'hump' of South-east England to the north of London. This is a region of rolling downs, gentle hills, lush valleys and floral excess. The British royal family's private home of Sandringham is in Norfolk with 2,800 hectares (6,916 acres) of parkland open to the public. The university town of Cambridge was founded by a group of Franciscans, Dominicans and Benedictines. The first college was founded by Oxford scholars who had fled their town after a disagreement with the authorities in 1209. One of the loveliest places in Britain are the Norfolk Broads, excellent for barge and boating holidays, being largely inaccessible to cars. Suffolk is Constable country. The artist's paintings of Suffolk landscapes are today a priceless part of the English heritage.

The West Country

This area embraces, from west to east, Cornwall, Devon, Somerset and Dorset. Cornwall, at England's westernmost tip, contains the aptly named village of Land's End. England's maritime heritage is enshrined here, an area of romance and dark history. Exmoor and Dartmoor are national parks with moorland evocative of mystery and evil deeds. Bodmin Moor in Cornwall is the setting for Daphne Du Maurier's *Jamaica Inn,* which still stands as a delightful pub full of the writer's memorabilia. Penzance and Plymouth exude the spirit of discovery and exploration from where Francis Drake, Walter Raleigh and the Pilgrim Fathers set out in search of adventure.

Wessex

To the south of London, Wessex is more a historical than a geographical description of Thomas Hardy country and other literary luminaries, once an ancient kingdom of the West Saxons that embraced what are now the counties of Hampshire and Wiltshire. From Winchester Cathedral's magnificence to the mystique of Stonehenge at Salisbury Plain, history permeates the whole region. The Victorian coastal watering hole of Bournemouth remains a very popular resort to 'take the air', as the Victorians did more than a century ago.

The Lake District

Britain's most visited area, the Lake District possesses the most stunning scenery within the smallest area: no more than 50 km by 30 km (31 miles by 18.5 miles). Nestled among gentle hills and dappled woodlands are sparkling lakes and shimmering tarns that mirror the magnificence of more rugged and misty peaks. The Lake District includes the western half of Cumbria and is distinctive for its beauty and charm.

Birthplace of William Wordsworth and Beatrix Potter, the Lake District is now increasingly congested with millions of tourists coming to soak up the poetic ambience. Kendal, Ambleside, Grasmere,

Did you know that there is a Japanese fan club for Beatrix Potter? It is rather amusing to see coach loads of Japanese men and women crowding into the local shop selling Potter memorabilia and carting them away in their Louis Vuitton and Prada. I am most anxious to see how Jemima Puddleduck translates on Japanese television, as it seems inevitable it will.

Windermere and Keswick are picture-postcard places— once you find a parking place.

The North

Immediately south of Scotland, the north of England embraces the counties of Northumbria, County Durham, Humberside and Lancashire, and the three ridings of Yorkshire. Here industrial grimness is cheek by jowl with stunning and wild scenic beauty, from the Yorkshire Moors and Dales down to the Peak District. Major cities include Newcastle-upon-Tyne on the north-east coast, and Manchester, Sheffield and Leeds skirting the Peak District National Park. The Pennines, England's backbone of hills, are topped by the long distance footpath of the Pennine Way, a formidable challenge to walkers stretching 400 km (248 miles) from the Peak through Yorkshire and Northumbria, finishing on the border of Scotland. The Roman emperor Hadrian built his fortified wall of 117 km (72.5 miles) from sea to sea to keep out the marauding Scots in AD 120. Yorkshire is reminiscent of the Brontë literary family. The delightful medieval city of York houses York Minster, the largest Gothic cathedral in England.

Much of the British countryside is a scene of pastoral tranquility such as the one shown in this picture.

Scotland

With its untamed landscapes, Scotland offers a mind-boggling number of ancient edifices to be explored, including some 4000 castles. Not a part of England, it is a separate county with a separate and distinct sense of pride and identity. Scotland is divided into Highlands and Lowlands, also described as Southern Uplands. Historic sites are Edinburgh Castle dominating the country's capital, which is surprisingly small but elegant; Linlithgow, the birthplace of Mary Queen of Scots; and St Andrews in the Kingdom of Fife, the birthplace of golf.

One of the most divine pursuits in Britain is quite simply to wander and meander through one of hundreds of parks throughout the country. Even season brings its own joy—the glorious awakening of life in spring amid daffodils, tulips and a thousand other blooms, the balmy, hazy days of summer, the magnificent russets and reds of autumnal fall and the crisp, clear air of winter.

Across the estuary of the Firth of Forth are the Highlands and the towering crags of the Grampian Mountains. Most of the settlement is along the coast. Major cities are Elgin, Inverness and Dundee with the major tourist attraction being Loch Ness. The monster's existence is still a hotly debated point.

Wales

With its impossibly complex language—the oldest in Europe—and lusty voices, Wales has a rustic charm all its own, and is known for being the birthplace of such luminaries as singer Tom Jones and actress Catherine Zeta-Jones. While South Wales is more industrial, North Wales is a country of exceptional beauty and rugged charm, especially Snowdonia that rivals the Lake District for scenic beauty. The Welsh are fiercely proud of their ancient heritage, unshaken in their belief that they are the true Britons. Due west of the Midlands, Wales lies beyond the Severn Bridge if you come along the M4 or A40 from London. The sign that reads 'Croeso i Cymru' means 'Welcome to Wales'. Cymru is the Welsh name for the country.

The Channel Islands

Guernsey, Jersey, Alderney and Sark are an autonomous democracy in their own right with their own currency; Great

Britain only looks after their foreign policy and defence. Little pockets of Gallic charm reflecting their historical links with France, the islands are less than an hour away by air. Only 12 km (7.5 miles) from the French coast, these islands are tax havens for the rich.

The Isle of Man

Like the Channel Islands, the Isle of Man has its own parliament, tax laws, currency and stamps. It is also a tax haven for the rich who don't like to pay British taxes. Lying in the Irish Sea midway between Northern Ireland and the Lake District's coast, the island is most notable for its Grand Prix circuit.

LONDON

Government

Since the abolition of the Greater London Council in 1986, the area has not had a single government body. It is divided into 32 borough councils, which have a status similar to

Britain Statistics

England
- Area: 130,000 sq km (50,193.3 sq miles)
- Population: 49.8 million
- Political status: Constitutional monarchy
- Capital: London, eight million residents swell daily to around 12 million by commuters, day-trippers and tourists.
- Language: English
- Currency: £ sterling, 100 p to the pound; £ 1 and £ 2 pieces, 50 p, 20 p, 10 p, 5 p, 2 p and 1 p. Scottish currency is also accepted. At time of press, the euro has not yet replaced the pound.

Wales
- Area: 2,080 sq km (803.1 sq miles)

the metropolitan district councils in the rest of England and the Corporation of the City of London. The Greater London Authority (GLA), inaugurated in March 1998, is now responsible for transport, economic development, strategic planning, culture, health and the environment, the police and fire and emergency planning.

Different boroughs have different political compositions and different priorities on expenditure needs and hence on revenue needs. Thus it can be twice as expensive to live in the Borough of Camden as it does in Kensington. Yet, the latter is a smart area with handsome houses amid leafy avenues, including Kensington Palace, and Camden remains congested, litter-strewn on most weekends and somewhat grubby.

The People

More than three million Londoners (of the total 12 million) belong to ethnic groups, the largest being the Indian community who have been here for more than a century.

- Population: 2.9 million
- Political status: Principality of Great Britain
- Capital: Cardiff, with 315,000 inhabitants
- Language: 80 per cent English, 20 per cent Welsh
- Currency: Same as England

Scotland
- Area: 78,000 sq km (30,116 sq miles)
  Population: 5.1 million
  Political status: Constitutional monarchy
  Capital: Edinburgh, with 445,000 residents
  Language: English with some Gaelic spoken in the Western Isles
- Currency: Scottish £. English and Scottish bank notes are interchangeable.

Today, the city as a whole plays host to millions of others, either refugees, job seekers from the EU and unaccountable thousands of others lured by the prospect of a (hopefully) better life.

There are no grim ghetto areas as such, though many ethnics choose to live close to one another. Income levels were once lower among these communities but in the last two decades, there has been much change where communities have become more affluent from sheer hard work and zeal. Racial problems are still occasional pinpricks but by and large, these are fairly isolated and do not constitute a national problem. The problem of wayward youth, nationalities notwithstanding, is a bigger headache like in every highly urbanized area.

The Lure of London

London lays bare the soul of the most stoic; one might be shocked, reviled, seduced or mesmerised, but few people remain unmoved by this beguiling city. It is totally pardonable to see London as a microcosm of England—Britain even—for its phantasmagorical offering of life, although people who live outside London would strongly disagree. It does, after all, have a little (or a lot) of everything that is good, bad, excessive, tasteful, shocking and pleasing.

I have rarely heard less ambivalent feelings about this sprawling city that provokes extremes in sentiment. Leaving this aside, and regarding London with the cool or feverish eye of one intent on getting under its skin, it provides an endless fascination and feast for the senses.

Shocks there are aplenty for the first-time visitor, but not always of a repellent nature. From its ancient beginnings as the Roman town of Londinium to the present-day metropolis that socks you with its sassy, trendy, eclectic, decadent, dignified, historical and contemporary elements, London is the object of a universal fascination that transcends race, language, culture and social divides. Metropolitan London

As a magnet to consumers bent on purchasing the latest, the best, the trendiest or plain kitsch, and the gawkers lured here by the city's irresistible charm, London has infinite capacity to accommodate millions.

that is, not the urban fringes of Greater London that seem like pastoral Utopia compared to the seething heart.

Seething Humanity

The millions still come to London as soon as the first shafts of the dawn light appear, drawn from the farthest corners of the globe. You reel from the first shock of lemming-like humanity moving about with desperate urgency to get somewhere; the push and shove, a herd-like instinct to answer some mysterious call, the seething humanity that can enthrall and frighten all at the same time. The streets, underground and pavements are a daily moving, bustling mass of people so intent on rushing that a strolling visitor is likely to be knocked off his feet. Like a boardwalk of shifting scenarios, it provides an enthralling vista of diverse humankind rarely found elsewhere. Even among those who commute to London to work, the city is the object of a never-ending love-hate relationship for many.

Entertainment

London is arguably the best city in the world for entertainment, with as much variety as you can ask for. It is a major centre for the arts with the South Bank Centre as the world's largest arts complex. Four major orchestras, two opera houses, 65 cabaret venues and some 65 new plays every month make London an entertainment mecca. Not cheap, with top show tickets going for as much as £ 45.

In the space of a few minutes strolling through the West End—not merely the shopping precinct but the hedonistic pulse—you can capture a splendid rainbow of life. Arab women covered from head to toe in black, American backpackers venting their youthful exuberance, European students chattering in a multitude of tongues, Japanese making a beeline for bespoke shops, vagrants, bag ladies, shifty-eyed, weasel-like men no doubt sizing up the day's purse-snatching potential, ladies who lunch, burger-munching kids—indeed it seems the whole world and a half are in London every day of the month.

The roar of ceaseless traffic is punctuated almost clockwork-like with screaming sirens of police cars heading for yet another crime spot. The pace is neither for the faint-hearted nor diffident. Observation of the rat-like scurrying pace of passers-by can leave you breathless, let alone with enough presence of mind to take in other splendid features of London's architectural and historical treasures.

The Old and the New

There are few places in the world that offer such an incredible juxtaposition of old and new, handsome and ugly, imposing and humble. A thousand years of history lie beneath the ancient streets, cobblestones, soaring edifices and traffic-snarled byways. While much building and refurbishing seems to go on ceaselessly, the heart of Central London has the patina of centuries that provides reflective wonderment amid the shocks of the teeming masses.

Surprises await the traveller at every other turn of the corner. Very much a walking city, the discovery of a quiet cul-de-sac (sometimes called a 'mews', originally an area of stabling now converted to chic housing) smack in the heart of a chrome, steel and smoked glass shopping area is sheer delight. Ancient churches nestle among gnarled old oaks like oases of benediction among the cacophonous surroundings of car-strangled streets. Minutes from the main thoroughfares and you're into the green lungs of Regent's Park and Hyde Park that allow you to luxuriate in verdance away from noxious fumes.

When wandering a village, town, city and especially London, one can often be too distracted by contemporary elements like shops and restaurants to notice the ancient history that lies beneath every cobblestone, gargoyle, steeple and archway. Do not forget this is a land that has a thousand years of history.

Day-trippers, by the very nature of their urgency, rarely pause to reflect on this startling contrast. Taking in London through the lens of a camera robs most of the pleasure of this feeling. As a resident, I use London's green lungs as a much needed respite from the daily shocks of crushing humanity and beleaguered transport systems.

London is a fascinating blend of old and new, ugly and beautiful, refinement and coarseness; in fact, it is the very essence of life.

The West End

There is much here that offers more shocks per minute than anywhere else in Britain. Pushers, hookers, conmen are never far from your shoulder. But look not merely on this side of life but at the fascinating faces of the place; its handsome theatres, cinema halls, shops, pubs and facades that make the West End what it is. London is a unique collection of historical buildings, timeless squares, quaint arcades, high-tech and faded with age, gleaming glass and ancient pillars, grubby pavements and pristine cobble-stoned alleys, shops rife with

London's offerings lie not just in the cash-for-flash genre but in the palpable aura of thrilling excitement; of simply standing, feeling and hearing the deep resonance of Big Ben that seems to toll of times past. Feel the sense of medieval mores while negotiating a cobblestone street between Tudor houses that belong to a time eons ago. Feel the heat of the Great Fire; smell the stench of the Plague.

the atmosphere of a time past and soulless chain stores. Within the little patch of land skirting the West End—Kensington, Bayswater, Paddington, Euston, Embankment, Westminster, Chelsea and Earl's Court—there is much that is entrancing, startling and mind-boggling.

Absorbing these places is an experience that touches most of the senses. Kensington is leafy, affluent and studded with handsome town houses even royalty are not ashamed of living in. Kensington Palace is a museum of court dress where occasionally Prince Charles, Prince and Princess Michael of Kent and some lesser royals host functions of various types. Yet, within a stone's throw of these exclusive residences lie the boisterous, sleazy, cosmopolitan district of Bayswater that possibly has only a little less low life than that in Earl's Court. The former is actually better known for its ethnic restaurants and the latter for its street hookers and red light areas. Paddington seems more like a souk out of the Middle East with a plethora of kebab shops and Lebanese eateries. And there, at the right turn of a corner, lies the wondrously green and peaceful Regent's Park.

Euston is a great maw of commercial buildings and railway stations, a source of bewilderment to visitors used, perhaps, to a more logical layout. Finding your way in and out of the bus, rail and train stations is an exercise to tax your heart and your patience. Embankment, Westminster and Chelsea are places where you can walk into history. But it may come as a shock to see soaring steel and glass high-rises that seem rudely out of place next to the Houses of Parliament. This is a juxtaposition that has not sat well on conservationists, and the battle rages on.

The High Life

London's Belgravia abounds with sumptuous houses belonging to blue bloods, chief of whom is the Duke of

Westminster, who owns practically all of Westminster. Most aristocratic homes (all over the country, not just in London) are open to the public for a small fee. This helps the families to maintain them. Many are heard to moan that it's a high price to pay, but the option is to ring to one's bank manager for a loan. So the high life still goes on where the family coffers and mansions are not in danger of insolvency. Millionaires abound in London but their flaunting of wealth speaks rather more of bad taste than impeccable lineage—something the British still set much store in.

The Low Life

The shock of seeing so many homeless sleeping rough in London never quite leaves one. Thousands of disillusioned fortune-seekers, tearaways and the gullible are drawn to London in search of whatever it is they cannot find in their suburban or rural patch. Most find the streets are far from being paved with gold, but are only a spectre of hunger and wretchedness.

It is not just youth who are so blighted in this sprawling city of so many faces where too few have time to care. There are thousands of old people, vagrants and bag ladies who wander the streets of London daily. Whatever the circumstances that have driven them to such degradation, there seems little hope of alleviating their depressing plights. In some cases, nothing can be done because they choose to live their shifting lives so. Drink appears to be a major cause but sociologists argue that they are driven to drink because of their miserable plights. Either they have no family, no home or have left welfare homes of their own volition.

A beholder does not have to be a poet to appreciate the multi-faceted nature of a metropolis that throbs and pulses to a thousand different beats. The exuberance of youth keeping up the frenetic pace of Piccadilly Circus; the seasoned mien of true Londoners seemingly untouched by the chaos as they down their pints of beer at quaint pubs; the splendour of St Paul's Cathedral and Nelson's Column dwarfing everything with their unbelievable majesty; the endless traffic choking every road, street and alley—

these are a few of the many scenes that make up London's unique ambience.

Fill your lungs with sharp air in the green parks of ever-changing floral displays. Or simply gaze at the splendid buildings that are divine examples of a flowering Renaissance centuries ago. Walking, seeing or taking in London needs singular concentration. A camera is for indelible mementoes but the mind is a much more permanent depository of all the things that make up London.

To embrace the shocks is to feel for London what a thousand snapshots cannot do. To live with them and perhaps feel a sense of involvement can make London so much more welcoming. There are many who have recoiled from London, perhaps having failed to do this. To be enamoured of London, once over the shocks, is to have a passionate love affair that can last a lifetime. To dislike London is to pass up a chance of life at a fast, frenetic, absorbing and utterly enchanting trot. Very few cities have this enigmatic appeal.

Take Time Out for London

It is a mistake to try and take in London in a few days–even a few weeks–as it tends to be with visitors. When you plant your stakes here, and if you want to get to know London really well, allow at least several weeks, preferably months, of protracted walking and copious note-taking to do justice to your task. Skimming the surface of any city is never satisfying—tourists are less concerned with in-depth knowledge than one-dimensional snapshots—more so with London than any other city. As I have mentioned, London is essentially a walking city.

Buy an all-day tube pass that entitles you to travel from 9:00 am to 12:00 midnight on all tube trains, buses and trains that service greater London where the tube does not reach. Taxis are murderously expensive—expect to pay up to £ 10 for a 10-minute ride, for which you might as well walk given the endless traffic jams. London is first and last for walkers.

Much of what's most interesting within metropolitan London is inaccessible by car, so you have to go on foot unless you're an avid cyclist; in that case, beware of the traffic. You take the tube and bus and then trudge to explore the nooks and crannies, giving you ample time to savour everything. An old building is never just an old building. The story behind its walls makes a fascinating study in architectural history.

These ramblings are an essential part of assimilating London if you are to feel a sense of belonging. Just like getting used to the train, bus and tube systems, they make for a much more meaningful stay. Champing at the bit when your bus is late does nothing for your mental equilibrium. Nor does it inculcate an indulgent fondness for London's idiosyncrasies, of which there are many. For it is this that separates the London lovers from the haters. You learn to rise above irksome feelings about the tardiness, the crowding, pushing, shoving and lack of grace because they are an integral part of the great maw that is London.

The Royal Albert Hall is simply breathtaking as an architectural curiosity—like a giant wedding cake. So is the much less somnolent Charing Cross Station. Both have their place in the complex heart that is London. Covent Garden—the covered market, that is, rather than the renowned and exclusive opera house—is brash, commercial and seemingly awash with tourists. But divorce your mind from the human multitude for a few minutes and cast it back to a time when it used to be the flower market that inspired *My Fair Lady*. Inigo Jones (believed by some to be Britain's greatest architect) columns take on totally different perspectives and you almost feel the noise fading away, as Eliza Doolittle's cockney tones begin to ring around the corners.

Alternatively you can skim London's surface, whinge about the noise, shove and push and go away knowing as little as when you came. Take time to gather in the ambience of the surroundings, above the neon-lit brashness of present-day commercial enterprises and you'll discover a new love for the place. Not just as a sprawling tourist trap where porcelain knick-knacks are a cheap affront to the innate beauty of the place, but a place full of surprising charm and quaint beauty.

Above all, London cannot be rushed even if its very pulse seems to race with the wind. Give it time and you'll grow a fondness for it that will make up for all its shortcomings.

Crime

Statistics make cold-blooded reading. For instance, in England and Wales for 2002, there were 835,000 violent offences, 48,000 sexual offences and more than 2 million petty thefts. But it is not so grim that visitors need to be constantly on their guard. The truth is, if one is vigilant and alert when moving about in city areas, especially at night, the threat of mugging and other petty crimes is no more sinister than in any other global city.

Of late, car jacking has earned high profile, and BMW and Mercedes owners are prime targets. People who wear or flaunt expensive designer watches and jewellery are particularly vulnerable, so the sensible thing is not to do so in public. The National Crime Squad (NCS) was established in 1998, replacing the six regional crime squads in England and Wales. It investigates national and international organised and serious crime. It also supports police forces investigating serious crime. The squad is accountable to the National Crime Squad Service Authority. [Contact HQ: PO Box 2500, London SW1V 2 WF; tel: (020) 7238-2500]

Parks

The city may be crowded, but London's green lungs make up for it. The Greater London area has 387 parks, 2,400 hectares (6,000 acres) of Royal Parks and 16,000 hectares (40,000 acres) of other parkland. For sports fans, there are 70 major sports centres, 12 football league grounds, 30 running tracks, six ice rinks and ten open-air swimming pools.

Housing

Property prices rocketed in 1989 but then plunged in the mid-1990s. While they stabilised for most of the late 1990s, prices went crazy again in 1999 and until now, there are no signs of a slowdown. The average price of a three-bedroom London home—previously in the region of £ 150,000—is now £ 250,000. So, if you had bought a three-bedroom semi-detached house in 1998 anywhere in London and in a few other major cities like Manchester or Birmingham, their value would have doubled today. Rents remain high in central

London going down to about half outside its perimeter. Expect to pay up to £ 100 a week for a no-frills room, and £ 200 per week for a three-bedroom flat.

Standard of Living

Londoners earn more than their counterparts in other British cities, but have to put up with a cost of living 36 per cent higher than the national average. A family of four living in a three-bedroom house spends 40.5 per cent more just to maintain a lifestyle comparable to that of a family in the north.

Homelessness

There are no accurate figures of the number of homeless sleeping rough in cities or shelters. The number is believed to run into the thousands, including the many drifters from provincial pockets who are lured by the golden hope of work in the big cities. An estimated 30,000 families still live in council-paid rented accommodation and hostels, swelled by a tide of refugees over the past five years. They form a mixed bag of peoples, mostly displaced peoples or refugees, such as the Kosovans, Bosnians, Turks, Kurds and Afghans.

Pollution

London has, in the past, earned the title of 'dirtiest city in Europe', with an exceptionally high level of carbon monoxide far exceeding WHO levels. Though the authorities have done their best to alleviate this, traffic pollution remains high and Central London, if not the greater area, still remains noxious during peak hours.

Transport

Some 1.7 million workers commute to London every day, about 500,000 by train, 400,000 by tube and 170,000 by car. More than two million cars crawl in Central London at an average speed of 18 km per hour. To alleviate traffic congestion and encourage the use of public transport, the government has recently introduced a 'congestion charge' of

Despite being one of the oldest in the world, the London Underground, commonly called the 'tube', is the best means of transport when you want to see as much of London as possible.

£ 5 for every car, van or lorry that drives into a designated area of Central London.

The tube service, despite hundreds of millions of pounds being spent over the past five years for upgrading, remains overused and overstretched. Tube fares are among the highest in the world, with an average fare of £ 1.90 for a 15-minute journey. This goes up to £ 2.90 during the peak hours before 9:00 am. The Paris metro is about 30 per cent cheaper.

RELIGION

Throughout the centuries, the history of Britain has been inextricably linked with religion. It is significant that the head of the Anglican Church is the head of state, that is the Queen.

The Church of Rome and the beginning of Protestantism
Britain was annexed by the Roman Empire in AD 44 and

after Christianity became the state religion of Rome in the 4th century, it began to spread rapidly. Rome, Catholicism and Britain flourished together until AD 410. However, Britain was left alone to fight off the marauding Scots and Picts from up north. By the 6th century, the defenders had established political power and the next six decades saw the growth of Roman Catholicism in Kent, Sussex, Essex, Wessex, East Anglia and Northumbria.By the time of the Plantagenets, the Anglo-Norman state was all-powerful. Henry II consolidated his power, made great reforms and established the common law system.

This was the beginning of the strain between Crown and Church. His archbishop, Thomas à Becket, was fiercely against his policy of punishing clerics for their involvement in secular matters, and was murdered by four royal knights on the altar at Canterbury in 1170.

When Henry died, his son Richard (The Lion-heart) took the throne only to spend most of his time in crusades abroad. His brother John's subsequent corrupt rule caused open revolt among the church barons but their plans to seize political power were destroyed by the Pope.

When John's son, Henry III, took the throne, feudal England was undergoing much upheaval. The king was beginning to lose his absolute power as Head of the Realm. By the time of his son Edward I's rule, England was a reformed nation with cohesion between Crown and Church. This was the era of great Christian buildings, at Lincoln and Salisbury and Westminster in London. More strife beset the nation after Edward I's death. His bungling son Edward II lost Scotland to Robert Bruce at the Battle of Bannockburn in 1314.

Baronial anarchy was largely suppressed during the subsequent reign of his son Edward III who died in 1377 and his grandson Richard II became king. Henry, the Duke of Lancaster, was eyeing the throne and, in the ensuing decade of plot and counter plot, killed Richard and proclaimed himself Henry IV in 1399. From then until Tudor times in 1485, England was ravaged by religious and political intrigue. Henry Tudor began to squeeze the Church for more money to fund his royal wars as Rome's influence dwindled. The Church was discredited and monks began to lose their discipline.

The more puritanical reacted against this laxity but the Church was still all-powerful and Cardinal Wolsey was the most feared churchman in England. He lived on a lavish scale in Hampton Court and controlled what was effectively the gateway to all professions. Resentment grew until the 1517 Reformation took place in what is now Germany. Henry VIII was obsessed with producing a male heir and when his first wife Catherine of Aragon bore him a daughter, his eyes soon fell on one of her ladies-in-waiting, Anne Boleyn. His request for a divorce was rejected by Rome and he passed a series of anti-clerical acts with the backing of the Reformation Parliament.

He also appointed his lawyer, Thomas Cranmer, as Archbishop of Canterbury who then annulled his marriage to Catherine and had her daughter Mary declared a bastard. Anne, meanwhile, gave birth to a girl, Elizabeth. The incensed Pope nullified Cranmer's annulment and excommunicated both. In retaliation, Henry decapitated Thomas More his Chancellor who refused to fall in with his plans, appointed Thomas Cranmer to the Privy Council and declared himself Supreme Head of the English Church.

He dissolved the monasteries, seized their vast landholdings and decapitated Anne for failing to produce a son. He married Jane Seymour who died bearing him the future King Edward VI. Cromwell introduced Protestantism into the English Church, and infuriated Henry so much he too lost his head in 1540. When Henry died in 1547, his enormous kingdom was expanding hugely but his son, the boy King Edward VI, was incapable of ruling.

When he died, his half-sister, Catherine of Aragon's daughter Mary, acquired the throne. A devout Catholic, she restored the Church to its former power, re-installed the bishops and began to close ties with Rome once again. In her brief reign she committed genocide in the name of Catholicism. But Mary was childless and when she died, Elizabeth, Anne Boleyn's daughter, seized the throne, thus ending the Catholic insurgence once and for all. She ruled for 45 years with sensible moderation. The new Puritans who had fled to the continent during Mary's reign returned. The English Church became more reliant on private interpretation of scripture, rather than ritual and episcopacy.

By the time James VI of Scotland became King James I of England, Scotland and Wales, there was tremendous pressure from Scottish Presbyterians. The sect had evolved from 'presbyteries'—local councils of elders under the authority of a synod who had no time for bishops and Anglican rituals.

Other Protestants clamoured for reform along the Scottish lines, demanded more say in the government and persisted in purifying the Anglican Church with its 'popish' rituals, ceremony and priestly pomp. The Catholics also began to push for a return to the old papacy of Mary. James I died in 1625 with his realm still in turmoil over religious, political and financial differences. His son Charles I had Catholic tendencies but was a weak politician. He hid behind the Archbishop of Canterbury and together they set out to halt Protestant reforms in his infamous Eleven Years of Tyranny. The demands became even more revolutionary and, by 1642, England erupted into civil war. The royal army was routed by Oliver Cromwell, a member of the Parliament that Charles had imperiously ordered dissolved.

The country was now in chaos and in 1649, Cromwell had Charles beheaded for treason. His son fled to France in exile. England was now effectively ruled by Parliament, fumblingly. Cromwell sacked the members and replaced them with his churchmen. This Parliament of Saints elected him Lord Protector in 1653. He died leaving the chaos in the hands of his son Richard. The exiled Charles II seized the opportunity to overthrow the incompetent Richard and restored the monarchy in 1660.

But the throne's power was now at its lowest ebb, though the Church of England was restored. When the Great Fire of London razed the city in 1666, it gave Sir Christopher Wren the opportunity to rebuild the great religious edifices. St Paul's Cathedral stands in magnificent testimony. Charles began to lean favorably towards the Catholics again, to the fury of Parliament. His brother, James, was a devout Catholic and heir to the throne. Catholicism was once again rearing its head in 1678 but before Charles could consolidate his efforts to stave off the threat, he died leaving the throne to the Catholic James.

In the Glorious Revolution, Protestants installed the Dutch William and his wife Mary Stuart in 1688. In his hatred for the French, William involved England in wars with France that lasted well into the reign of Anglican Queen Anne. Many rebellions were to follow for the next few decades and 18th century Britain saw much wealth and flowering of the arts. Cities mushroomed; the East India Company and the Bank of England accumulated vast resources, the result of hard-working precepts laid down by the earlier Puritans.

The two revolutions between 1740 and 1780 were neither religious nor political. They were the Agrarian and Industrial Revolutions which had great impact on Britain for hundreds of years to come. James Watt invented the steam engine, John Wilkinson invented new uses for iron and the country saw a burgeoning of building, manufacturing and farming. The old Puritan values of thrift and hard work became the national ethos. Children working 16 hours a day were a common plight. The Anglican Church did little to help these wretched people. In fact, Anglicanism seemed to have burrowed under ground.

Religious ferment was kept under wraps while Britain pursued commercial, industrial and colonising aims. But the American colonies began to champ at the bit and proclaimed themselves independent after the 1783 victory. The Methodists, who supported the American cause, began to stir the lower classes. They had in fact caused an anti-Catholic riot in 1780.

The next three decades were to see Europe in bloody turmoil again. The French Revolution of 1789 had the English aristocracy quaking in their satin boots and lacy jabots. Louis XVI lost his pompadoured head, Napoleon Bonaparte was a bloodthirsty little general and it was Horatio Nelson who began to turn the tide in 1804 with his spectacular victory at Trafalgar. His statue now takes pride of place above his soaring column in London's Trafalgar Square. Napoleon was finally defeated at Waterloo by Arthur Wellesley, the Duke of Wellington.

Midway through Queen Victoria's reign, murmurs of church reforms began to surface. The Oxford Movement wanted a return to the ritual of Anglican service which had languished for the last hundred years. The Puritan dissenters began to push for their own churches. Quakers, Congregationalists, Baptists, Presbyterians and Methodists did not want to conform to the Church of England. Reforms by 1833 were to have far-reaching effects. The religious intensity of Christian socialism was aimed at bettering the lot of women and workmen's colleges.

Today

The Church of England—its members are called Anglicans—has kept certain marks of its previous Catholic identity. The church has bishops headed by the Archbishop of Canterbury and his deputy, the Archbishop of York, who under them have 40 assistant bishops. There are 69 dioceses, each with 200 parishes, and every parish is under the religious leadership of a priest. He may be called a rector or a vicar, all of which mean the same thing.

Bishops are appointed by the Queen from nominations presented to the prime minister. The bishop lives from the donations of his congregation and a stipend from the central church. Financial matters are handled by church commissioners.

The Church of England is one of Britain's major landowners and all church expenditure comes from this revenue. It also has 18,700 church buildings to maintain, which takes a big chunk of the income for many of them are hundreds of years old and require not only constant care but delicate refurbishing. The Church of England is not funded by the state, though it is ultimately answerable to Parliament and cannot legislate without Parliament's sanction.

Foreigners exposed to English literature have come across the vicar most frequently, and perhaps labour under the misconception that only sleepy villages have vicars. Witness the Agatha Christie mysteries that invariably have a vicar popping up somewhere. But urban cities also have vicars who preside at public worship. Most parishes have an Anglican church, some two, depending on the size. An Anglican

You will often hear reference to High Church which implies the type of service and not, as you may think, a class distinction or architecture. A High Church service can be elaborate with ceremonial use of vestments, incense and candles as opposed to a simple one with the minimum of trappings.

vicar is licensed by the state to perform marriages, baptism and funerals—in short he is the local community shepherd. He's also sometimes known as the parson. Marriage ceremonies in other denominational churches are attended by a state functionary, or preceded by a registry office ceremony, since it is only the Church of England that is licensed in this way.

A Magnificent Testimony

Cynics might say—and they're backed in no small measure by church leaders—that this is a misnomer. There has been a general decline in Christian faith and church attendance in Britain over the past decades. This can be attributed to many factors: breakdown of extended families, moral laxity and general disillusionment brought about by unemployment and urban stress. The rising tide of secularism is very real according to religious leaders. Some church practices can be hide-bound and younger people may find it difficult to relate Christianity to their daily life. Whatever the religious inclinations of British people, thousands of churches and cathedrals built over a thousand years still stand in magnificent testimony to the Christian faith, attendant upheavals and bloody wars in the name of Christ.

Visitors from non-Christian countries and those with minimal Christian communities will be awed by the well-preserved antiquity and grandeur of these historic buildings. Places of worship they may be but, as tourist attractions, they lure millions of people to gasp and gawk, and perhaps to pray.

That this patronage helps to fund the religious organizations running their churches is undeniable. Each is run with efficiency, giving visitors comprehensive information about its history and service schedules. The architectural beauty and ecclesiastical ambience of Christian churches in Britain provoke different reactions in different people. If your inclination is to reach for your camera, check first to see if photography is allowed.

Apart from those that are in ruins, standing only by the grace of God and the preservation council, churches and cathedrals are first and foremost places of worship. The unending queues of tourists with fingers poised on cameras can be a headache to church elders trying to conduct services. Service times are usually listed on the door outside the main chapel together with information on what areas are out of bounds and whether photography is permitted.

It would be disrespectful to flout any of these, remembering that, whatever the tourist attraction; the church remains a sacred place. This fundamental observance must also apply to all religious places, even a heap of ancient stones where a church stood centuries ago. All over Britain can be found such founts of religious practice, pagan and Christian. Each is sacrosanct and must not be sullied by littering, graffiti or uncivil regard.

Don't simply traipse through clicking at every architectural detail and marble sarcophagus. Where a church has had a particularly long and interesting history, an area will be designated for visitors to browse and soak up the unravelling story via pictures and text.

Ecclesiastical postcards, religious artefacts and other literature are on sale at many churches and cathedrals of a certain age and historical import. It's one of the best ways of boning up on British history that for hundreds of years was inextricably entwined with Christian evolution.

More pertinent to the foreigner is an understanding of British Christian history and the terms of references used in the community. In 1990, total church membership in the United Kingdom was 65 per cent, with active church membership at Trinitarian churches—those believing in the Holy Trinity in unison with God—a mere 14 per cent, or 6.7 million people. Of these, 1.82 million were Anglican, 1.95 million Roman Catholic and 2.92 million of other Protestant denominations. Membership of non-Christian religions has more than doubled from 1975 to 1990, with 1.74 million active adherents in 1990, the largest group being Muslim.

You will come across all types of churches in Britain, from the little country chapel in a tiny village to the awesome cathedrals which tower imposingly over one whole city.

Great Churches

There are far too many to list, this being a random pick of the more handsome and better-known examples.

Westminster Abbey and St Paul's Cathedral, both in London, may have become the best-known symbols of tourist and religious Britain, but are by no means the most grand. Westminster Cathedral, in Victoria, is a Roman Catholic church built in 1890 in a rather eclectic style reminiscent of Byzantine and Italian styles. The Anglican church of St Martin's-in-the-Fields, built in the early 18th century, became the prototype of dozens of others in New England in America.

As for St Paul's, it rose out of the ashes of 1666 London after the Great Fire had razed the city to the ground. Its Italian baroque reflects St Peter's in Rome, but was, and still is, dedicated to the Protestant faith. It is the venue for most regal ceremonies. Wessex is known for its twin offerings of Winchester and Salisbury Cathedrals—both dating back to Norman times.

Not far from these is the mystical Stonehenge; the purpose for which the stones were erected remains a fascinating mystery. Believed to be the site of pagan sun worshipping by the ancient order of Druids, it still draws modern day druids by the thousands each Midsummer Day.

Canterbury is the cradle of English Christianity and the cathedral drew many pilgrims for centuries. It was built largely between 1100 and 1400 with some parts dating back to ad 602. Its stained glass windows alone are worth a visit. Dotted all over the countryside are remains of Roman ruins and St Augustine's College, near the ruins of its ancient abbey, trains Anglican clergy today.

Exeter Cathedral is Devon's most imposing building in the West Country. Built between the 11th and 12th centuries in Norman Gothic style, it has the largest surviving group of 14th century sculptures in England. Among its treasures are the 14th century *Bishop's Throne* and the *Exeter Book of Old English Verse*.

York Minster is Britain's largest cathedral, appearing to float above the medieval capital city of Yorkshire. Alas, in 1984, it was struck by lightning and nearly burned to the ground. Artisans had a monumental task restoring the 8,000 pieces of 12th century stained glass that had fractured into 50,000 fragments. Tintern Abbey in Gwent, Wales, was fittingly eulogised by Wordsworth for its extraordinary beauty. Built by Cistercian monks in 1131, it is still the most complete of ruined British monasteries.

Scotland is known more for its castles than churches, but Glasgow Cathedral is the only medieval building not destroyed during the carnage of the Reformation. It dates from the 12th century and houses the tomb of Glasgow's patron, St Mungo.

East Anglia comprises the four counties of Suffolk, Norfolk, Cambridgeshire and Essex with Cambridge being its best-known ecclesiastical and academic attraction. It was founded in the 12th century by Franciscans, Dominicans and Carmelites but it is Ely Cathedral with its unique lantern that stands out. This feat of engineering, a huge octagon of wood and glass, reflects the rays of the dying sun with awesome magnificence.

Norwich has more churches than you care to count—32 medieval ones within its ancient city walls—and Norwich Cathedral remains one of the most handsome examples of Saxon architecture. Stone for it was quarried in Normandy, France, and brought up river so its spire could rival that of Salisbury.

HOUSE OF WINDSOR

Much as Britain considers itself a modern democratic state, preoccupation with, and affection for the monarchy, despite much public outcry and emotional upheaval after the death of Princess Diana, still remain strong. There was a general feeling a few years ago that Britain veered close to becoming a republic but the ensuing poll proved otherwise with a respectable 53 per cent wanting to keep the Windsors on. So for the moment, it looks like Buck House (a.k.a Buckingham Palace) is not going to be converted into luxury apartments.

The royalist sentiment is that the royal family should remain detached, aloof even, and keep the certain mysticism that is intrinsic to being royal, much like imperial Japan. Somehow the glamour is tarnished if one of them is seen doing things normal people do—like shopping in a supermarket or engaging in rowdy behaviour in public. But such is the abiding love of the British people for the royals that scarcely a day passes without the papers coming up with some story or other about the royal goings-on. Love 'em or hate 'em, the British royal family sells newspapers, magazines, and television et al. For one thing, unlike practically all of European royalty—the late Dutch Queen used to cycle about without anyone turning a hair—that seem stored in mothballs, the Windsors still thrive on pomp and pageantry.

Given that the attraction of British royalty brings in unaccountable tourist income, Prince Philip's rather wry remark that 'We are not a family but a firm' is understandable.

Every single day, rain, shine, sleet or snow, the gates at Buckingham Palace are thick with tourists hoping to catch a glimpse of the most famous personage in the country. Or any lesser royalty. Or even the Queen's beloved pet dogs. Or not. They just want to show folks back home they'd been here, done it and with 1,001 pictures to show for it, even if none of them contain a single member of the ruling house.

The truth is the British royalty live a charmed life as, whatever disenchantment some sectors of the public feel about them, it is still in the minority albeit the occasional outcry that 'they're nothing but spongers' living off the public purse.'

Despite stories about royal spending habits, size of the Privy Purse and allowances that seem unreal in a world of increasing inflation, there really isn't a palpable reason for them to be removed. The republican voice waxes and wanes and seems to have little lasting effect. In the past two decades, despite the tradition that royalty never respond to public criticism and mud-slinging, some younger royals have been less than tight-lipped. The Queen herself has always maintained a magnificent stance of remoteness and indifference to any adverse comment and she never gives interviews.

The winds of change have come about especially with the younger royals who are not above appearing on television or speaking to the press, but not always with circumspection. Even the Queen herself has bowed to change and takes advice from the palace spin-doctors on various issues. The brouhaha, and the various unsolicited tomes with regard to the late Princess Diana's life and tribulations, does not seem to subside despite the passing years. The Diana camp, it seems, is determined to prove that her death was the result of murkier plottings.

When Princess Anne was divorced from her husband and then remarried, the tabloids had a field day. So, too,

Royal Quirks

Whether you care a hoot or not, royal behaviour makes interesting, and often mildly shocking, reading. Some of the trivia that sneaked out of the Palace:

- The Queen feeds her corgis herself with fillet of beef from a silver salver and with a silver fork. A royal 'pooper scooper' attendant takes care of the afters with a different sort of salver and gets paid to do the job full-time!
- The Queen travels with her own toilet seat and feather pillows. She is the only person in Britain who travels without a passport. And the only person for whom Harrods used to close its doors to the public for one day a year so she could do her Christmas shopping. But she doesn't carry money even though bank notes have her picture on them.
- Prince Charles has his toothpaste squeezed for him by a valet
- Wherever he travels within the UK, he only eats his own vegetables organically grown in Highgrove estate.

with the very public divorce of Prince Andrew and Sarah Ferguson—Fergie to all. Perhaps mindful of murmurings and resentment over their lavish lifestyle amid so many jobless and homeless, the royals' aloofness and their being out of touch with the common people, the second generation has been visible and audible over television. Prince William and Prince Harry, now young adults, are constantly hounded by the media. With William now very much in the public eye as a handsome young man, and most likely heir to the throne, every move he makes is closely shadowed by the media.

Royal Ancestry

Largely, the British regard their monarchy as a useful institution, a symbol of national identity by its ancient roots and apolitical stance. The Queen can trace her ancestry to the first King of England, Egbert of Wessex in AD 829.

She is also Queen of Scotland and this lineage goes back to Kenneth MacAlpin who established the Kingdom of Scotland in AD 839. Though British monarchy is not the oldest in Europe, it is certainly the most continuous and the most high-profile with only an 11-year break between 1649 and 1660. This was when the infamous Oliver Cromwell and his roundheads chopped off the head of King Charles I and the Puritans ruled briefly.

A Darned Good Show

Whatever the reasons for the monarchy's endurance and endearance, it's the showbiz side that has the crowds cheering for more. 'A darned good show' as American tourists put it. The pomp and pageantry are very much a public relations exercise.

So are the social activities of the young royals whose every action is minutely reported in the daily tabloid press. This is the side of royalty that visitors first encounter, whatever the truth of the matter. The British tabloid papers are notorious for sensational headlines. Like when Prince Edward offered to work in Andrew Lloyd Webber's theatrical enterprise, the press went to town. They dubbed him 'dishcloth Doris' and claimed his apprenticeship amounted to no more than making tea for Lloyd Webber!

In the past year, the murmurs of speculation about Prince Charles and his long-time paramour Camilla Parker-Bowles became a veritable crescendo. The question that hangs heavily is whether she will ever be queen, being a divorcee—a situation that the Constitution would never have accepted in the past. Anyway, they got married without too much public furore and seem settled—for the moment. Other questions still pop up now and then—will the Queen abdicate, will Prince Andrew and Fergie ever reconcile? These and a hundred posers sell the tabloids and magazines by the millions every day.

From inside the palace, minor royals have been heard to moan that it's a pain being a blue blood. They have little privacy in public and every minor gaffe, social slip or plain youthful high jinks is chronicled and often blown out of proportion. When Prince Charles made a flip remark that he talks to his plants, the press made him out to be something of a nut case. He was certainly not amused but resigned to the fact that every little twitch he makes is going to cause waves.

Princess Anne has been called horsey, bossy and a bitch. Now the feisty lady has redeemed herself by working tirelessly for her Save the Children charity, travelling thousands of miles around the world raising money for the underprivileged children. Even with her marriage about to collapse, she was thousands of miles away in Central America. And on television—an act that would have been unthinkable a decade ago—she excelled herself by answering questions from the audience with a disarming, self-effacing wit that won her even more fans.

The constitution does not abide the Queen's abdication for reasons other than ill health but public sentiment seems to echo that Prince William should be crowned king, sidestepping his father as by the time the Queen dies—and given her rude health she could live to a hundred and more—Charles will be to decrepit. And so the royal soap opera grinds on.

When young Prince Harry, obviously for a lark, spotted a Nazi swastika emblem on his arm for a costume party, it made world news and caused much consternation to the family. Naturally, the tabloid press, cutting its teeth on anything newsworthy, went to town and the prince had to make an abject apology. If the Queen was exasperated with her children's marriages going not only awry, but increasingly weird, she made no public comment. One wonders what her feelings are about her grandchildren's behaviour.

I found myself being more absorbed each day with every story about the British royals, as you no doubt will. The media certainly know how to package them and they sell like no other. Even after her tragic death, fascination for Princess Diana has not waned. The Queen Mother, affectionately called Queen Mum, died in 2002 at the ripe old age of 102. This was not long after the death of her younger daughter Princess Margaret who, after a series of mishaps and illnesses, never fully recovered. It was a sombre time for the family and a particularly trying one for the Queen who lost her beloved sister and mother within a few months of each other.

That the younger royals are not seen to have any kind of real job does not go down well with the chattering masses. Even Prince Edward's attempts to run a film production company had landed him in many a controversial situation. And even his wife's attempts at running her own public relations firm turned sour and her company had to quietly shut down, succumbing to Windsor family pressure, after a series of questionable actions. The pair, now parents of a baby girl, devote all their time to royal duties.

So the wheel turns and the public continue to lap up such coverage. Nary a day passes that the press does not have a story or another about the goings-on within the royal ranks. As a visitor, you will no doubt find it fascinating reading (as do the Americans who do not have a monarchy) and when Hollywood stories are less than biting, the British Royal Soap Opera as it were, never fails to entertain.

Anti-Royalists

In truth, the band of fierce anti-royalists is small even among a large republican mass. At worst, royalty is thought of as being irrelevant and a waste of public taxes. Some grudgingly concede that much tourism revenue would be lost without the royal show. The irritant seems to be the Privy Purse paid out of public funds. What, for instance, do Prince Edward and Prince Andrew do each year to earn hundreds of thousands of pounds?

The Queen's allowance runs into millions but most of it goes into maintaining the royal lifestyle—which brings the argument back to tourist revenue. Just how much of state and private money is spent maintaining the royal status of an ever-growing family is a fact that the media are not prepared to explore to the full. In any case, the Queen is now paying taxes just like everyone else.

By and large, public murmurings are just that. The press may occasionally question the justification of minor royals taking six months out of a year to go on holidays and being paid for it, on top of that. But as the palace never comments on press stories, ambivalent public feelings simply dissipate.

Royal Riches

The Queen is deemed to be one of the richest women in the world, if not the richest. But it is highly unlikely that she could ever liquidate her priceless paintings, jewellery and property and hop it to live in grand style on some private island. Most of the royal abodes and property belong to the state and the Queen actually owns only Sandringham in Norfolk and Balmoral Castle in Scotland.

She may own priceless crowns and jewels but they're a part of the monarchical repository and she could no more sell Buckingham Palace than the American President could the White House. For all being surrounded by galleries stuffed with priceless masterpieces, the Queen remains a countrywoman at heart and is happiest walking her dogs and checking on her stable of horses.

The press often remark about the Queen's taste in clothes, despite the obvious enormous cost of having a new outfit for each formal occasion—and there must have been thousands during her reign—but Her Majesty has never subscribed to fashion for its sake, preferring instead to wear what she deems to be suitable to her station in life. In short, grand and opulent without the need to be faddish or even fashionable. Whatever their foibles, the fairy-tale existence of some and the common touch of others, British royalty is an integral part of British life and likely to carry on for the next 1,000 years.

BRITISH PEOPLE

'One is inclined to feel the British set a stiff upper lip when things go awry, and thus Rule Britannia. Well, it's all EU now and stiff lips, upper and lower, simply would not curl around Brussels (sprouts) sic!'
—Terry's journal, April 1984

STEREOTYPES

When Britannia was ruling the waves and the 'Made in England' stamp had a definite prestige during the Industrial Revolution and right up to the 1960s, the Briton was as archetypal as his picture-postcard backdrop: the pudding-basin black bowler hat above a sober, stiff upper lip echoed by his tightly furled umbrella. His backdrop? Any one of the historical sights millions of tourists flock to Britain each year to gawk, photograph and marvel at. You can take your liberal pick from a Georgian mansion to an Elizabethan cottage, from Westminster Abbey to Canterbury Cathedral. This chocolate-box perfection was the arch lure for tourist revenue in untold millions right up to the 1980s.

This scenario has shifted inevitably with the passing of time, the stereotype now relegated to the pages of history, replaced by not so much another singular iconic element but a montage of different ones. There has been some diffusion for there does not exist today any such distinctive identifiable image. The pearly kings and queens of cockney London and the serving wenches of 16th century Tudor Britain are brought out of mothballs only in organised commercial functions to satisfy tourist appetites for such historical throwbacks. You won't see them walking the streets of Britain.

What of the rosy-cheeked farmers of rural patches? Many other traditional images remain but only as rustic pockets of rural Britain and then only in the architectural sense. These villages of old may seem to exist in a time warp but the reality is they are very much in the mainstream of the 21st century with the aforementioned 'farmers' now being IT literate and more at home with computers and high-tech than ploughs and horses as most farming is mechanical.

The 'red hair' description that Orientals are wont to give all British, indeed all Europeans, could not be further off the mark. There is no such thing as the average British national in terms of hair and skin colouring. One language is the common denominator. Fundamentally, Britain has much more of a multi-racial mix today than ever before and it is difficult to picture any archetypal Briton. Even typical advertising posters might include an ethnic mix of people as representative of Britain today— and it is not mere tokenism.

You will find that English people are not necessarily tall, fair and blonde as normally perceived. In fact they run the gamut from stocky, dark and swarthy courtesy to tall, fair and blonde and many hybrids in-between courtesy of Celtic, Nordic and intermarriage origins. They could look continental, Middle-eastern or even Asian.

THE FIRST BRIT

The origin of the British is rather more genetically mixed. They are descendants of the ancient Norman, Celtic, Saxon and Nordic tribes which settled here from 2000 BC until the 11th century. Even before the Celts came, swarthy Mediterranean peoples had lived in Britain and founded cities like Canterbury and London. The Celts actually came 1,000 years later—from Brittany in France and the Alps. Many moved north to Scotland and across the seas to Ireland, laying the foundation for the Irish and Scottish national parties which promote the revival of old Celtic languages.

The Cornish people still speak affectionately of their Breton cousins. Around 55 BC, the beady eyes of the Romans were cast on Britain and they conquered the Celts. However, the Roman Empire collapsed during the 4th century falling prey to the newcomers—the Angles, Saxons and Jutes hailing from Germany. They in turn were conquered by the fierce Vikings who ruled by their blood-stained swords till the 11th century. William, the Duke of Normandy, with the help of Norman soldiers descended from Scandinavians, ascended the throne after the fateful Battle of Hastings in 1066. Norman castles still dot the countryside. The Romans left their road systems, and ancient tongues pepper the spoken English today. Modern English emerged from a mix of Celtic, Norse dialects, Anglo-Saxon, Latin and Norman French.

By the early 19th century, Jews fleeing the pogroms of Eastern Europe flooded into Britain settling in the East London area of Spitalfields. They prospered through the fur and clothing trade, and by the middle of the 20th century, another wave of immigrants moved in. Bangladeshis fleeing the poverty and strife of their crowded homeland stepped into the trades left by the departing Jews. A house of worship that still stands today in Brick Lane in East London reflects this demographic change. It was a French chapel dating back 300 years, then a Wesleyan church, a synagogue, and is now a mosque.

The Bangladeshis are themselves part of a larger community of people from the Indian sub-continent who began migrating here in the 1950s. Sikhs from the Punjab, Gujeratis, Ismailis and others from Kenya, Tanzania, Uganda and Malawi jostled for a living. They sought work in Leicester, Birmingham and other Midlands areas, moving later into London's Southhall. Walking down the high street of this area evokes a palpable feeling of being in India.

From the 1950s too, West Indians came here in large numbers to take on jobs the British did not want—mostly menial and lowly paid. As Commonwealth subjects and regarding Britain as their mother country, they were not prepared for the shock of social rejection and often-overt racial discrimination. Settling in the inner cities of London, Birmingham and Manchester, and working on railroads and other service industries, their lot was not a pleasant one, what with bad wages and anti-black

In one road near to where I live in northwest London, there are at least four greengrocers, two fishmongers, two butchers, three hairdressers, three fast food joints and various newsagents—and every single business owned and run by Iranians, Afghans, Blacks, Kosovans and Asian Indians–and not a single English person among them.

feelings. Among the younger immigrants, anger became the common stance, often exploding in riots.

WHAT MAKES THEM TICK

It is not possible to categorise Britain as a whole because you meet so many different psyches in relation to a foreigner in their midst. Britain today has a racial mix that reflects a global melting pot. In areas where ethnic communities are thin and scattered, a sense of isolation can permeate, as most English people are slow to warm up to strangers whatever their ethnic origin. The Welsh and Scots are generally more forthcoming. Visits up north confirm this. A Scottish friend often moans about the unfriendliness of his southern compatriots.

Certainly, people in London—whether visitors or locals—seem less friendly than those in the counties and villages. This is mainly the result of the push-and-shove big city life and one can get sucked into this pattern unwittingly. Despite the pluri-ethnic population, and difficult though it is to generalise, there are traits common to most people in the nation. Where they come from, whether country or urban, and what their education and social backgrounds are, have a great bearing on their behaviour as a whole.

People from the counties and rural folk who live quieter lives are usually more polite, friendly and helpful when a stranger asks for help. In the highly urbanised cities, a request for help does not always elicit warm response. A brusque dismissal is more likely. Though this is true of most countries with highly urbanised city centres, public abrasiveness is particularly pronounced in a city that attracts more people than space can allow.

Likely as not, the person you approach to ask for help is in a great hurry, trying to get on the train or tube and, therefore, disinclined to waste precious minutes answering a query. Just as likely, he is a visitor who knows as little as you do. But by and large, the local Brits are helpful should you ask for assistance. They are not so ready to warm up though, if you ask too many personal questions. What might seem like a normal query, such as "Which part of the country are you from?" may be construed as nosiness.

The 'minding one's own business' syndrome has unfairly given the British an undeserved reputation for coldness. True, they are disinclined to make the first move, but once you take the first step, you'll find the coldness thawing perceptibly—as long as you don't poke or pry, naturally. You'll find the stiff upper lip visibly thawing.

Tradesmen in busy city centres are also likely to be offhand and brusque when approached for assistance. They are among the first people new arrivals meet, usually outside a railway station. You must understand that you are likely to be the 100th person to ask him where Buckingham Palace is. In the counties and suburban areas, people will go out of their way to direct you to a local attraction. For one thing, they don't get thousands of visitors everyday. For another, pride for one's local scene is deeply entrenched.

SILENT COMMUTERS

The British are notoriously tight-lipped during commuting, whether by train, tube or bus. When a train stops between

When you attempt to chat with someone at a bus stop or while waiting in queue, and you get monosyllabic answers, leave off. The apparent lack of curiosity about other people's lives is simply a greatly cherished sense of privacy and a fear of being perceived as invading others' personal space.

stations for any reason, even for as long as half an hour, you can almost hear a pin drop for the ensuing silence. Few, apart from friends, are inclined to make casual conversation even as relief from the tedium of waiting. The only sound in a carriage of 30 people will be the rustling of newspapers. Visitors used to public bonhomie usually end up embarrassed when their remarks provoke only silence and weak smiles.

The occasional sight in tube trains of drunks and vagrants singing and swearing would only make the British turn the other way and pretend this embarrassment is not there. The only people staring and smiling with bemusement are likely to be visitors.

When you are among many of your own people, the tendency is to mingle almost exclusively among them, cutting against the grain of integration. Let us take a typical urban town in a county where there is a visible mix of English, blacks, Chinese, Greek Cypriots, Indians and other ethnic minorities. You live in a terrace house near the high street where kebab houses, pizza places, Chinese takeaways and Indian newsagents jostle with English supermarkets and West Indian greengrocers.

This eclectic community typifies many towns in Britain. The best opportunity to make friends and foster good relationships is via the trade. Business people are by design more forthcoming, cheery and less private. From here, you build a certain foundation in the understanding of different cultures, echoing much Britishness at the same time. I often shop at West Indian greengrocers that feature unusual produce not found in Chinese specialist stores and supermarkets.

Most shopkeepers warm up to regular customers but are loath to be too friendly for fear of being called nosy, unless you make the first move in striking up chumminess. There is a common ground to inter-relate with them if you take

One place where you will make friends is at the greengrocer's. The street market also has a friendly atmosphere and the stallholders tend to be more garrulous.

the first step. On home ground, poking your nose across the fence to make conversation is likely to elicit a certain reluctance to be friendly. Yet, the same person at the butcher or fishmonger will be more ready to engage in conversation over the relative merits of chicken or cod.

In many ways Britain's high streets of burgeoning ethnic shops and a growing interest in ethnic cuisines among even the conservative British have provided a conversational springboard. The same human bonds are less easily forged at department stores, bus stops and other public areas. Perhaps it is the fear of the unknown, here dispelled on the cosy ground of domestic routine. Somehow, picking, choosing and waffling over market produce creates an instant bonhomie; a conducive atmosphere that brings out the friendliest face of humanity.

VALUES
The Scots
The Scots are not all dour as rumour would have it and are in fact very warm, extremely cultured and philosophical. As

for being tight-fisted, it is an undeserved reputation. Who can generalise about such a personal trait? It is a fallacy that probably goes back to antiquity and notionally offensive, though the Scots are the first to make jokes about this underserved reputation. While self-deprecating, they are at the same time fiercely proud of their Scottish heritage.

The Welsh

Likewise, the Welsh will take umbrage if you should mistake them for English. A friendly, poetic and musical people, they join forces with the Scots to poke fun at the English. But then much of the basis of national humour takes a leaf from this free-for-all when someone takes a pot shot at another with tired old jokes by simply changing the nationality.

The Chinese

The Chinese from Hong Kong—now swelled by droves from mainland China—take umbrage at being labeled 'Hongkies'. There are now a second and even third generation of these Hongkongers who are practically all-British but for skin colour and good-humouredly dub themselves BBC—British Born Chinese. Working with the older generation, of whom many still speak little English, can be trying as they can be brusque and dismissive if you don't speak Cantonese.

This generation is being rapidly replaced by their local-born progeny of restaurateurs and shopkeepers—the majority are still in these trades—who are largely English-speaking. Many are now in other trades and it is not uncommon to be served by a Hong Kong Chinese in post offices, transport facilities and hospitals. Not surprisingly, Mandarin is rapidly becoming the street language of Chinatown, as there has been an influx of migrants, refugees and illegals from China. The 2001 census for Chinese population shows the figure of around 200,000.

The Vietnamese

Once the newcomers to London's Chinese enclave, and inadvertently rubbing up the Chinese the wrong way as much for the historical hostility of several centuries ago as for competition in business, the Vietnamese tend to be low key. They have not yet made their presence felt to any large degree and any presence is manifest mainly in restaurants. Most are actually ethnic Chinese, but for the reason mentioned above, are still regarded with suspicion by the Hongkongers.

The Thais

About 20 years ago, the Thai community was relatively small and reflected by no more than a dozen Thai restaurants throughout the UK. Today, there are more than 500 Thai eateries, with new ones opening every other week and far-flung at that, from Scotland down to the South coastal towns of Brighton and Eastbourne. Thai cuisine has been eagerly relished by the British public and hundreds of Thai chefs have since been decamped from Thailand to work and live in the UK.

The Indians

Collectively known as 'Asians', they number more than 3 million and are scattered all over the UK. They represent the largest single group of non-whites and have their roots in the sub-continent, Pakistan, Bangladesh, East Africa and Sri Lanka. The groups are increasingly becoming more high profile in all areas of endeavour. Very much in the news lately have been the achievements of these British citizens of Indian descent who now hold influential positions in industry and the government.

In cities like Leicester, Leeds, Birmingham, Bradford and London, there are high concentrations of Asians. Strolling down the high streets of Wembley and Southhall in London for instance, you might think you are in Mumbai given the number of Indian enterprises.

Black Caribbean and Black Africans

Once known to be forthright and sometimes aggressive due to historical reasons of being imported labour early this century and not treated very well, they have more or less integrated into British society. There are still a few who have

Centuries of colonisation and immigration have turned Bristish society into a very cosmopolitan one. Tolerance and respect for each other's culture have helped many foreigners integrate fully into British society, although tension is never far from the surface in deprived areas.

chips on their shoulders, but generally, the one-million-plus community has learnt to live in harmony with others. The Rastafarian sect is no longer seen as some sinister element for all their dreadlocks and swagger—more a fashion statement than tradition.

Others
As for the Americans, Canadians, Australians, fair-skinned Middle-easterners and Europeans, they mostly blend in and

are almost indistinguishable from the locals, given their Caucasian features. The Japanese are now less big spenders than they once were given their economic downturn; Koreans stick to their enclave and are relatively low profile, as are the Malaysians and Singaporeans, although these last two groups do not live in specific enclaves.

While many of Britain's foreign residents are still transient businessmen or students, more have become permanent residents, assimilating into the British way of life and even opting for citizenship. If asking neighbours over for a meal elicits no response initially, probably because they find foreign food off putting—and many British do—ask them in for tea. This is a social habit close to their own heart. Basically the British are more than curious about foreign cultures and lifestyles, but do use subtle persistence to convince them you're totally sincere and do not expect any reciprocation. They are not inclined to hand out casual invitations to their homes and, for this reason, often refuse yours.

> In the first few years that I had a garden and a common fence with my English neighbours, I found that offering the occasional gift of food or snack helped tremendously to cement friendship. Thus have my curry puffs, samosas, spring rolls and satay paved the way for warm neighbourly bonds. It may be food we take for granted but for most British, they are a fascinating treat.

It is more than making nodding acquaintances across the garden fence. It's making the effort to convince the conservative, wary British that foreign residents, whatever their pigmentation, basically want to be accepted even if sometimes they don't quite understand the need for assimilation. When you meet a neighbour further afield and not sharing a common fence, a cheery good morning and cursory conversation about the weather and other light observations will widen your social register.

It's knowing what makes the British tick. The safe ice-breaking subjects are the weather, pets, gardens, children and their antics, community welfare—such as what to do about loud music from an unreasonable household—and problems that draw neighbours together to fight a common cause. It shows clearly that you care about the welfare of the community.

AT WORK

The office you work in will probably have a large proportion of British staff, so make a supreme effort to be on their wavelength. Office procedures all over the world are quite similar, but you can look into their culture in a number of ways, for example by sharing their lunch pattern. British workers often have a rather simple lunch routine: while factories and industrial units may have a workers' canteen serving a complete, carbohydrate-full lunch or dinner, for many workers, sandwiches and soft drinks augmented by chocolate bars are the order of the workaday week.

Joining in local lunch arrangements will repel the likelihood of isolating yourself in an all-British environment and you will win your colleagues over with your genuine keenness to share your culture. Convincing them that you're an anglophile is not the best way to win British friends either. The British have a healthy regard for aliens who preserve their own culture and yet have a healthy curiosity about theirs. It endorses the fact that you are not a passenger among their midst and nothing demystifies the 'inscrutable' or insular tag more than when you show cursory knowledge of British culture. It can become an invaluable cue for the Brit to break out of his rigid reserve and tell you all you want to know; be it the best way to brew a cup of tea or which pub has the best ale.

Even if the organisation you work in has a reputation for being egalitarian and anti-racist, the balance of minority ethnic working among the majority of British can be fragile. Curtail your hypersensitivity about the jokey peccadilloes that might come your way. Innocent ribbing is a good basis to form warm working relationships if you don't read too much into it. Unless you know for sure it was said with real venom, take it in the right spirit of cheeky ragging. Incidences of outright racism within a working environment are relatively rare and, if they persist, take the matter up with the proper authorities.

OF LAUGHTER AND LAMENT

Strange bedfellows, yet the slight paradox of being custodian of a jut-jawed stiff upper lip and a wry sense of humour is very British. Here, there must be some qualification as Scottish, Welsh and English people each have their own laughter medicine. Fundamentally, all have a similar self-deprecating sense of humour that is refreshing. It's often bandied about that if Americans laughed at themselves more often, they wouldn't spend so much time on a psychiatrist's couch. Supposed national characteristics are woven into the jokey pattern—Scottish meanness, Welsh romance and English coldness.

It's humour that's pervasive, spilling out over just about every aspect of life. You'll notice that most British advertisements, whatever the selling message, usually have a tongue-in-cheek touch. You'll be hard put to meet a nation more ready to laugh at itself. Brought up as I was on absolute filial piety, rapping with my elders was simply not done. Here, I have met many elderly friends who are uproariously funny and not afraid to show it. Naturally, in the beginning I was most reluctant to say anything that might be regarded as impudent. But they soon put me at ease with their cracking good humour, some positively blue!

> I knew a friend's mother who had a colostomy bag for many years. Far from being coy about her predicament, she had a marvellous sense of humour. When I once asked how to change a colostomy bag, she replied: "Make sure you keep the receipt before you bring it into the store!" It took me all of two minutes to fathom her wry sense of humour.

The great British put-down, as they say, is almost always aimed inwards and you see this more markedly on stage and television than anywhere else. In the characterisation of a drab person, replete with curlers in the hair and bedraggled clothes, no punches are pulled. This funny image of a charlady (cleaner to you) is something you don't often see on American TV, where glamour is all-full make-up in bed, etc. In fact, this sense of honesty has enshrined many characters as national symbols—the charlady forever in her pinafore, the tramp, the frumpy housewife, the henpecked husband, etc—not just as fiction, but a reflection of real life. The charlady image has become so much of an institution that it spawned many TV sitcoms and even a current West End musical called *Acorn Antiques*. The star of the show is called Mrs Overall on account of what she wears and played by no less than Oscar winner Julie Walters.

Nothing is sacred when it comes to squeezing a laugh. Not even the priesthood, as evidenced by one of the most popular sitcoms of the 1990s and still showing—*Father Ted*. It chronicles, rather irreverently, the shenanigans of a rag tag group of Irish Catholic priests and no one takes offence. Even eminent politicians and royalty are not safe from the barbs of TV humour.

Yes Minister is a highly satirical programme that shows no mercy in tweaking the British political system and even the prime minister and members of the British royal family have been frequent subjects of such razor sharp humour. It is believed to still be one of the Queen's favourite programmes although most of the cast are now dead. As for the other face of the British psyche, the indomitable spirit not to break down in the face of disaster is most admirable. You read often about tragedy—the past decades have seen the King's Cross Fire, the Paddington rail disaster and other major motorway accidents. The aggrieved families rarely show anything but the bravest, most stoic face. Even when Princess Diana died, the Queen and her family appeared to show the kind of stoicism that had the public baying for blood.

It's a trait you see again and again where people touched by tragedy prefer to bite their lips in public than crumble in a heap. Carrying on regardless is what they call it—as epitomised in the hilarious series of British comedies regarded as classics of British mores.

Making a scene is not being British at all, which also explains why you rarely see them complaining about bad service. If a customer is upset about anything, he will not make a public fuss. He will make a polite comment and leave it at that. Consumer watchdogs in the past few years have been getting at the British public for this reticence to complain, thus perpetuating the bad service.

Whether it's good or bad is not the point here. If you were to become vociferous about some injustice, you would get the feeling you were being uncivilised by the curious looks of other customers. It is a good thing when you can complain without histrionics as you often see in other societies not given to the same diffidence.

This understanding of their psyche is important if you are never to feel at odds among British people. Nor should you take offence when they make jokes about you for it is meant to be taken in this light. If anyone were to be deliberately vicious, racist or otherwise rude, he wouldn't bother to make a joke of it. Learn to take it in the same spirit and you'll find them warming up to you as a mate. Indeed, one of the best compliments you could be paid is to be regarded as a mate.

FAMILY

The British family unit is no different from its counterpart elsewhere in the world: one, and increasingly, two working parents, children (an average of two), a house or flat on mortgage and a basic social lifestyle built around the local pub, weekends and the annual two-week holiday. The rich differ only in their choice of residence location, leisure pursuits and holiday destinations: perhaps Greece or Italy instead of Torquay or Torremolinos, Disneyland instead of Brighton Pier.

The system of contributing to the family kitty is much less customary in Britain for the simple reason that financially independent young people tend to fly the coop as soon as they are able to. In this, the British are different from the Southern Europeans who still live in extended families.

When a family goes out to dinner, the bill is often split between parents and working children. The system where the father pays for the whole family is not for them. But the winds of change are blowing. Recent research shows that more and more single men are opting to stay at home with their parents until they set up their own families. It has a lot to do with the cost of housing, bachelor pads being expensive, and coming home to dirty laundry and cold canned food: not exactly a warming prospect. Sceptics may say this is mother-smothering and likely to be the cause of marriage failures because of the inevitable comparison. Like 'nobody cooks like Mum does'.

But whether the trend is likely to spread depends on economic factors, i.e. cost of bachelor pads, studios, and availability of services where one works and lives. The nurturing of independence away from the family fold remains the norm rather than the exception. This encourages an early maturity that can only stand the young people in good stead when they strike out on their own. Hence the Gap Year between final year A levels and university where young students are encouraged to test the waters of the great wide world.

British parents are less likely than other races to be aghast if their children decide they want to 'bum' around for a bit before getting work. As long as they do not ask for handouts. The British are generally more relaxed about the need to live a useful and productive life and not wasting one minute. It's not so much indulgence as the understanding that young people have to find their own feet and direction. Spending time without actually earning money is not frowned upon as being prodigal. Many middle-class parents actively encourage their grown children to explore life, soak up things if they can, especially travelling, before deciding on a job. There is much less parental pressure in this direction, unlike in more structured societies.

British youths have been accused of being indolent but this is an unfair generalization. The few years of a teenager's life before he embarks on adulthood are often spent in the pursuit of ideals. But whatever decision he makes, deep down, every parent, especially doting mothers, would probably rather their children stay at home as long as they're not married—if there is enough room.

This philosophy applies to most people, rich or poor, but of course the rich can be more indulgent and forgiving of their children who drag their feet about being independent. However, you read of many cases where self-reliant young people carve their own niche in life rather than live off the fat of affluent parents. It's different kinds of society with different attitudes to what constitutes closeness and strong family ties. Close proximity does not always make for unity. The fundamental difference in the British is that they do not subscribe to clinging. Again, it's the self-reliance factor that ultimately sees them through their twilight years.

MARRIAGE

One in three marriages end in divorce in Britain. But cold-blooded statistics do not take into account that many people simply do not bother with the legalities and rituals of a marriage ceremony. They simply live together and raise children. Sociologists say that the institution of marriage in Britain has all but lost its meaning. However one has to see the situation in the contemporary light before passing judgement about moral decay. Given that laws are currently flexible in dealing with entitlements when a relationship breaks down, marriage or no marriage, young people already disenchanted with conventional and religious unions are less likely to bother about rituals and legalities.

In short, what is moral turpitude and decay to some is grist to the mill of life to the British. A young unmarried girl getting pregnant does not necessarily send her family into shock. More often than not, they are supportive and close ranks. There are few hang-ups about sexual infidelity and preaching about the wages of sin. Of primary concern is ultimate happiness, a realistic appraisal of what counts.

If you don't love someone any more, you leave him and you won't be tarnished as a scarlet woman. Wayward children are forgiven time and again until they go over the brink, which is sad, but it is not in the British to mete out hellfire and brimstone for something that might cause a person to be ostracised in another society.

This does not reflect that marriage as such is out of fashion–the white wedding with full trimmings is still a big business for couturiers and caterers—it reflects a rather fatalistic attitude towards life's losing dice. Many simply live together until such time they feel it imperative to make

Increasingly, people refer to each other as 'partners', which immediately infers that the couple have not been through a civil ceremony. Given the traditions under which most Asians have been brought up, this may seem a little startling. But the laws here advocate partners have similar rights as married couples, if they can prove their relationship.

it legal. Others would hastily call it quits when a few cracks appear in their union, arguably giving up too easily rather than salvaging the marriage, and dusting off the broken pieces in order to go through the whole routine again perhaps with another partner.

So another marriage bites the dust but fewer and fewer people go into hysterics about divorce. Even with children in the middle of the trauma, husbands and wives revert to single status without too much dragged-out agony. For many, the sensible attitude of remaining friends rather than bitter foes provides some balm for the children caught in between. In a strange way, this very fatalistic stance makes life easier for divorced couples to remain amicable.

It's by no means an across-the-board situation; conservative people in smaller towns probably suffer less stress because of less distraction and strain on their marriage. For a woman who is content to stay at home and child-mind while her husband brings home the bacon, there is less reason for discord or chafing at chauvinism. For a dynamic couple in a big city, career demands often mean putting off having children, little time together and a general absence of quiet weekends. The bonds of marriage can get threadbare.

Divorce and Settlements

There is a move to make divorce even easier than it already is. The customary period of a two-year separation as grounds for a decree is likely to be trimmed to one year. As for settlement, under the British law, the divorced woman gets half of all joint assets and the court is more likely to grant child custody to the mother, unless the court can prove she is an unsuitable mother. Maintenance and child support vary depending on the father's circumstances. Even in cases where a couple is not married, the parting of ways is not clear-cut. The court can exercise the power to force the man to settle on paternity grounds, married or not.

Single Parents

Britain has an alarmingly high percentage of single parents, many of whom seem to make a go of it without too much moaning. I personally know several people whose marriages have failed but who are also determined to carry on without breaking apart. One is fiercely determined to prove she can cut it without a husband and has decided to go ahead to bring up her baby who was barely weeks old when he left her. Is she bitter? Angry? A little at first but now simply determined to make the best of her lot.

British parents are generally very supportive of their children, especially gullible daughters barely out of their teens, who get into trouble and become unmarried mothers. While statistics tell a grim story of abandoned babies (by girls as young as 14), many parents give their helpless daughters all the help they can muster without unending censure.

Because Caucasian children tend to be physically precocious at a young age—liberalism and relaxed mores being the major causes—they marry or enter into relationships young. Seventeen or eighteen is very common with financial security not being a problem because of the welfare state. In other words, two young people barely out of their teens play house without the attendant sense of responsibility and find they haven't got the maturity to handle relationships or parenthood. Most single parents are in this age group.

> The Asian Indian community still holds dear their traditional values, even by those born here. Many are happy to have their marriages arranged but there have been increasing numbers of young people committing suicide rather than subject themselves to loveless marriages.

It would not be fair to pass sweeping judgement that the British are morally lax. Urban stress, disenchantment, cynicism and a general sceptical attitude about the till-death-do-us-part vow all lend to the situation. For someone brought up in a traditionally Asian environment, it would seem a shocking state of affairs to read, daily, about relationship breakdowns, a casual attitude towards sexual indiscretions and disregard for marriage formalities.

I Just Called To Say I Love You

But the extended family does exist, though perhaps not in the same way as in the East. Young people are fairly mobile in their pursuit of ambition. Leaving the family home at 18 or whatever age a young person begins to seek his niche in life is not the need for independence per se. The job scene may be depressed in his hometown and the big city beckons with glamorous promise. So the fledgling leaves home, perhaps forever and only keeps in sporadic touch with the parents.

Sadly, many end up in the streets of big cities, especially London, seeking the proverbial pot of gold or simply hoping to get a slice of the action that was missing back home. It is easy to be critical without understanding the situation. I know that friends who see their parents once a year or even less frequently are not any less filial than children living with their parents. Nor do many of the cardboard city dwellers do so by choice. Family closeness is not measured by the yardstick of contact frequency or gestures. Some of the most loving families I have known see each other rarely—sometimes once in several years.

British parents are not inclined to hover over and smother their offspring like those in Oriental societies. Nor do they moan much about infrequent contact when the offspring leave home. I was touched by the obvious closeness of families when they did meet at Christmas and the refreshing lack of nagging from the oldsters. The old 'you don't visit often enough' moan is usually low-key, if at all. Even with feeble parents who find it difficult to cope without help.

The umbilical cord gets severed quite early in life here. Children are thrust out into the world to cope even before they are out of their shorts. Like in boarding school. Whatever argument for or against, a child of eight soon learns self-sufficiency when there are no parents around to gather the loose ends. Of course you get the indulgent parents, especially with kids in day schools and living at home, but relatively few are spoilt rotten, even with wealthy families. Kids of ten are encouraged to earn their pocket money with paper rounds or other odd jobs, even among the affluent.

Nothing Comes Free
In a country where cost of living is relatively high, earning extra pocket money does not come with any stigma. Dog-

walking, baby-sitting (even for your own relatives) and Saturday clean-up jobs are taken up eagerly. Generally, British parents are careful about giving generous allowances to their children.

British males tend to marry young—the average is 22, and even younger for females, around 18. With the problem of immaturity, financial inadequacy and the arrival of children, family units forged on adolescent passion and not much else often break down. Sociologists tend to point at these circumstances when cases of child abuse are reported.

By and large, the typical family unit is one of cosy closeness with father working and mother as a homemaker, or working part-time when there is a granny around. British fathers do not generally display chauvinism, happily tackling division of labour for household and parental chores. The weekly supermarket shopping trip with mum, dad, baby in the pram and clinging toddlers paints a fairly cosy picture. For one thing, domestic help is beyond most people, barring the charlady who comes in to clean once or twice a week. The British working wife today is unlikely to let her husband get away with outright chauvinism like her sister of an earlier decade who was financially dependent on her husband.

Among many families too, there has been a trend to live in houses with the possible extension of a 'granny flat' within the premises, but yet private enough to give the old privacy and dignity. I know one couple who invited me to a champagne evening to celebrate the granting of building permission for their granny flat.

> When I first heard the reference to 'granny flat', I had no idea what it meant. What it is seems the best option to an extended family, something that is lacking in British society. If a couple has an aged parent or parents that they want to accommodate under the same roof, and to preserve the elders' sense of independence and privacy, they convert a part of the house into a self-contained flat. Or apply for planning permission to extend a part of the house.

Marrying for Residential Status

If you're a man from another country marrying a British woman, the Home Office does not automatically grant you residential status, even when you prove the marriage is genuine. Even a shared address and a joint bank account are not sufficient proof. Home Office officers do spot checks on such couples and, if residence is granted, it could be for a provisional period of one year. By and large, the Home Office is very discretionary about its decisions and not bound to explain the reason for granting or not granting residence.

Even for a foreign woman marrying a British man, residence is still not a breeze. The same rules apply, but they are more relaxed. There has been a racket going on for years where a foreign man marries a British woman purely for residential status. Many women make a real business out of charging for such arrangements, and the press has reported many cases where a woman contracted multiple marriages, each time for thousands of pounds.

RETIREMENT

The official retirement age for men is 65 and 60 for women—though recent claims of sexual discrimination may change this difference. Both sexes receive a 'freedom pass' when they reach 60 and this entitles the holder to travel free all over Greater London on the tube, bus and train. All over 60s do not pay for medication and are also entitled to special discounts for train travel all over Britain. Among the socially conscious tradesmen, there are schemes whereby OAPs (old age pensioners from the age of 65) get certain discounts. Like dry-cleaning every Wednesday at half price or the cinema every Tuesday.

The old and infirm living in homes and in trust estates when they have families seems to reflect a certain callousness. This is not necessarily so. In many cases, the old people are fiercely independent and prefer to be on their own, especially if they are couples. In some cases, the married children simply cannot accommodate them. Often young people move away from their hometown by force of circumstances and their parents cannot or will not follow them.

Look through your local directories (there's *Yellow Pages* and *Thomson's directory* that list among many things, sheltered housing places.) Shop around if you are looking for such a place and make a visit to determine the quality of service and standard of accommodation. They vary widely.

The older generation is fiercely independent and does not cling to the children for support. Many AOPs (old age pensioners) live alone and see their children and grandchildren only a few times a year.

Many of these 'sheltered housing' apartment blocks are run privately and can cost upwards of £ 1500 a month per home for the elderly who can afford it.

Don't forget too that most British work until they are in their sixties, or even seventies, so leaving their home and work place is out of the question. Working grandparents is now more of a norm than an exception—among most of the working classes which constitute some 90 per cent of the population. Even the landed gentry have to work to keep up their lifestyles and maintain their inherited premises, albeit in a different way. Running a stately home as a living is as much hard work as any other job.

PETS
Cats

The British have long been a nation of dog lovers. Cats come a close second. However the feline tide has caught on and cat ownership now represents some £ 450 million a year on cat food. Even the business of feline private business rakes in some £ 40 million a year! More than being a flavour of the month or even a fluffy Christmas present that too often got dumped when recipients went off them, cats are now pets of the moment.

Statistical forecasts have it that if every one of Britain's six million cats visits the vet once a year, vets would be £ 60 million richer. Feline analysts have a theory for this trend. Yuppie professionals have made them a sort of lifestyle pet—more suited to their urban stomping ground. All you need is a cat-flap, a litter tray and you can sail blithely out of your flat without worrying about mess. You can't do this with a dog for it is not in its nature to respect the difference between a plush carpet and a mound of earth.

Feline owners will go to any length to pamper their cats. Diamante studded collars and cat toys are also million pound businesses. And if your tom is suffering from neuroses, refusing the designer cat food you put before him, why, there are many numbers of behavioural consultants to get to the root of the problem. Would you believe Perturbed Urban Stress Syndrome—PUSS?

Cats don't need to be taken for walks—a daily chore busy people have little time for. Every tom with alley cat instincts will simply vanish through his flap for his prowls and return home when satiated. Often days later.

In many a typical British suburban home, the sight of an extremely fat cat stretched out on top of the TV set, or wherever it chooses, is a cosy picture. Besotted cat owners will forgive their cats anything–even when their precious rugs are clawed to shreds.

Dogs

Much as the urban professional may love dogs, it doesn't suit his lifestyle to have one—even a small breed. Dogs are more the old age pensioners' devoted companions because they have all the time in the world for endless walks, and are able to pander to the messy nature of a weaning dog. There are about six million assorted dogs in Britain. Many have transformed the lives of blind people, acting as guide dogs—especially the golden retriever breed.

Dogs are used in old people's homes to comfort the elderly, are therapeutic to the sick, and scientific tests have shown that simply patting a dog can reduce stress. Cats don't take kindly to being bundled in a designer tartan torso cover—they'd rip it in seconds—and are too aloof to provide the misty-eyed devotion which a dog can lavish on its owner.

Nonetheless it seems shocking to see an old age pensioner stinge on her diet to feed her dog—biscuits and milk for mistress and chopped liver and canned food for Fido. A rather misplaced priority you think, but the companionship a dog can give to its owner far outweighs the human need for more than basic sustenance.

A Dog's Feast

A friend once related to me the strange lifestyle of her old age pensioner neighbour. She was some 80 years old and devoted to her equally mature little Yorkie Terrier. As my friend shared a common kitchen with the old lady, she was privy to her eating habits. Every few weeks her garbage bin would be put out and for every empty fish finger pack, there were half a dozen 'Pedigree Chum' cans. In short, she subsisted on meagre meals so that her dog could dine well on chicken, rabbit and beef.

Not too shocking a state of affairs when you consider a dog can often make the difference between a purpose in life or slow insanity. The great disparity between animal and human diets is initially astonishing. But with many old people living alone, a pet, be it a mangy cat, flea-bitten dog, goldfish or budgerigar can provide comforting companionship and a lifeline. Many old people utterly alone slide into senile dementia much faster when faced with nothing more than four walls and fading memories. Also a barking dog can provide a sense of security when there are unwelcome visitors.

Even mongrels are not left out in the cold when it comes to dog pampering. In response to the annual dog show *Crufts*, which is a national showcase for pedigree dogs, some people have organised an alternative for the un-pedigreed—*Scruffs*. The organisation, while serious in its intent to give mongrels some media mileage, has come up with rather jokey classifications. They range from 'Dog Most Like Its Owner' to 'Lamp Post Specialist'! No doubt the haughty French poodles and Afghan hounds will look down their doggie noses at such displays.

Pet insurance is big business in Britain as vet treatment and surgery for animal ailments can be expensive. It is a high profile business with almost daily advertisements on television offering many schemes for insuring against illness for your tabby and fido. For something like £ 15 a month, you are ensured that should your pet break a paw or get roughed up in a fight, your pet policy will cover most of the hospitalisation costs.

About Keeping Pets

What you must never do is to let your dog foul sidewalks. It will bring the wrath of the neighbours on your head, not to mention a likely fine. Take it for a walk in a park or any

Dog Lovers

Here are a few reasons why a dog is indispensable in alleviating a few shocks:

- When out walking in a park in the company of a dog, you feel that much safer. At home, every dog, no matter how small, is an effective burglar deterrent.
- Guide dogs, hearing dogs and dogs for the disabled have all been lifelines to the handicapped in Britain.
- Meeting a fellow dog owner is one of the best ways to make friends. Canine introductions will invariably bring a smile to a British at the end of his dog lead, no matter how dour he is.

patch of grass not used as public thoroughfare. If your dog is at all skittish about strangers, make sure it's on a lead. Most dogs in Britain are used to humans and unlikely to be snappy. In housing estates where houses have open front gardens, make sure your dog does not foul others' property if you let it loose for a run.

Vets are not expensive here and regular visits will ensure your pet keeps in good tick. Most supermarkets have a pet product counter, as prominently displayed as human consumer items. It is NOT advisable to keep a dog in a flat—not even a little one—unless you have the time to take it out twice a day. A yapping dog in an empty house is not only a nuisance to the neighbours, it also draws attention to burglars who are professional enough to know whether your dog is a mere titch or a great fearsome hound.

Expect to spend in the region of £ 15 a week for animal upkeep, including medical attention, grooming and other necessities. Unless you absolutely have no liking for animals, keeping a dog or cat in Britain is more than affluent indulgence for all the reasons mentioned below.

- A dog is good for children, giving them a sense of responsibility. It also provides great companionship, especially if you live in an area where it is difficult to meet other kids.
- Pet shops abound, should you want to own an animal that is generally in good health. And no license is required any longer.
- If you are less fussy about the lineage of an animal, give a home to an abandoned cat or dog of which there are thousands in animal homes. While most British are animal loving people, there are many who treat pets with callousness when they outlive their use. Or when the novelty wears off.

INSTITUTIONS

Not, as you might think, great edifices of academe but reference to the dyed-in-the-wool things that reflect the very soul of Britishness. Without the need for a single word or protracted prose, these give the British their sense of identity and uniqueness. Some have been embraced by commercialism and traded in for profit, perhaps all to the good, and often thrust upon the world as 'touristy collectibles'. The pragmatic will say it can only mean immortality but others deplore the consumer-orientated fate of their beloved icons. Many of these have been miniaturized into tourist kitsch.

Just what these are, a foreigner may not know immediately but will begin to understand in time why some things never change in this country. For many conservatives, these are the very things that give them the emotional security in a world that seems bent on spinning itself into the frightening sphere of mass production and homogeneous multiplicity.

Burberry Raincoat

As British as Big Ben and for which hordes of Japanese tourists gladly fork out hundreds of pounds. What set out to be a practical wet weather garment has now been elevated to the hall of fame, not quite in the same way as the kimono is to the Japanese, but nearly there. In a style that has remained unchanged for decades, beige with check interfacing, wearing one reflects not mere fashion but the epitome of Britishness. By a stroke of economic necessity, Burberry's has been sold to a Japanese conglomerate.

Wellington Boots

Who would think a pair of humble black, or the more upmarket green rubber boots for tramping around the garden would become an institution? Yet, they are, for a few pounds, as British as can be. Named after the Duke of Wellington, Wellies, as they are called, are essential to the true Briton to venture into his garden in slushy weather. The Duke would turn in his grave to see the many versions of his Wellie—from porcelain vases to moneyboxes.

Paddington Bear
A cuddly toy, nay, much more for it always wears a classic duffle coat that is the uniform cover for millions of British school kids. A character much loved by young and old.

Earl Grey Tea
Not just any tea, Earl Grey marks a gentleman and reflects an elegant tradition. Earl Grey tea in fine bone china—who needs coffee?

London Taxis
These deceivingly lumberous black cabs, though typical of London, have come to be an internationally recognised symbol of Britain for their stolid dependability and comfort.

Tartan
Really Scottish of bold checks, each design is the symbol of this clan or that. Tartan pure wool scarves, skirts and kilts have remained untouched by the flights of fashion for centuries.

Oxford Brogues
Stout shoes of the English country squire genre that no true Brit would be without.

Travel in comfort in the London taxi; spacious, it gives you a lot of leg room and allows you to bring big pieces of luggage on board.

Tweed

This spawned the 'tweedy set': conservative and countrified. It is usually worn by people of refinement. A true classic in any wardrobe, it has remained untouched by the changing trends of fashion.

The Ritz Hotel

In London's Piccadilly, it spawned the very epitome of style–hence the word 'ritzy', meaning everything classy.

Wedgwood

Which visitor has not succumbed to buying something of Josiah Wedgwood's? The classic blue or green alabaster china in myriad forms of ornamental or functional use is so distinctive you cannot miss them.

Fish and Chips

No longer wrapped in newspaper, and more often in brown paper, fish and chips are still the lifeblood of hungry Britons seeking cheap, familiar and beloved sustenance. As a general rule, the further north you travel, the better they are.

The Great British Invention: with a liberal sprinkling of vinegar, fish and chip wrapped in newspaper makes a delicious meal for thousands of people.

Sausages

Fat, pork or beef sausages are the very soul of a British breakfast, cooked and served a million times across the country each day. They are also called bangers, as in Bangers and Mash—sausages and mashed potatoes, a British salt of the earth meal.

Roast Beef and Yorkshire Pudding

If English (the Scottish and Welsh set much less store on this national dish) cuisine has a representative, this is it. If you cannot make a decent roast beef and Yorkshire pudding, you might as well not be English.

FITTING IN

'Say "top of the morning guv" and be warmed to the bosom of the street trader. Or counter with "I say old chap" when hit in the face by an upper crust toff's rolled brolly. The class divide still exists, but only just, among brolly-carrying gents.'
—Terry's journal, August 1984

CLASS CONSCIOUSNESS

Firstly, despite current egalitarian mores, some of British society still set much store by the class system either out of insipient snobbery, mind-set or sycophancy—you name it. The truth is the notion of classes, whatever its merits, is politically incorrect in terms of reference. One can think of oneself as upper class (royalty, inherited titles, dubious lordships), middle-class (Rolex-toting, Mercedes-driving) or working class (salary men and women and everyone else struggling to pay off their mortgage). This historical and social pigeonholing is antiquated and is only whispered among serial traditionalists. Anyone flouting it in a self-serving way is likely to be slammed by the media.

Whether the upper and middle-classes, generally better educated, are better mannered is debatable. You are likely to encounter totally different types of manners as a foreigner first thrust amongst British mores. Whether asking someone for directions, dealing with service staff or simply passing the time of day with a fellow train passenger can be fascinating insights into the spectrum of British manners. A working class chap will answer almost dismissively, "don't know, mate" when asked for directions. And likely as not, with a cheery smile and an accent reflective of his roots, be it northern, cockney or Welsh.

On the one hand, there are the working classes who believe in a backslapping bonhomie that precludes the need

to mind one's Ps and Qs. And still come across as warm, friendly people. On the other, the posh middle classes who breathe refinement could imbue politeness with a cold superciliousness.

You see this contrast all the time in Britain. The great divide between a ruddy-cheeked innkeeper in the country and the forbidding, sullen mien of a concierge in a posh hotel can be a chasm. This is class by inclination, not birth right. Perhaps they act from the basis of their trade's requirements. Manners are usually the result of upbringing and education. And intrinsic good breeding that cannot be taught.

Which is not to say which set of manners is right or wrong. Just different. You might find the rough and ready manners of the street stallholder more enchanting than the upper class ooze of mellifluous diction. Your bed and breakfast landlady can be all charm in her barking admonitions to her staff. Yet, a housekeeper at a five-star hotel who says, "Hortense, the linen on the breakfast table this morning left a lot to be desired" could strike fear into the hearts of cowering chambermaids. Both have the same desired effect but it speaks volumes for the difference in tone and possible effects on others.

Neither is it true any more that the well-mannered do not swear or otherwise employ salty language. They just do it with sharper articulation and more linguistic pungency. You hear much the same thing, saltier even, in every pub, bus stop and some television situation comedies or dramas.

Some boisterous members of the upper classes seem bent on destroying their patina of refinement with a vengeance. When a titled lady called an airport staff 'a silly cow', it made headlines for days. The insult is traded everyday in the supermarket, the street and homes, and nobody turns a hair. You see, it's not so much what manners are employed but your station in life that dictates how it is perceived. In short, when invited to a home you know to be fairly refined and privileged (by virtue of money, title, etc.) you'd have to watch your language or risk never being asked again.

> When visiting someone for the first time, you take the cue from your host's behaviour. Not to mean you can be rude, but the odd 'silly bugger or cow' in jokey reference is less likely to turn a hair if that is the tone of his language within his family fold.

HOW TO BEHAVE AS A GUEST

When invited to a function, no matter what your host's station in life, you should observe a certain etiquette. It can only reflect well on you. When given tea, do not clank your spoon vigorously. Always pour milk in first, and then add sugar. Sip quietly. And don't hold the cup with the palm of your hand as if cradling it. Hold it by the handle with your thumb and forefinger, with the saucer in your other hand.

Dinner can be a problem if you are unfamiliar with the mode of eating. You can be disarmingly honest and profess to be ignorant, and chances are any clumsiness will be indulged with amusement. Or you can observe what your host is doing and mirror the actions. These days, elaborate table layouts are rather passé except for grand formal functions and there are any number of etiquette books to bone up on.

Expect some time to be spent on pre-dinner drinks and light conversation. It is also a trend for people to have pre-

Having a meal with the family in the kitchen is a most enjoyable experience, particularly if it is in an old country home.

prandial drinks at a pub. This is sensible as it saves the host or hostess the bother of washing up innumerable glasses. It is also an opportunity to be amid a typical British ambience. Don't refuse to go along, even if you don't drink. Nurse an orange juice for an hour if you have to. Weekend social occasions of this kind tend to operate on flexi-time and many a time I had to quell my stomach rumbling because my hosts did not seem to want to make a move about food!

If it's a buffet, wait to be asked by the host before you dig in or when handed a plate. And do not sit on the floor, even if the home is small and there doesn't seem to be enough chairs around. Stand and eat and find a handy counter—fireplace mantel or occasional table—for your drinks. Do not insist on helping with the washing up if the host demurs when you

At a pre-Christmas lunch once, a friend steered all her guests towards the local pub at about 12:00 noon, saying drinks first and then food. Well, we were in the pub until nearly closing time at 3:00 o'clock and my stomach was really growling. She paid no attention to my polite hints. Such is the importance of pre-prandial drinks, food becomes secondary.

offer. Some people are averse to relative strangers in their kitchens.

Unless you're with very good friends, ask before you use the telephone, bathroom, etc. Don't, whatever you do, blunder about opening doors and poking into private quarters. The British are particularly averse to people doing this or asking them the price of artefacts in the home. If asked to be an overnight guest, abide by whatever is laid on for you, even if asked to sleep on a couch. Most people who have overnight guests often have a sofa bed. Come breakfast time, change into proper clothes. It is simply not done to eat in your pajamas unless it's with close friends.

> I was once invited to the home of a former Singaporean now married to an English Lord and committed the faux pas of not asking where the toilet was and simply wandered around looking for it. This is simply not done in Britain. You must politely ask and wait to be shown where it is.

THE LOCAL SOCIAL SCENE

If you've lived here long enough, or made enough effort to make friends among the locals, your social diary can be rewarding. You don't have to be whooping it up at nightclubs or doing the town. Relatively tame outings like sharing a car to drive out to the country, getting together to swap recipes and generally jaw a weekend away–these are the do's that make for easier, faster assimilation into the British mainstream of leisure activity. It is imperative that living among different races and nationalities, you'd want to be a part of their social calendar even if it's something alien to you at first. When asked to join them at a pub, don't demur that you don't drink. It's more than having a drink–it's a national British pastime.

At formal functions, the invitation usually states '7:30 pm for 8', which simply means there is a passage of time that allows people to be late given the distances that are involved with a country as large as Britain. There is the tradition of pre-prandial drinks before dinner.

The trend these days are for corporate functions to be less intimidating and formal. These are usually held in hotel function rooms and the meal structure is almost always

Western style, waiter service. Buffets as such are not a British favourite form of service.

GIFTS
Weddings

There is penchant among the British people to give affectionate names to objects and people. Hence, presents are 'prezzies'; Paul Gascoigne is Gazza; if your name is David or anything beginning with a 'd', you are Del; sandwiches are 'sarnies' etc.

Wedding functions may be simply a reception with finger food and grand dinners such as the Chinese hold them, are rarely held. At weddings, there is almost always a church service and this is when everyone dresses up to the nines, with hats as almost de rigueur. Most people blend church and reception on the same day and preferably at the same location. Wedding gifts are dependent on how close your relationship is with either bride or groom or if you are handed a bridal shower list, meaning the type of gift is suggested to avoid duplication. Getting drunk at weddings is not deemed overly rude but go easy on the champagne anyway.

The Dearly Departed

Funerals are generally sombre affairs with a church service followed by refreshments and a light buffet at either the widow/widower's home or a function room. You offer your condolences, have a light meal and leave. Gifts as such are not a part of commiserations and the best things are wreaths, flowers and condolence cards.

Visiting Someone

Depending on your relationship, a gift is not necessary when you visit someone on a casual basis. If you are getting a dinner, it is customary to bring a bottle of wine or some other comestible but not a gift as such. Good items are fruit baskets, some scented candles or a small basket of flowers. One thing you should never do is call on someone without warning, no matter how close your friendship is. In fact, it is considered intrusive and antisocial to even phone someone after 10:00 pm. The British as a race are not wont to be receptive to unsolicited visits.

NORMS OF BEHAVIOUR
In a Shop
You'll rarely see sales persons hovering around unless it's a small shop. Peruse till you find what you want and then go to the checkout counter. Or ask if what you want is not on view or in a different size not displayed. Most shops have expensive things like leather goods wired to electronic alarms; so if you want to try something on, don't simply pull it off the rack. And you wait to be served, do not jump queues or demand attention from passing staff.

In a Restaurant
Always state your name if you have a reservation and wait to be seated. Never walk in and find your own table—even in the humblest place. Restaurants dislike this as they have their seating plans worked out for reserved places. Don't clank your cutlery for attention. The ratio of waiting staff to customers in Britain is not very high and some waiting is inevitable. They will get to you in time.

Unbecoming behaviour will only cause waiters to either ignore you or to be rude. Don't make repeated orders for different things at different times. They would rather you take your time and give it all to them in one go. It is now illegal for restaurants to put a mandatory tip on the bill though some still do it. The customary amount is 10 per cent of the total and it is at the customer's discretion. If you should refuse to tip, you are within your legal rights but do not make a fuss. Simply say that the service wasn't up to scratch and leave quietly.

At a Pub
As patronage is usually brisk at pubs, often two or three deep on weekends, wait patiently at the bar counter till served. It's not done to barge your way in through other customers or rap the counter for attention. Depending on the bar staff, you might get a rude response.

Communication

Public service offices are notoriously overburdened with enquiries and every call you make is generally held on queue (increasingly automated), sometimes for as long as half an hour before it is answered. Be patient. Ringing off and trying again will put you back at the end of the queue. Don't be impatient when you are put on hold. This is a fairly big country with departmental divisions that handle specific enquiries. Unless you can be specific, your call may be routed a bit before you get to the person you want to speak to. Don't bark at the person at the other end who may not seem to understand your needs. If you explain clearly, you will usually get some help and re-direction.

DYED IN THE WOOL HABITS

The British are, by and large, creatures of rather fixed habits. The following must be viewed in general light and not as a statistical study. It is not possible to pigeonhole individuals and cite specific numbers. Attitudes are changing all the time, but it is my personal observation—and that of many Brits I have met—that this conservatism is more the norm than the exception.

A little old lady will dine on the same day each week, at the same table in the same restaurant of the same dish for years and think it perfectly normal. Psychologists say it's a fear of the unknown, especially for old people who lived through the hardship of the Second World War. The very familiarity of steak and kidney pie every Wednesday serves to calm an old person's fears by its very predictability. Others, even the younger set, are wont to eat three times a week at the same restaurant, more or less at the same time and preferably at the same table and off the same menu! Conservative? Yet he may be eating something quite exotic for an Englishman. Lasagne is exotic for an Englishman, a dyed-in-the-wool chap not given to impulse.

Suggest to an Englishman to do something quite mad like walking down Oxford Street in his pyjamas and he will probably have a fit. Yet, paradoxically, Britain has produced the most idiosyncratic people and the most adventurous; the first to scale Mount Everest, the first to dive under the South Pole or some other derring do. After all, when Great Britain ruled the waves, the British were everywhere from wildest Africa to the jungles of Borneo.

Most old age pensioners live out the rest of their lives in a well-ordered manner because their incomes do not stretch to rash, impulsive spending. Yet, it is not the thought of spending more money than they can afford but doing something out of the ordinary that they baulk at. Every Saturday night at the same pub, drinking the same amount of the same brew seems to be comforting assurance.

People will spend their holidays in the same places at the same time each year—quite often traditional holiday camps like Butlin's or Pontin's where everything is run on the same well-ordered lines. Assembly line activities and food are grist to the Englishman's leisure mill. Recently a retired couple was given a special treat by the hotel they had been staying in for the last 30 years every year at the same time!

Going up a notch or two, the Briton will holiday in the same European country, usually Spain, year in year out. The thought of anything more foreign than that is distinctly unappealing. It also helps to understand why the Spanish authorities bend over backwards to provide the comforting sustenance of typical British food in Majorca, Costa del Sol or wherever the millions of British spend their holidays. The numbers of British who venture further afield are a pin drop compared to the masses who make their annual exodus to well-tried and tested spots.

It took me a while to cotton on to why on certain days; backyards are awash with drying laundry. The routine of a particular day for doing laundry best exemplifies this entrenched sense of regularity. It matters little that it's pouring with rain on that day. Wash day is wash day and not even the foulest of

A typical case in point is the current controversy about fox hunting, an ancient sport that the landed gentry are determined to adhere to. Others are baying for the rights of the poor fox not to be torn to shreds by a pack of hunting dogs. The pro-groups contend the sport (if you can call it this) creates jobs in the country. The protestors say it is downright cruel and the battle rages on, with a possible ban in a year or two but no one will bet on the eventual outcome...

inclement weather can nudge the ritual among many. The clothes simply dry indoors.

To be fair this is only typical of the average family with working husband, housebound wife and small children. There is diffusion when it comes to single people and those living a more peripatetic lifestyle. Even so, some will faithfully drag their dirty laundry on a given day each week to the laundromat.

Manufacturers of household goods, via their advertising agencies, thrive on this predictability and are reticent to change their creative platforms. Perhaps the most visible adherence to unchanging habits is in the royal family's lifestyle. The Queen has not changed her hairstyle since the 1950s and magazines defend that her tiara can only sit on such coiffure. Nor did she change her couturier for decades until her favourite Norman Hartnell died. Then she opted for someone just as traditional, Hardy Amies. As a result, her dress preference still reflects a time two decades past.

Prince Charles was coaxed out of his boring grey suits by his late wife Diana, but he still sticks to his ageless garb. More significant is the fact that he is rarely seen in jeans. Some royals are known to eat to live and will happily dine on smoked salmon every day of the year. Perhaps they are privileged in being able to indulge thus, but it serves to illustrate the British penchant for familiarity and the comfort therein.

In every sphere of life, this slowness and reluctance to adapt to change has been detrimental to the smooth running of public organisations. Changes to the transport system, be it newfangled turnstiles in the Underground or a new colour for telephone boxes, usually meet with some resistance, or even vehement outcry. When British Telecom began switching their traditional red phone boxes for more high-tech yellow, green and gun metal ones, you could have heard the public howl of protest clear across the country. Rich Americans have been known to buy these red phone boxes to be converted into shower stalls!

The argument that history is being compromised for technology—usually regarded as dubious at best and

The traditional red phone box, a symbol of the past.

downright sacrilegious at worst–is spat out with great vehemence. The technocrats are usually unmoved and the authorities invariably go the way of progress. Lobbying for reversal can become quite fierce and for every defender of the high-tech, there are dozens of protestors against unfeeling change.

A sympathetic observer might see it all as a concerted effort to preserve nature's handiwork. But with relevance to progress and development, such outcry often seems out of proportion to the importance of the defended object. Prince Charles has even published a book with critical observation of what architects have done to the British landscape. His description of a high-rise block minces no words. He wants all development to be along the lines of historical buildings and at the moment he isn't thought of too kindly by most forward looking architects. Again, it's the thought of change that both frightens and bewilders him. The argument against him in its most valid form is that he has little knowledge of what it might cost to engage artisans for all those curlicues and sculpture he thinks all buildings should have. But this is simply one example of an entrenched attitude against change that has received media blowout because of who he is. The commoner too is often heard to bemoan that modern houses are nothing more than little boxes. But a box with minarets, turrets, gargoyles or even a modest portico will drive housing prices even higher than they already are. And he would be the first person to object to this if he is in the market for a house.

If you decide to have an impromptu party and invite friends over at short notice, don't expect any sort of turnout. For one thing the British plan things way ahead and chances are your friends would have fixed up their social calendar weeks, if not months, in advance. Even if they are not otherwise occupied, doing social things on impulse is basically against their nature.

> When I moved into my first converted flat within an old Victorian house, I dropped invitation cards through the mailboxes of all four other flats. I did not get one single response. And it wasn't because I was going to serve *mee siam*—the British simply do not respond so quickly to a newcomer in their midst. By the time I moved out after two years, I only got to know the name of my immediate neighbour on the same floor. And he never got to taste my *mee siam*.

It's inexplicable but that's the way most British are—something I had to get used to after frustrating attempts to coral people at last minute's notice. This explains why many things have remained the same for hundreds of years. It took me months before I could find a stove wide enough to accommodate a Chinese wok and a pot at the same time. Then again it was Italian.

POLITICAL ISSUES
Racism

Britain must rank as one of the most aware nations of the insidiousness of real or imagined racism, and the British authorities are extremely sensitive to the needs of the ethnic minorities. When an issue, be it racism or any of the dozens of sensitivities that are never far from ethnic social fabric, is whipped up on the flimsiest premise, bureaucrats freak out. This happens often and can reach ridiculous heights. The most recent issue was over a baby's photograph in his passport. It showed him naked from waist up and the Muslims deemed it offensive. This is PC gone mad surely.

In schools, offices and other organisations where ethnic minorities work among the majority of whites, this sensitivity is never far from the surface. Until about 15 years ago, relatively few Chinese worked outside the catering industry. Today, you are very likely to see Chinese postmen, bus drivers, bank tellers—in fact in any field of endeavour that they were never involved in less than two decade ago. The fact is instances of anti-Chinese feeling are so rare they almost do not exist and the community is rarely involved in any racial brouhaha. They are generally regarded with respect for their diligence. A century ago, when the first Chinese arrived to work in the docks in the East End of London and in Liverpool, as now, this same diligence won the respect and admiration of the British.

West Indians and Indians from the sub-continent, who make up the two largest ethnic minorities, are more liable to bear the brunt of racism and bigotry, however isolated. West Indians, especially because of initial cultural differences of the first arrivals, and a historical justification for being uptight, having arrived on British shores as indentured labour, suffer more ignominy.

The seeds of racism need but little pellets of fuel to spread. So the vicious circle spreads. It seems incredulous that such colourful entertainment as *The Black and White Minstrel Show*—the mainstay of early vaudeville both in America and here—was axed in the seventies amid cries of insensitivity. No matter how politically correct an incident, product or entertainment element is, there will always be one or a few voices raised

To be fair, given the penchant among Britain's tabloid press for sensationalism, the most inconsequential story gets over played and goes on to stir national feelings. Reports of young children fighting become the cause celebre for anti-racism sentiment. There's nothing quite as normal as a seven-year-old bashing the head of a six-year-old with his Bob the Builder lunch box. The fact that one is black and the other white becomes an issue.

The changing face of the British bobby: an Indian policeman.

in protest. On the other side of the coin, bigotry exists among individuals who must not be seen as reflective of a national attitude.

Racism takes strange forms as in one incident related to me by a friend. One of his father's acquaintances refuses to watch any television with blacks in the cast! "I will not have a coloured person in my parlour!" is his incredible stand. This is an isolated but nonetheless, alarming, case of blinkered bigotry. Time and time again, I have reached out first with a genuine interest in British mores and put all superciliousness and chauvinism in the background. Yet, when confronted with such posers as "Do you eat dog?", it is extremely easy to get huffy and drive the wedge in further.

By and large, Britain has a harmonious polyglot society even in the most remote of counties and towns. Witness at least one Chinese takeaway and Indian tandoori restaurant in every other town or village. The Chinese are not as numerous as the Indians with a total population of some 300,000 as opposed to the three million plus of the former.

There are, however, still problems of non-assimilation that was cause for concern back in 1984. The Home Affairs Committee published a report aimed specifically at the Chinese community to try and alleviate the problem. Indians have been in Britain much longer; first from the sub-continent and later, from post-Idi Amin Kenya. They have assimilated much better, given that for most the lingua franca is English, unlike many Chinese, even new arrivals today, who speak little or no English. Today, Indians are fairly spread out in every trade, from professions like dentistry, accountancy to newsagents and retail. In high ethnic density areas like Leicester, Wembley and Stanmore in London, some supermarkets' entire checkout staff are Indians.

While London is not a yardstick by which to judge cultural cohesion, racial harmony in this great maw rubs off well on other communities. A recent threat that members of the Neo Nazis were planning to desecrate sacred Jewish ground (there were a few isolated incidents) resulted in a national stand against all racial prejudice.

Today, aggression and resentment are not only issues involving skin colour. The last two decades have seen an influx of enormous numbers of displaced Afghans, Kosovans, Kurds, Iranians and others from Eastern Europe who could easily blend in with the British as most are of Caucasian types. But there is still anti-feeling about anyone not deemed 'British-born' and Britain's immigration policy is currently under tremendous public criticism for being totally skewed. A recent survey found that of some 25,000 illegal immigrants discovered, only 4,000 were repatriated. All this is a strain on the social services and it is understandable that locals are angry about the drainage of cash and services.

Britain welcomes anyone who has the legal right to live, work or study here. Probably, this welcoming attitude has resulted in many from halfway across the world seeing it as a proverbial pot of gold. Not too long ago, thousands of Chinese came illegally, hidden in containers on ships and there was a terrible tragedy when one container-load was discovered to contain mostly dead people. They had perished from lack of air after an appalling journey.

I know of two women from mainland China who emigrated here some 30 years ago. Their children, born here, speak fluent English down to regional accents. The poor mothers can hardly string together two sentences. One managed to make her nationalisation proclamation and got her papers. The other failed and has made no attempt to cross this linguistic divide and bone up on English. She does not attribute this to her indifference to a fundamental requirement, but that the Home Office is biased! More seriously, her social activities are much curtailed as she cannot read English, especially signs on the Underground and train platforms.

Individual incidents of racial intolerance must be viewed in singular light. It is not easy to quell the anger provoked by racial bigotry, but so is that of any other human misdeed. Vandalism, muggings, robbery are all blights of urban living, not racism, though the accusation is never far from the surface in communities where migrant populations are extensive. One must put these in proper perspective or run the risk of perpetual inward-turning anger that is detrimental to peaceful existence in a foreign country.

By and large what racial prejudice exists does so in the mental pockets of individuals who, for historical or personal reasons, will not condone non-English amongst their midst. But they are in the minority and do not reflect a national attitude.

The Black and White Issue

Every year for the past two decades or so, London's Notting Hill Carnival, Europe's biggest street festival, a sort of mini Rio, focuses attention on Britain's considerable Caribbean population. Come late August, this area explodes in a frenzy of noise, colour and pulsating rhythms.

The carnival used to be a sparkling festival of music, gorgeous costumes and frenzied camaraderie. In the past several years, it erupted into violence and even death, and when white police went into action to stem the fray, the old problem of harassment surfaced again. Another instance of using the racism tag to drive the wedge in between black and white.

The Carnival Entertainment Committee took no chances and at every carnival now, thousands of policemen are drafted to supervise the three-day event. With the number of people expected to attend numbering some 500,000 a day, anything can—and usually does—happen. It did among a handful of those, probably with too much alcohol and too little common sense, and when the police shut down the festival at 7 o'clock, fury erupted.

Still, leading black figures see the area as a vehicle for black enterprise. The organisers contend that carnivals can be big business—both from catering and spin-offs—and enormous potential for community development. They see it as an economic base obviating the need for local government funding eventually. Sponsorship is welcome but it is a shot in the arm of black pride if the carnival becomes self-sufficient. The objective is to channel the money spent back into the community pot. There are conflicting views of the carnival. On one side, the murmurs accuse it as a 'capitalist sell-out'. On the other, it is seen as a gathering of the arts, an example of public safety, community enterprise and good management. Recent carnivals have been relatively incident-free and the public look forward to this fun-filled and colourful festival that is a brilliant burst of colour and spectacle.

Unlike in the Caribbean where extended families embrace single parents without reprobation, it is not the same case in Britain. A youngster growing up in a disruptive environment is likely to view society with scepticism and some anger. In his book *Behind the Front Lines—Journey Into Afro Britain*, Ferdinand Dennis, who won the 1988 Martin Luther King Memorial prize, concluded one thing: black leaders must demand that their communities take greater responsibility for their own development. Only then will the crisis of all black families in Britain be recognised. Only then will cries of white harassment and other imagined putdowns be seen in their true light of racism fanning.

Violence

Well-meaning though the responsible British media mean to be, their reporting of crime can sometimes paint an uglier-than-the-truth picture of violence. One bomb does not make London or any other city in Britain an explosive site. Fatalism aside, Britain is no more a statistical horror story of criminal carnage than any other country with the same urban sprawls and attendant problems.

The tabloid press, on the other hand, tend to overplay every little eruption, and indulge in sensational headlines that often tell a different story from the meat of the article. This is irresponsible journalism however you cut it and can frighten the public out of their wits. It's easy to be frightened when you read of someone being mugged for £ 3 but the circumstances need to be considered in depth.

Petty thievery exists everywhere where affluence juxtaposes uncomfortably with joblessness. And it's often the carelessness of the public that creates it. Tourists are usually the easiest targets. With camera, bags, shopping and all the jetsam of buying sprees weighing you down, and being less alert than usual after a day's tramping, you might as well wear a sign saying 'Pick me, I'm all yours'. As cautionary notes:

- Never keep your wallet in your back trouser pocket— pickpockets in urban areas are very professional as I found out to my dismay, twice.
- Do not place handbags within easy reach of the person next to you on a train or tube.
- Do not fumble in your bag looking for items in a crowded place, as it is an invitation to bag-snatchers.

There are something like three million jobless in Britain in addition to the thousands of others from the EC and elsewhere with no particular set moral codes about where their incomes come from. The finger of suspicion points only too easily to those most likely to turn to crime. The real reason lies in the lure of millions of visitors to these shores, usually with plenty of cash and valuables practically on public display.

The jobless of course cannot defend themselves because they do not have a strong enough collective voice. In any case, it's easy to tarnish the entire lot for the misdeed of one. They're a handy pincushion for all of society's accusatory pricks. On the whole, petty crime—and this constitutes the major cases—does not simply occur if circumstances are not conducive.

Britain is a country where passionate causes garner tremendous support. But great passion, political, religious or artistic, can be a two-edged sword. There are followers and detractors. Depending on the degree of emotional upheaval, there will be spit and blood. This is what makes the country interesting. Whether you simply observe or get involved, your destiny lies in your own hands. From simply avoiding potential petty thievery to a religious imbroglio, common sense, fatalism and plain luck all play a part. You also have to sharpen your alertness and sense of self-preservation.

Often crime and violent behaviour are the result of frustration. You see a gang of youths 'steaming' down a train from carriage to carriage with time on their hands, perhaps penniless and angry at the whole world. Their criminal bent stops short of actual physical violence because at the heart of their volatile behaviour probably lies a crying need for attention. It may seem like so much psychobabble but keeping this mental stance has helped allay my fears that I might be a victim.

When you see a group of youths looking huddled in a sinister manner, you could be wrong or your imagination could be on overdrive. They could just as well be clean-living people having a social chitchat. I

Reading about bombs in department stores, in parks and through the post, you can get paranoid about even going to a public toilet if you let it worry you. The truth is Britain is not the hotbed of violence it appears to be from all the pulp press stories. Political causes, suicide bombers, personal vendettas and great railway robberies generally do not touch the lives of the masses unless you happen to be in the way.

make this point because of the 'stigma' of being a member of minority, black, displaced etc in this country. In some minds, one black is aggro, two spell trouble and a group you had better avoid. This is an injustice to the community and fuels racism no end.

However, to avoid trouble, there are a few rules to observe when you settle in Britain:

- Avoid getting into an argument with any angry looking youth. He may be looking for a punch bag for his anger at the world. Or your affluence serves to aggravate his deprived situation.
- If you have to travel by tube or train at night, make sure you sit in a carriage with several other people.
- If you have to get off at a lonely station, keep your wits about you and run like hell if accosted.
- Don't flaunt your jewellery no matter how tempted you are to display designer labels.
- Give up your few pounds to avoid being hurt. Unless you're in the position to defend yourself against knives and other lethal weapons, it's more than your life's worth to retaliate. For all your civic-mindedness your principles are no match for a switchblade or gun.

Rape is another matter altogether. There are no easy solutions to this terrible crime. The same rule of thumb must apply. Avoid being in a situation where you are alone with a stranger—respectable though he may appear to be.

British Rail has talked about introducing 'women only' carriages, as many women have to travel alone at night. Whether this will come about or will be an effective deterrent remains to be seen. Again, reading about one rape case does not mean it happens all the time.

Don't follow anyone who accosts you with the promise of a real 'bargain price' leather jacket just around the corner in his car! It could be fatal for he could be a mugger. Nine times out of ten, this sort of conman is simply selling stolen goods. Even so, you run the risk of the goods falling apart in no time.

Last but not least, carry some sort of makeshift weapon like a rolled-up umbrella or a mace spray. At least you can

ward off attack if you're big enough. Otherwise pray that it's only your money the criminal wants. Unless you provoke a fight, you are unlikely to be involved in physical violence of any kind. Of course it happens but only you can help prevent the odds of it happening to a great degree.

Out in the country, crime rate drops sharply because there are few pockets of urban crowding that breed crime. Still you read about women drivers who, because of a car fault, stop at a motorway point only to be assaulted by some sexual or criminal opportunist. The police warning is that, should your car develop problems, do not walk away further than you need to. All motorways have emergency phones dotted at convenient distances throughout Britain. If this is not possible, either flag down passing motorists or wait till daylight or the police to arrive, if the problem crops up at night.

The Best Insurance

The first thing you do in Britain is to insure yourself properly. Everything from your entire household down to your winter coat. Insurance premiums are low in this country where it is huge business and paying around £ 30 a month to cover all your worldly belongings makes for easy sleep. Most banks and building societies will give you complete advice on what is the best package and what coverage you need. For a low monthly outlay you know that, if your roof caves in or an expensive antique is stolen, insurance will cover the cash value, if not the sentimental. The latter can only be protected by adequate burglar alarms which every home should have. It can range from heat-sensing lights to an alarm that will wake up the dead should a trespasser trip it. Whatever system you need, there are plenty of security systems firms listed in your local directory or the *Yellow Pages*.

FASHION

Fashion pundits of the European market sharpen their needles in the constant battle for trend-setting supremacy; the clamorous claims of Milan, Paris or London being THE sartorial capital hyped up by such glossies as *Vogue*, *Cosmopolitan* and the various rag mags. Despite the likes of such stellar designers as Alexander McQueen, Christian Lacroix—French to the tips of his well-manicured fingernails—and enfant terrible Jean Paul Gaultier who gave chic to punk street fashions, English designers defend to the death the far-reaching influences of their designs.

An inadequate overview perhaps, but London—as the undisputed fashion capital, at least of Great Britain—does gobsmack one within a few minutes of strolling down Oxford Street and any suburban high street as multiple chain stores and their smaller cousins stock the very latest, be it outrageous neon-glow pedal pushers or drop-dead chic.

Given justifiable human vanity—the British male of the species having more or less shaken off their staid pinstriped suit and conservative image—the stores and boutiques create somewhat conspicuous spending and a constant dilemma. It takes the most dyed-in-the-wool not to be affected by such elegant offerings, the other dilemma being to spend £ 25 for chain store jeans or its upmarket designer relative for ten times as much. I found the most refreshing aspect of dress codes being a liberal attitude of what is or is not suitable work-wear.

Apart from such serious professions as banking, law and high finance where the sombre suit (the bowler and furled-up umbrella being rather exclusive to an antiquated era), the British pretty much dress as they please. It can be difficult to tell whether a be-jeaned, pony-tailed hunk is an artistic director or businessman as he is likely to be either! Jeans are not a reflection of sloppiness nor a single earring dangling on a male earlobe a glinting hint of decadence. Freedom of expression, in its widest interpretation, is a fundamental right. Unless of course your employer lays down his particular guidelines.

Britain does open the closet doors wide for people who have lived and worked in more restrictive societies where even trousers on women are frowned upon as being too bold. Peculiarly and even paradoxically, certain clubs still cling to this rule much to the angst of British women who shout very loudly about sexism. A few hallowed bastions of

Almost anything goes when it comes to fashion and hairstyles. Individuality and freedom of expression are the guidelines.

exclusive male clubs have given way to women membership with resigned sighs.

Living in a country where daily wear is highly dependent on the vagaries of weather can present a few problems. You can make some awful (and expensive) mistakes in your early months here but will soon learn how to buy shrewdly. Unless you opt to take yourself out of the fashion rat race altogether, putting together a wardrobe to do battle with biting winter winds, stifling summer heat in the underground or unpredictable wet/dry changes can be fun. What is comforting is that chain stores are up to the minute with seasonal wear at affordable prices. After this, it's all a matter of keeping a close ear and eye to daily weather reports.

I used to muffle a chuckle seeing someone swamped in a Chaplinesque great coat several sizes too large. The person inside it had the last laugh when a sudden chilling blast hit me in my ribs covered only by a short, cheap bomber jacket purchased more for its style than function. As for those who

Wardrobe Tips

As a practical guideline, if you are staying over a year, your wardrobe must have the following, whether designer label or budget:

- Winter coat, either in wool or fully-lined with water and wind-resistant fabric. This is one item you should not stinge on if it's going to see you through several years. The latter is more practical as it doubles as rain and cold wear.
- A light spring/summer short coat with plenty of pockets. Not only are they useful for keeping cheque books, wallets and passports, they are warm duffles for your hands when there is a sudden chill.
- A woollen scarf for those parts of the anatomy garments cannot cover, such as your neck, chin

persist in refusing to invest in a winter coat—three borrowed cardigans only single you out as a visitor and therefore clumsy fodder for snatch thieves—they aren't half as effective as a second-hand duffle coat.

There are any number of second-hand shops usually run by charitable organisations such as Oxfam, which has hundreds of outlets throughout Britain, and street stallholders. The temptation (especially if you have spare cash) is to go mad and buy a new coat every year. It will soon dawn on a visitor that most chain stores sell the basic garment year in year out with but the subtlest changes in design features. All this is consumer seduction that costs you in terms of outlay and wardrobe space.

Winter garments used about four months of the year take up a lot of space of which there is a premium in most English homes. The weather being what it is, you really need two sets of clothes—spring/summer and autumn/winter wear. Of course the store and catalogue companies, and increasingly television shopping channels, will hit you with

and ears. Biting winter cold can really hurt those exposed bits.

- A pair of fitting gloves that do not rob your fingers of feeling when you're rummaging for your tube pass or small change. Leather is a good buy as it lasts for ages.
- Comfortable jeans and woollen trousers for the two seasons.
- Good walking shoes and thick socks because cold gets to your feet first.

Outside (or rather inside) these basics, it matters little what you wear next to your skin as there are but a few months in Britain that you can walk about in open-necked shirt and open-toed sandals.

new goods every season and resistance can go weak in the face of glitzed-up selling messages.

Every decade since the post-war years has seen fashion trends taking root across the nation that in turn influenced what you could buy, even if some were so impractical you could not wear. The 1960s perhaps made the most imprint with psychedelic bell-bottoms, mini-skirts, winkle-pickers (pointy-toed, high-heeled shoes for men), back-combed hair and fringed jackets just to name a few. If you are into retro at all and were not around during that period, you'd probably know the 'look' immortalised by Twiggy and Mary Quant, The Beatles and films of the genre. Their influence was global and who did not have a pair of bells that picked up more dirt than compliments?

Forty years on, fashion is pretty much an important priority among most of us though there is a marked absence of that 'total, pulled-together' look. One finds one's own style amid the welter of clothes churned out by the industry with much wider-ranging styles. Since the 1970s, the emphasis has been on individuality rather than prescribed fashion dictates. In short, you rummage among department stores, street stalls and the inner recesses of your wardrobe for your threads. Cast a beady eye on street fashions and the rest depends on your individual panache or whatever you deem suitable for work or play.

The very term 'street fashions' is no mere description per se. In Britain, it dictates the industry to a degree that unwise indifference to it can be disastrous. As a first-time observer, this mode à la public is captivating and bewildering. Are spiky green hair, hob-nailed boots and torn jeans a must for parties? Or are cycling shorts in luminous purple what you wear for a summer picnic? Up the market, do you need a designer dress for an executive meeting or a £ 3,000 bespoke, custom-made suit to impress your interviewer? Then there are the 'street fashions' in as much as they are what you see in great profusion on the thousands of people scurrying to work, catching buses, cycling or simply clack-clacking down the high street in no particular hurry.

Judge not the strange looking chap in leather trousers, ripped T-shirt and half a ton of jewellery as a symbol of indolent youth. He might very well be an off-duty civil servant simply indulging in his own sartorial fantasy away from office constraints of neat shirt, trousers and tie. By the same token, a woman wearing something that appears to be layers of mismatched tablecloths could be a high-powered executive on her way to an acid house nightclub.

One thing I have learnt after 22 years in Britain is to rid myself of self-consciousness about wearing something a little unconventional. It's great for self-confidence because nobody gives a hoot. However, I haven't quite got the nerve to spot a gold stud in my left earlobe, even if Harrison Ford has a diamond one. Never mind that my neighbour's daughter has studs in her earlobe, nose, tongue and eyelids.

In the service industry (hotels and department stores in the main), all staff, if not in uniform, are sharply togged out in suits or dresses. Manager or minion, designation and name tagged, package themselves thus. And they travel by public transport.

As a final analysis, people should not be judged on what they wear because it can be highly erroneous and even offensive. In a sense, fashion forges egalitarianism in Britain because every individual enjoys the freedom to dress as he or she pleases, outside whatever parameters that preclude total freedom set by employers.

By the Buy

Chain stores and their several sales a year are a comfort. Sales in Britain are, praise be, not the token 10 per cent off affair, and if you have a keen eye, you can pick up great buys like a carpet for a fraction of its normal cost.

Sales at clothing stores are particularly chaotic, though, and you should be prepared to jostle and snatch at what you're after with all the elbow power you have. People have been known to queue up in the wee hours of the morning just to pick up a winter coat slashed from £ 300 to £ 30. Alas, such bargains are usually one-offs with a thousand other people casting the same beady eye on that garment.

There is no time for dithering as Britain is awash with professional bargain hunters highly skilled at swooping down and hanging on to a cut-price item even as you are diffidently fingering it. At sales time, queues at checkout counters can last forever and there are many pitfalls to look out for.

Many items are less than perfect and trading practices disallow any exchange for sale goods, so beware of factory faults like odd sleeves and torn linings that, given the cost of labour in Britain, can sometimes set you back more than what you have paid for a new garment in the first place.

The key factor really is what you can afford and whether you need a particular item. And don't think that street stalls and factory outlets offer you cut-prices at no expense to quality. The rag trade is a dog-eat-dog world where saving thread in one garment times several thousand units can make all the difference in retail pricing. And profit. As such, it is not a 'sale' but more a con.

Department store sales are generally above board and are used to get rid of end-of-season lines. Throwaway chic, as the term goes, dictates sales and prices are slashed simply because a large percentage of the mass buying simply would not buy something considered passé. Never mind that the same people swoop down on the same things when the prices are trimmed drastically. If 'FREE' is the most powerful word in advertising, 'CUT PRICE SALE' comes a close second in consumer seduction.

In the past decade, manufacturers with a sharp awareness of consumer habits have made fortunes by producing masses of all kinds of clothing and other accessories, thereby reducing unit prices and putting hitherto expensive things within reach of the budget conscious. A case in point is a nation-wide jewellery chain store that got rid of intimidating shop ambience (it was after all gold and precious stones that they were selling), created bright shop windows without glitz and brought prices down to affordable levels for the masses. In short, the whiz kid businessman got into the head of the consumer and came up with a money-making solution that his predecessors thought beneath them. Trays of gold jewellery, watches and accessories were displayed without the least pretension and people walked in knowing exactly how much they could spend. Also, they were not greeted by the frosty tones of a toffee-nosed salesperson used only to clients making appointments before visiting the store. To cut a long story short, the same chain became a business success story that has rarely been topped.

This concept has pretty much set the trend for clothing retailers as well, and suddenly, it is as chic to buy from them as from a bespoke boutique that probably charges much more because of smaller turnover.

The most visible clothing store chains that specialise in middle-of-the-road prices are Top Shop, Next and Gap (for youngish and trendy fashions), Burton (for suits) and Zara (for women's fashions). You cannot miss them as there is an outlet in virtually every city and town of any size throughout the country, with new ones opening all the time. Then there are the department stores with clothing on high key like Marks & Spencer, John Lewis, D.H. Evans and British Home Stores. John Lewis has a particularly attractive sales pitch under the umbrella catchphrase of 'never knowingly undersold'. In other words, if you can buy a similar item from any other store in the country for less than the John Lewis price tag, they will give you the difference. No doubt professional shoppers thrive on such delicious offering.

Many stores, will exchange goods with no questions asked within a week, should you be unsatisfied with what you bought. Of course you should show your receipt, and the garment's innumerable tags (anti-theft, washing labels, manufacturer's codes, etc.) should not have been removed.

> I have never seen more tags than those on clothes sold in Britain. It gets downright bewildering sometimes to know which ones to snip off and which ones to retain so dry-cleaners know what to do.

As of going to print, middle-of-the-road (for basic wear from chain stores) prices are £ 25 (trousers), £ 15 (shirt), £ 40 (dress), £ 120 (suit), £ 100 (winter coat) and £ 35 (leather shoes). This is a rough guideline as there are too many variables, like where you shop, type of fabric, etc. Rather more 'high class' than high street to use a somewhat antiquated term, are names such as Jaeger (brand as well as store name), Aquascutum, Burberry (their raincoats are practically collector's items) and The Scotch House. They all represent top quality whatever their country of origin or manufacture, even if made in Hong Kong, and prices can be mind-boggling.

A Burberry raincoat with signature checked lining and immaculate finish can set you back £ 1000 or more. The option of a similar-looking one with similar (not on close scrutiny) finish in a department store can cost £ 50 if you are not into the designer tag. Personally, it makes no sense to pay a lot of money for designer this or that when ten million people can be seen sporting the same thing! Throw in the 'Made in Thailand' fakes and you've got a real quandary. Still, you've got the snob who refuses to buy anything unless it has someone's name on it or better yet, it comes from a specific store in Knightsbridge.

Harrods is not just a London store; it has been for long, an institution, a hallmark for quality, style etc. It's a whole image, brimful of undisputed panache or so it seems. I know they sell tat as well but, as a friend says, 'at least it's Harrods tat.' You can't argue with this kind of consumer logic. Even their shopping bags in green plastic are a status symbol. If it so pleases you to fork out £ 45 for a scarf with the Harrods label deftly displayed to full advantage, then enjoy. A high street store one lasts just as long, keeps you just as warm for perhaps less than half the price.

Getting the low-down from my rag trade friends, I discovered that there is still a bias against the 'Made in Hong Kong, Japan, Manila or Singapore' tag. Never mind that cost of labour in Britain has driven just about every manufacturer to seek stitching skills from the East. Although it is required by law to state the country of manufacture, the tag is usually so well hidden that it gets missed among the half dozen or so others. The other ploy is to place the 'Designed in...' tag prominently. If it is a country like Italy or France, chances are the country of manufacture will matter less.

Many British designers have actually set up factories in India, China and the Far East especially for intricate bead and sequin work which craftsmen and women are famous for. And the price tag can be equivalent to a year's wages in Asia! Whatever your tastes in clothing are, Britain is a treasure trove of fashion finds. Trendy, conservative, way out or plain outrageous, there's something for every taste and pocket. I have never seen people appear more comfortable in clothes that make you feel uncomfortable just looking at them!

If you're on a budget, putting together a wardrobe for the changes in temperature requires forethought and a strong will. Everywhere you turn, you are seduced by magnificent window displays that are an art unto themselves. Fashion window display experts are highly skilled in creating an aura that is irresistible. Of course when you actually go into the shop and see racks of the same items, the glamour wears off a little. But you're already halfway there, enticed into the shops as the displays are meant to do. But ultimately, common sense must prevail if you don't want to end up owning something that will not see the light of day because you haven't the nerve to wear it.

Street Creed

Britain has earned the reputation of being the world's trendsetter for fashion in the broadest sense. British inventiveness is matchless, even if marketing falls short of American go-getting. Nowhere is originality, ingenuity and all the other -ities you can think of, more visible than on the streets in London and only slightly more muted in other cities and towns. The ancient, the quaint, eccentric and plain outrageous all co-exist in wonderful pastiche. Individual right is the sacred cow and cries of repression will explode if one so much as decrees a no-no, be it in dress code or architecture.

Only in the area of historical heritage will people close ranks and oust the kitsch and contemporary misfits. Given the variety of styles hobnobbing on the streets, a first-time visitor is apt to get eyeball fatigue. In a packed train, orange hair, nose studs and black-streaked cheeks cause no more than a cursory glance. As much the British penchant for politeness and minding their own business is the fact that it is not deemed decadent. Outlandish maybe. My neighbour used to spend hours putting war paint on her daughter's face and waxing her hair till it stood up like a foot-high pyramid just so that she could attend a party. It was a startling introduction to a different culture and set of values. Causes, religious sects and other British eccentricities use the streets to draw attention to their public displays and, hopefully, win more people over to their side.

Pop Culture

Whatever the current pop culture, British streets provide the most colourful backdrop for the inevitable spillover. Ever since the 1950s, Britain has exerted the most powerful influence in trend setting, each new cult—usually riding on the backs of teenagers—being greeted with consternation by parents, great glee by the popular press and a little alarm by the authorities.

From the 1950s Teddy Boy era with their drain pipe trousers and natty jackets to the sequined spectacle frames that Elton John sports, street creed (short for credibility) has always reflected the mode and behaviour of these role models. And they strut in their threads as if on mobile parade reflecting the same merchandise in store windows. British youth have always thrived on the personal freedom of sexual fusion. A strapping six-footer may be seen wearing full make-up, ribbons, bells and it seems everything he could lay his hands on from his sister's cosmetics kit. And he won't be looked on as a freak—just an individual with strange taste.

Over the past three decades, the pop bandwagon has taken on and unloaded the lot—drugs, fashion, promiscuity, a spectrum of music from the sublime to the ridiculous—but its manifestation on British streets today is less cohesive. What with the constant need for revivalism, the 1960s strut exists in tandem with 1980s yuppies chic and 21st century mores whatever shape or form they take. Today, anything goes and whatever trend the pop stars like Beyonce, Justin Timberlake, television icons like Sarah-Jessica Parker, Matt LeBlanc and the big screen goddesses like Nicole Kidman and Leonardo di Caprio seem to be endorsing, its fair game for the public to ape.

DIRT

Nothing comes more as an initial shock when arriving in a country than its state of public cleanliness—or rather uncleanliness. Britain suffers the ignominy of being the paradoxical idyllic pastoral backdrop to one of the dirtiest cities in the world. This is London today and this grimy state of affairs does not seem to have changed much in the 22 years I have been here. To be fair, it is one of the most visited places on this planet and this popularity comes with an avalanche of crisp wrappers, coke cans and the endless jetsam of urban life.

Just what has made this city so filthy? The finger of blame is firmly pointed in the direction of the takeaway purveyors, usually of food. Containers by the millions are simply chucked indiscriminately on the streets, on trains and buses and from them. Vandals and graffiti artists add the blighted backdrop to this heap of greasy fast food jetsam. Residents blame visitors and civic-minded visitors blame those who have no such inclination.

But accusations come to naught because little action has been taken until now, when the debris from years of littering has reached epic proportions. Parliament is now preparing to pass a Green Bill that will give ordinary citizens the power to take councils and public bodies to court for despoiling public areas. Anti-litter laws have been around for a long time but are hardly ever implemented. The law is usually too busy with more urgent matters like sniffing out drug merchants and hunting real criminals. Now councils intend to impose a minimum fine of £ 10 on litter louts, and serious offences might have a hefty tag of £ 1000.

> It isn't just litter because litter begets grime which in turn becomes dust. I have seen Japanese men and women walking around London wearing curious nostril covers as protection, no doubt, against the polluted air. They, after all, come from a country that sets complete store by cleanliness, both at home and in the street.

It will come as an alarming sight to see, especially in London, people blatantly littering not only streets but public transport and in full view of dozens of other people. Few have the nerve to say anything because the litterbug is often abusive when taken to task. Some even become violent. As a rule, if you see an individual hurling a beer can across a tube carriage, let an alarm bell ring in your head that he could be deliberately calling attention to his bravado. It could be dangerous to confront him, however diplomatic you may be. It is a different matter if an organisation falls foul of litter laws. You can report this to the proper authority.

Much more really depends on the individual and how he responds to the inculcation of civic-mindedness. Thousands of visitors and migrants to Britain come from countries where public hygiene is either feeble or non-existent. Throwing away a can onto the street is simply an echo of a rural habit.

Garbage collection also plays a part in the accumulation of this filth. In most city centres, this is done every day and in the suburbs, it is more often than not weekly. In theory that is. I have been through as long as three weeks where my garbage remained uncollected and building up putrefying matter and smell. Scavenger dogs and cats complete the job by spreading it around the neighbourhood, but not before leaving the bulk in my driveway.

You simply live with the knowledge that in any given month, your garbage may not be collected more than twice. Even the regulation black garbage bags given to most households by their respective boroughs cannot provide enough insulation against rotting food. As for the city centres, even multiple daily collections cannot keep up with the volume, and uncollected rubbish usually ends up as dogs' dinners spread across pedestrian malls and streets.

In windy weather, litter bags and unwrapped rubbish go their own merry ways fouling up even more than a pack of scavenger dogs can do. Restaurants are the biggest culprits here as their swill can amount to a small lorry load every evening. Even tied up in bags, swill can ferment remarkably fast in summer. Takeaway joints have no jurisdiction over what their customers do with their empty burger boxes but they have given them the ammunition to add to this junk food. Perhaps 'junk food' is an apt name because the junk refers not only to what you put in your stomach but also to what is thrown away.

THE PRACTICALITIES

CHAPTER 5

'Buying a house is like tripping through a minefield
of acronyms. Witness: des res, dg, ch, osp.
Read: Desirable residence, double glazing,
central heating, off street parking.You soon get
the hang of it and learn to say: fmah, nem.
Find me another house, not enough money.'
—Terry's journal, April 1984

FINDING A HOME

Looking for the right accommodation is a veritable minefield of rules and regulations, not to mention that finding a house to suit one's needs perfectly is well nigh on impossible. My personal experience of having to move three times in 15 years was fairly typical. The fundamentals are almost always the same.

First of all, you go to an estate agent, of which there are usually several in any town centre of any town. They are usually well placed and every agent has a large picture window on which are displayed their properties for sale. There will be a picture of every house or flat, the asking price, the basic structure/description like semi, three bedrooms, tow bathrooms, garage, own drive, freehold etc.

Most estate agents will immediately ask you if your property is put up for sale. Most are anxious that you have a confirmed offer/buyer for your present property before you can make an offer for a new one. There is always the spectre of being gazumped—the word meaning a sale does not go through after you have made the offer because of several reasons. Your buyer has let you down. Or someone else with cash has pipped you by offering more than you did for the property you had made an on offer for. It is the most dreaded word in the property market. When all things go smoothly, you will then be asked to contact a solicitor who takes over from here to handle all the paper work.

The sequence in property buying is as follows: (It may all seem very complicated but isn't really. It's all a matter of precise organisation.)

You put your house up for sale, either with sole agency or multiple—the choice is yours.

If you need a loan, you go to a building society who will explain the whole process very clearly; there are dozens of types of loans and can be complicated. You need building insurance and household insurance. Your solicitor or building society will advise you on this.

When an offer is made on your property, the estate agent will then put up a sign outside your home with all the basic details, except the price.

When an offer is made and you accept, the sign will then display 'On Offer' to deter other potential buyers. When all offers are in place, your solicitor will then let you know when there is, what is called, 'an exchange of contracts'.

There will also be other technical needs like a survey of the property, a search to determine if there is going to be any development that might affect the value of your property etc. All these things will be looked into by your solicitor who will keep you informed.

When the contracts have been exchanged, it simply means all obstacles and technicalities have been taken care of and all the monies will be paid and cleared.

The last stage will then be the completion, and your solicitor will advise you of the actual day. You would then make all the moving arrangements as you will have to move out by a certain time, and more than likely, move into your new home on the same day.

Keep a file of all the legal documents like survey results, search results etc. Upon completion, you will need to contact all your utility suppliers like electricity, gas and phone and cancel on an appointed date. You will also need to contact the same or new suppliers to install them at your new home. They may or may not require documentary proof of your employment/credit rating etc depending on whether this is your first property or you were an established customer.

When you purchase things like furniture and appliances, they usually take six to eight weeks for delivery. Fully fitted kitchens will take up to several months.

All landed properties are freehold and flats are leasehold, ranging from 35 years to 999 years. In many cases, if you are buying a flat that has been converted within an old mansion or large house, you will be a leaseholder or you can opt to buy out a share of the freehold. All repair costs of such flats are borne by every flat owner whether or not the repair is directly related to your fat. Which means if the roof needs repair, you still have to bear part of the cost, even if your flat is on the ground floor. The same applies to exterior walls, damp proofing etc.

If you are coming to Britain directly from abroad and shipping personal items like furniture, do not make the usual mistakes most people make. That is bring over basic things that you can buy here. I made the silly mistake of shipping over (at considerable cost) things like pine wardrobes (there are thousands of better ones in Britain), dining table (unless it is an antique or of sentimental value), chairs, carpets, rugs, pots and pans etc. When it comes to setting up home, Britain is hard to beat for furniture, appliances—every conceivable thing you would need. It's really pointless to bring things you

A typical suburban home.

can buy easily, unless, as I said, it is irreplaceable. Clothes to bring shoud include:

- Jumpers and at least one good winter coat, preferably of wool or cashmere.
- Good walking shoes or trainers as Britain is a walker's country.
- Summer wear is pretty much what you like but the temperature rarely goes above 30°C, even at the height of summer.
- A good raincoat as British rain is unpredictable.
- Slippers are mainly for indoor wear.

RENTING ACCOMMODATION
Service Flats

It is not advisable to arrive in Britain for any extended stay without making prior arrangements for accommodation. Nor is buying a house sight unseen. So rental makes the most sense for the first few months. Chances are you will not be able to organise this straight away, so it's best to stay in serviced accommodation (unless you have friends who can put you up for a few weeks) until you sort it out. Check if there are agencies in your home country which can do this for you. Generally, in Central London, expect to pay upwards of £ 600 a week for a studio flat depending on the locality. In Greater London (as a rough guide, this is the area outside the Circle Line on the Underground map), you can get a two or three-bedroom flat with basic amenities for cooking and laundry for about £ 200-£ 300 a week.

Houses

These can be quite expensive, especially in Central London and in affluent counties. Some estate agents (there is at least one in virtually every high street of every town in Britain) will have a list of houses for rental if the area you choose to live in has a largish foreign community. You cannot rent council accommodation until you establish residence and, in any case, there is a long waiting list.

If you are renting through an agency—in most cases it is best to leave all the paperwork to them—you are less likely to run into problems with the landlord. Agents will only handle premises that pass muster and provide comfortable and well-oiled facilities. If you rent on your own through local advertisements, landlords can be elusive creatures and when utility services break down, you could wait a while before they get fixed. Saving a little money by renting thus (agents' fees are added to your weekly rent) could cause more headaches than you bargained for. Many houses in Britain are old and problems arise with cold weather. Rising damp, frozen pipes, condensation and chilling draughts are just a few likely gremlins.

A house usually comes with a garden and the maintenance required to keep it from becoming a grubby patch. Unless you want to undertake this yourself, make sure that it is mentioned in the contract that it is the landlord's responsibility. Few landlords want to do this for obvious reasons. It is invasion of your privacy and not a logistical exercise. If you haven't done gardening before, a trip to a garden centre will soon set you on the right path and you'll discover the joys of this most British pursuit.

A garden requires care and maintenance. But nothing beats the joy of plucking the sun-ripened fruit from the tree or shrub.

What the landlord should undertake is the maintenance of your central heating system and other utilities, should they go on the blink. Leave no area uncovered: who supplies cleaning materials, electric bulbs, extra heaters, laundry of drapes and other non-personal haberdashery items. Once a contract is signed, a landlord cannot evict you on any grounds before the period of stay expires. What is important is a harmonious agreement whereby your landlord is accessible and amiable about certain grey areas.

> Few landlords will rent you a house on a month-to-month basis. The minimum contract is for six months, usually a year. After this, you may opt for a month-to-month. The norm for payment is one month deposit (for repair bills) and two months in advance. The sacrosanct rule is once you are a tenant, the landlord has no right of entry without your permission.

For example, if you cause a breakdown of your washing machine, who pays for the repairs? In most cases, professional landlords will have adequate long-term maintenance contracts for such equipment. Apply this to all electrical appliances to make sure each is covered by an extended warranty. You will only have to phone the service engineers. Also, does your bill cover the cost of utilities? If so, up to how much? Telephone bills are always the responsibility of the tenant.

Rents for houses vary greatly depending on the locality. A three-bedroom cottage in Wales may cost a mere £ 150 a week and a small two-bedroom terrace in Central London £ 1000. You decide on your budget and narrow down the choice within the area you want.

Flats

These are less expensive (again depending on location) but basic rental guidelines still apply. For instance a posh two-bedroom flat in London's Mayfair could cost up to £ 800 a week. What you get is the privilege of living among the affluent classes, perhaps a porter and 24-hour security. Or a bed-sit in Scotland for £ 100 a week where you share a common toilet and tiny kitchen.

In the suburbs, flats are much less expensive if they are basic. There are not that many high rises in Britain outside the cities as the British are generally averse to apartment living.

Increasingly, developers are building low rise apartment blocks with two and three-bedroom flats but these can go for anything from £ 300 a week to £ 1000.

If you do find a flat that suits your needs, go through it with a fine tooth comb. Are the electrics sound? Is there double glazing, central heating, well-lagged boiler and immersion heater? The latter is a backup hot water system should your central heating go on the blink.

Unlike in a house where you are buffered against noisy or difficult neighbours, flat-living comes with some problems that are best avoided. Check who or what your neighbours are like, not just next door, but below and above you. Transport, banking, school and other facilities must be looked into for their proximity if you don't own a car.

Who pays for what is again crucial in the area of repairs, carpets and maintenance.

Decoding the Language

Trying to find accommodation through the classifieds is a protracted exercise in decoding that by the time you make any sense of it, you are too late. Try this: 'Rm, ch, bt entr in des. res. off st pk.' What they really mean: Room, central heating, basement entrance, in desirable residence, off street parking.

Council Tax

In 1993, the Council Tax replaced the community charge levied by each local council. Liability falls on the owner-occupier or tenant of a dwelling which is their sole or main residence. Council tax may be reduced because of personal circumstances and there are discounts in the case of dwellings occupied by less than two adults. The tax relates to the value of each dwelling and there are eight valuation bands ranging from £ 30,000 to £ 424,000. The tax you pay is thus very variable, but on average, expect to pay about £ 150 per month for a three-bedroom semi-detached house.

Whether your contract takes the council tax in as the landlord's responsibility is subject to agreement, but few landlords will agree to this. As for rent, generally flats go for an average of £ 60 per room counting living and dining areas. In other words, a two-bedroom flat with sitting and dining rooms will cost around £ 240 a week. But there are too many variables in a country as diverse as Britain where property prices range so widely. In the depressed areas, you could probably get a whole mansion for the same price as a flat in London—if it is in a fit state to live in. The common nightmare among flat tenants in Britain, especially in the urban areas, is the lack of regular maintenance. When you rent direct from landlords, especially in a large house converted into many small flats, the chances are they are only interested in the revenue and not much else.

Rooms

These are even more difficult to find in any major city with a thriving economy. Most are rented out on a direct first-come first-served basis without agents and you negotiate directly with the landlord. The best kind of room to rent for single people is that in a house where the family lives. Perhaps a child has grown up and now lives away and the family needs

Choosing Your Home

- Many supermarkets and newsagents have a window where people advertise their flats and rooms (rarely houses as estate agents deal with these larger transactions) with a phone number or email. Act quickly as these are taken up very fast.
- Always see the accommodation at first morning light as semi-darkness can hide a multitude of sins like dampness, mould and leaks.
- Ask to check every electricity point or mains and determine how old it is or if it needs repairing.
- Once you have rented a place, the landlord has no right of entry without your permission. Never allow trespassing under any circumstances.

the extra income; or the company of another human being if it's a single aged parent.

The amount of rent again varies, but generally a room cannot be had for less than £ 50 a week inclusive of amenities, but not the phone bill. Most landlords in this situation will ask you to make a note of the numbers you call, and then pay him a lump sum every quarter when the breakdown phone bill arrives. Thank heavens for mobiles!

Renting such a room is more hassle-free and, as long as you pay your rent regularly, you are pretty much left on your own. But check that you do have the run of the house, use of the kitchen or whatever the landlord stipulates. Take nothing for granted—even watching TV in his sitting room. Check first that your agreement covers this.

Most room tenants provide their own cutlery, utensils, etc, unless the landlord has offered you the use of his equipment. The cardinal rule with living in a rented room, as opposed to a flat or house, is abide by the house rules. You may be asked to help out in vacuuming the house once a week, do the laundry or generally upkeep the areas where you have common use.

Are you allowed visitors and to what extent? Who provides such basics as toilet paper, detergents, etc.? No area is too small to cover for it pays in the long run to clarify household expenditure. Ask for a rent book and agree on the amount of deposit (against breakages) and advance. The norm is two weeks' deposit and two weeks' advance.

Last but not least, should you run into major problems, contact your local citizens advisory bureau who can help you sort out legal and other matters of unfair treatment. Your local council office will have the telephone number and address.

STANDARD OF LIVING

Londoners earn more than their counterparts in other British cities, but have to put up with a cost of living 36 per cent higher than the national average. A family of four living in a three-bedroom house spends 40.5 per cent more just to maintain a lifestyle comparable to that of a family in the north. London is at the bottom of the list where quality of life is concerned, with Scotland heading it.

Homelessness

There are no accurate figures of the number of homeless sleeping rough in cities or shelters. The number is believed to run into the thousands, including the many drifters from provincial pockets who are lured by the golden hope of work in the big cities. An estimated 30,000 families still live in council-paid rented accommodation and hostels, swelled by a tide of refugees over the past five years. They form a mixed bag of peoples, mostly displaced peoples or refugees from Africa, Eastern Europe and Asia.

FOR THE KIDS

A large variety of services and activities are available for children. Two good ones worth checking out are:

- **Essex Children's Information Service**
  Tel: (01245) 440-400
  Email: cis@essexcc.gov.uk;
  Website: http://www.childcarelink.gov.uk
  Offers information for parents on looking for childcare with registered child minders, pre-schools, day nurseries, playgroups, working families tax credit, holiday schemes, signposting local early years and childcare services, crèches, breakfast and after school clubs.

- **Home-Start UK Office**
  2 Salisbury Road, Leicester LE1 7QR
  Tel: (0116) 233-9955; fax: (0116) 233-0232
  Email: info@home-start.org.uk
  Website: www.home-start.org.uk
  Home-Start is the leading family support charity in the UK. Home-Start volunteers offer friendship, support and practical help to families with at least one child under five years old. There are many reasons why parents and families go to Home-Start. These reasons include bereavement, children's behavioural problems, disability, relationship difficulties, single parenthood and postnatal depression.

Look out for the publication *Time Out for Children* (£ 9) available in most book shops and newsagents and is a most comprehensive guide. Check out Parentline [tel: (0808) 800 -2222] that gives confidential free advice or Simply Childcare [tel: (020) 7701-6111] for childcare listings. Relevant websites are http://www.parentline plus.org.uk and http://www.kidslovelondon.com

Childcare is expensive and not widely available but there are agencies in London that have several thousands of babysitters, mainly nurses, nannies and infant teachers who charge between £ 6.90–£ 35.20 an hour. Always ask for references. Check out:

- **Childminders**
  6 Nottingham Street, Marylebone, London W1U 5EJ
  Tel: (020) 7935-3000/2049
  Website: http://www.babysitter.co.uk

- **Universal Aunts**
  Tel: (020) 7738-8937 (daytime child minding)
  Tel: (020) 7386-5900 (evening child minding).
  A well-known agency established in 1929 that provides not only child carers but also those who will meet lone children at airports, train stations and boats and also take them sightseeing. Agency fee: £ 15 and rates from £ 8.50 an hour.

Children will also find a lot of fun visiting farms as animals are known to provide therapeutic vibes when you stroke them. Most of these places are well run, clean and feature menageries of goats, sheep, chickens, ducks and other farmyard animals that children will love to commune with. For a complete list of city farms in around London, contact: The British Federation of City Farms [tel: (0117) 923-1800; website: http://www.farmgarden.org.uk].

Maids

Domestic labour in the UK is extremely expensive and live-in maids are practically non-existent. Most part-time domestics like cleaners and child-minders are generally recommended by word of mouth or are advertised in local supermarkets' notice boards and newspapers. You will not find this service in normal employment agencies and your best bet is still to scan the notice boards of supermarkets and newsagents.

Food

As for food, there is much on offer for young children. Belgo is a London-wide chain where children actually eat free if accompanied by parents or adults [website: http://www.belgorestaurant.com]. Also seek out similar child-focus chains like Café Rouge, Café Uno, Nando's Pizza Express, Sticky Fingers and Yo! Sushi.

Theatre

Little Angel Theatre has a world-wide reputation for puppetry and is an important training ground for puppeteers. The tiny proscenium arch stage is the only permanent performance space in Britain for traditional long-stringed marionettes.

14, Dagmar Passage, Islington, London N1 2 DN;
Tel: (020) 7226-1787.
Website: http://www.littleangeltheatre.com
Cost: Tickets average £7 per child

Theme Parks

Chessington World of Adventures features thrilling rides for intrepid stomachs. Brave such as Samurai, Vampire and Rameses' Revenge. Also interactive adventures for the younger set, like Hocus Pocus Hall, an animated mansion teeming with goblins, Carousels, Crazy Cars in Toytown and Professor Burp's Bubble Works.

Leatherhead Road, Chessington, Surrey KT9 2NE;
Tel: (0870) 444-7777
Website: http://www.chessington.com
Opening hours: April–August, 10:00 am–7:00 pm daily.
September and October, days and times vary.
Admission: £ 15–£ 25 and other concession rates.
Train station: Chessington South
By car: M25 or A3 junction 9

Legoland

The place features scaled down Lego versions of Buckingham Palace and the London Eye. Take a trip on Lego Safari and chase Lego Dragons. The beauty of this park is the creativity that the designers have put into the use of the adaptable plastic bricks. Anything is possible, from fantasy castles to space exploration. No white-knuckle rides here but it will leave kids enthralled just the same.

Winkfield Road, Windsor, Berkshire, SL4 4 AY;
Tel: (0870) 504-0404
Website: http://www.legoland.co.uk
Opening hours: April–August, 10:00 am–7:00 pm daily
September and October, days and times vary.
Admission: £ 19–£ 23 and other concession rates.
Train station: Windsor & Eton Riverside, Windsor Central
By car: J3, M3 or J6 off M4, B3022 Windsor-Ascot Road

Thorpe Park

This is as close as you can get to Disneyland in Britain. For stomach churning thrills, try Nemesis Inferno, a high-speed suspended roller coaster, Colossus Loop and the Detonator, a 75 mph drop from 100 ft up. Gentler attractions include Amity Cove, which goes downhill through a mini tidal wave, Neptune's Beach, resident goats, llamas, cows and pigs. Altogether, it makes a fantastic day out for the family.

Staines Road, Chertsey, Surrey KT16 8PN;
Tel: (0870) 444-4466
Website: http://www.thorpepark.co.uk
Opening hours: March–October, days and times vary
Admission: £ 19–£ 26, and other concession rates.
Train station: Staines then the 551 Bus
By car: M25 Junction 11 or 13

EDUCATION

Formal education in England and Wales is administered by Local Education Authorities (LEAs), by Her Majesty's Inspectorate of Education (HMIE) in Scotland and the Education and Training Inspectorate (ETI) in Northern Ireland. Together with the HEFCs (Higher Education Finding Councils), these boards provide adult education suitable for local needs.

The State System

All early years services in England, including pre-school education, now come under the Sure Start banner. Sure Start programmes increase the availability of childcare

SCHOOL AND SKOOL

for all children, improve health, education and emotional development for young people, and support parents in their role by increasing their opportunity to work, train and study. Check out their website at: http://www.surestart.gov.uk.

Pre-school education for children from two to five years old is not compulsory, although free places are available for four-year-olds if so required, and the provision of free education for three-year-olds is increasingly common. In Wales, a free part-time place in a maintained or non-maintained setting is available for each child of three years of age. Northern Ireland has a compulsory school starting age of four.

Primary education begins at five years in England and four in Northern Ireland. In all regions, children generally enter secondary school after 11 years of primary education. In Scotland, the primary school course lasts for seven years and pupils transfer to secondary courses at about the age of 12. Primary schools consist mainly of infant schools for children aged five to seven, junior schools for those aged seven to 11 and combined junior and infant schools for both age groups. Scotland has only primary schools and no infant and junior schools.

Secondary schools are attended by children aged between 11 and 16 and for those who choose to stay on until they are 18. Most secondary schools in England, Wales and Scotland are co-educational. The largest secondary schools have more than 1,500 pupils and the average size of classes is 25.5 pupils.

In England and Wales, the main types of maintained secondary schools are comprehensive schools, whose admission arrangements are without reference to ability or aptitude; and deemed Middle Schools, for children aged between eight and 14 years of age. These then move on to senior comprehensive schools at 12, 13 or 14; and in England only, secondary grammar schools with selective intake, providing an academic course from 11 to 18 years of age.

Independent Schools
These establishments charge fees and are owned and managed under special trusts, with profits being used for

All schools have a uniform, usually in a neutral colour which is quite easy to buy new or even second-hand.

the benefit of the schools concerned. There is a wide variety of provisions, from kindergartens to large day schools and boarding schools, and from experimental schools to traditional institutions. A number of independent schools have been instituted by religious and ethnic minorities. There are a total of 2,300 independent schools in Britain, educating over 630,000 pupils, or seven per cent of the total school age population.

The Independent Schools Council (ISC) founded in 1974 acts on behalf of seven independent schools' associations and there are 1,279 schools in membership of the ISC, mostly being privately owned and termed 'public schools'.

Preparatory (Prep) Schools are so called because they prepare pupils for the Common Entrance Examination to senior independent schools. Most independent schools follow the same examination system in England, Wales and Northern Ireland.

Boarding Schools

Boarding is a choice dictated by several reasons. You may want to enrol your child in a particular school at all costs but it's too far away for day attendance. Generally, those British parents who send their children to boarding schools want their offspring to become independent, learn self-sufficiency and other spartan values that are considered to be good for character development. It is also expensive, with some top boarding places charging up to £ 20,000 a year.

All in all, boarding schools can be prohibitive with investment not always justifying quality of education. There have been a few stories of how some boarders actually suffer emotional trauma from being forced into early independence and others resorting to drugs or getting thrown out. Conversely, boarding schools have also been excellent for others. There are two sides to the coin and all a matter of making the right choices and praying that your child will not succumb to bad influences.

Special Education

Where possible, children with special needs are educated in ordinary schools, if their parents so wish. LEAs in England and Wales and Library Boards in Northern Ireland are required to identify and secure provision for the needs of children with learning difficulties, to involve the parents in any decision and draw up a formal statement of the child's special needs and how they intend to meet them.

The National Curriculum

The National Curriculum was introduced in primary and secondary schools between 1989 and 1996 for the period of compulsory schooling from the age of five to 16, mandatory in all maintained schools. Revised in 1995, 1996 and lastly in August 1999, it was introduced in September 2000. Education policies in Britain in the past were fairly flexible. Most schools could set their own curriculum, time tables and methodology, albeit under supervision of one of the 104 Local Education Authorities (LEAs).

The Foundation Stage was also introduced in 2000 for children aged 3–5 setting the six areas of learning:
- Personal, social and emotional development
- Communication
- Mathematical development
- Knowledge and understanding of the world

- Physical development
- Creative development

The Statutory Subjects

The statutory subjects at key stage 1 (5–11 years) are English, Mathematics and Science (core subjects), Information and Communication Technology, History, Geography, Music, Design and Technology, Art and Design and Physical Education. At key stage 3 (11–14 years) a modern foreign language is introduced. At key stage 4 (14–16 years), pupils are required to continue studying the core subjects, Physical Education, Design and Technology and Information and Communication Technology.

The Education Act of 2002 extended the national curriculum to include this Foundation Stage and established a single national assessment system called the Foundation Stage Profile. Religious education must be taught across all key stages.

The introduction of a modern foreign language as an entitlement was seen as a positive step away from hidebound and often whimsical decisions by school heads to teach or not to teach a foreign language. Until now, French has been dominant. Yet, six out of 10 end up knowing only the most rudimentary French. Most drop French at 13 or 14 years of age. English is so widely spoken in other countries that there has been little compunction to learn even the rudiments of a foreign language. Many British, though, harbour more than a little envy of people who speak more than one language.

It is expected that European languages will dominate. Then again, it could be Russian, Urdu, Gujerati or any one of the Asian languages spoken by Britain's ethnic groups. What is significant is the British Government's decision not to take part in the European 'Lingua' programme. This would have required all member states to offer two EC languages in their schools. For the moment, most British baulk at having to study even one!

Qualifications

In 1988, a single system of examination, the General Certificate of Secondary Education (GCSE), which is usually taken after five years of secondary education was introduced.

This continues to be the main method of assessing performance of pupils at age 16 in all national curriculum subjects. In 2002, eight GCSEs in vocational subjects were introduced, based on an eight-point scale of A to G:

- Art and design
- Applied Business
- Engineering
- Health and Social Care
- Applied ICT
- Leisure and Tourism
- Manufacturing
- Applied Science

Primary school students from now will have to grapple with the mechanics of high tech. Parents fear their children will be highly stressed from all this. What happened to Nature Study? All that healthy rambling among flora and fauna should be preserved. For the moment it's too premature to assess how this will affect students in the long term. But the previous systems obviously had too many flaws and many British children who learnt their 3Rs under the comprehensive system could not even spell simple words. It has been a standing joke among the British themselves. Regional dialects only compounded the confusion among younger children who were taught to pronounce a word one way in school only to hear it in a totally strange guise at home.

Choice of Schools

What concerns you if you have school-going children is more immediate. Which school? State or private, fee-paying or not? Are there other ethnic children? Will he or she adapt? When we arrived, our son was 11 and at the most crucial stage of his education. We asked all these questions, checked with dozens of schools and the education authorities.

At the end of the day, there was one major consideration that tended to overrule the others. The school's proximity to home. Of course you could do it the other way by finding a school first and then deciding to buy or rent accommodation. Except that your choice of home is equally important and sublimating it to choice of school could be a disservice to your whole family. Once you have decided, it is a simple matter of enrolling with the school before the start of each school year in September. Obviously, the earlier you register the better chances you have of securing a place.

The other problem was the option of private schools—paradoxically called 'public' in Britain—that offered quality education. There are thousands of schools in Britain, both state and public. There are bad public schools just as there are good state schools. But a fee-paying public school has the autonomy to structure its education policies with a much freer hand. Most are well-funded and facilities are less likely to be stretched as in state schools.

By the same token of numbers and facilities, state school students can expect a more raucous time in most extra curricular activities. A foreign student in a big school with a small ethnic population may feel a greater sense of isolation. How he mingles, makes friends and establishes himself is largely dependent upon himself. Of course there will be the odd bully, bigot or nuisance element. There is no ready answer to this problem. Only personal grit and determination not to be intimidated.

My son's primary public school (called a prep school) only had ten or 11 pupils in a class. Compare this with some 30–40 in a state primary school, naturally there is more individual attention. What is fundamental is that parents want the best for their children, within the boundaries of their financial capabilities, and assiduous checking will help you determine which school you like best.

The student population in many schools is also a worry. Up to a thousand is common in a comprehensive compared with several hundred, or much less, in a fee-paying school. If you decide to send your children to a public school, be prepared for fees anywhere between £ 700 and £ 2,500 per term, for day school, and about twice this for boarding.

Qualifications

The GCSE differs from its predecessors in that there are syllabuses based on national criteria covering course objectives, content and assessment methods; differentiated assessment (i.e. different papers or questions for different ranges of ability) and grade-related criteria. All GCSE syllabuses, assessments and grading procedures are monitored by the Qualifications and Curriculum Authority to ensure that they conform to the national criteria.

Students are increasingly encouraged to continue their education post-16 and for those who do so, there are General Certificate of Education (GCE) and Vocational Certificate of Education (VCE), Advanced (A-level). The new Advanced subsidiary (AS) level qualification represents the first half of a full A-Level qualification. The new A-level qualification consists of six units (three AS units and three A2 units). Students who go on to complete the full A level will be assessed on their attainment in all six units, which may be taken either in stages or at the end of the course.

General National Vocational Qualifications (GNVQ) requires candidates to be more systematically tested; at present, the advanced GNVQ certificate is comparable with the A-level certificate to some extent. Key skills qualification involve instruction in communication skills and the application of number and information technology.

The Top Ten State Schools at GCSE

- Brooke Weston City Technology College:
  Corby, Northamptonshire
- Thomas Telford School: Telford
- Emmanuel City Technology College: Gateshead
- The Cooper's Company and Coborn School:
  Upminster, Havering
- Millais School: Horsham, West Sussex
- Lady Margaret School: London, Hammersmith and Fulham
- The London Oratory School: London Hammersmith
  and Fulham
- The King's School: Peterborough
- Old Swinford Hospital: Stourbridge, Dudley
- The Hertfordshire and Essex High School: Bishop's
  Stortford, Hertfordshire

The Top Ten State Schools at A level

- Colchester Royal Grammar: Colchester, Essex
- King Edward VI Camp Hill School for boys: Birmingham
- Chelmsford County High for girls: Chelmsford, Essex
- King Edward VI Grammar School: Chelmsford, Essex
- Lancaster Royal Grammar School: Lancaster, Lancashire
- Colyton Grammar School: Colyton, Devon
- Colchester County High School for girls: Colchester, Essex
- King Edward VI Handsworth School: Birmingham
- Pate's Grammar School: Cheltenham, Gloucestershire
- King Edward VI Camp Hill School for girls: Birmingham

The Top Universities in Britain

- Cambridge
- York
- Imperial College, London
- Oxford
- London School of Economics (LSE)
- University College, London
- Nottingham
- Durham
- School of Oriental and African Studies, London
- Warwick

The Top Universities for Research

- Cambridge
- Oxford
- LSE
- Warwick
- Imperial College, London
- University College, London
- Edinburgh
- Lancaster
- UMIST

Security and Safety

With Britain's seasons, and increasingly erratic weather because of global warming, journeys to and from school can be fraught with dangers from the elements as well as criminal intent, especially for younger children. Not all schools, state or public, can provide transport and even then, pickup points are not always convenient.

The fundamental has to be parental care in accompanying younger children, even for a short distance. In winter, when it gets dark by as early as 3:00 pm, this is particularly important. Snow, ice, blizzards and fog are all potential dangers, and proper clothing is important. It is best, if you can, to find out if other children living nearby are going the same way. Arrange for them to keep each other company for there is no better deterrent to evil intent than groups.

Where dangers lie in the school itself, possibly from bad hats and bullies, the only recourse is to switch schools or make effective reports to the school head. Unfortunately, if you send a child to a school with hundreds of pupils, this can be a tricky problem. The problems in this quarter would have been more or less eliminated during your choice of school. The most important is to talk to the school head, ask to be shown around and look at everything before you decide. Talk to friends who have children in those schools and ask the children themselves about the school conditions, whether they encounter racism, prejudice, etc.

> Make sure the journey between home and tube or bus stop is safe i.e. does not pass through dark alleyways or other areas where a child might be mugged or otherwise interfered with by trouble makers. Check out the school students if you can by spending some time observing them from a distance.

Racism in Schools

Even the most innocent of childish ribbing can be misconstrued as racism. Of course it can happen in any institution where there is a mix of nationalities. It is not an easy problem to eradicate, only that parents should not overreact to complaints of such schoolboy jibing. You can only hope that your children's schoolmates have been brought up with values that proscribe prejudice against colour, race and creed. If there are racist taunts directed at your children because of rubbed-off values from unenlightened parents or individual bigotry, the best way is to speak to the headmaster and determine the seriousness of the problem.

Of late, reverse bigotry has been making front page news. The pernicious 'special needs' doctrine of the 1976 Race Relations Act has turned the minds of many Asian Indian parents. At one school in Birmingham where only 12 of the 600 students are of ethnic Indian origin, an English school-teacher was sacked for not speaking Urdu!

Many of the parents have not learned English despite being in England for more than a dozen years. There has obviously not been the integration necessary for them to assimilate and learn enough English to have useful parent-teacher relationships. The English-speaking Asian parents are vociferous in their objection to such an attitude, but the seeds of the problem have been too deeply sown. They are aghast that many in their community have not learnt even rudimentary English and, worse, actually resist

At school, your child will make friends with children of various races.

learning. Boroughs with high ethnic population have been pushing hard on anti-racist education that often goes over the brink of sensibility. Educationists have hit out at this as intellectual nonsense knowing that some half a million ethnic immigrants, perhaps much more, are functionally illiterate in English. In this light, accusations that Britain is a racist society seem grossly out of step.

In defence of the National Curriculum, it would appear that an overbalance of ethnic language and cultural education threatens to undermine the status of English. They are after all living in an English country. And with something like 150 different languages spoken, such race lobbies can only upset the delicate balance of an educational system. Not to mention the enormous cost if public affairs are to be conducted in different languages. The question of bi-lingual schools has so far not been mentioned by the education authorities, the argument above negating this step.

Whatever form it takes, racism is a sensitive issue and rightly or wrongly, decision makers are naturally chary of taking remedial action. One good point made was that many ethnic children are already saturated in their own culture 18 out of 24 hours. What is the rationale of urging their school to celebrate such culture when they are there essentially to be educated in English and ultimately to become British citizens in the fullest sense?

My feeling is there is enormous goodwill and tolerance in this country, blighted occasionally by the outbursts of racial bigots who see themselves as victims, fuelled by race lobbies. In this sense, the Chinese are different in that they spend almost all their time working hard and making their fortunes. Hardly any of them are involved in race lobbies and they prefer to steer clear of any racial arguments. It is also significant that many second and third generation Chinese speak perfect English, accents and all, and yet are fully conversant in their native tongues. Even if they are not, their parents are generally not bothered, and if at all, in a resigned way. As for Chinese not being part of the curriculum, their solution has been to organise Mandarin and Cantonese classes through their community associations.

Religious Faiths

There are independent schools for Catholics, Methodists, Quakers and Jews, with many having links with the Church of England.

When to Register Your Child

At least a year or even two in advance, if the school is popular, particularly day schools in London and other cities.

The Headmaster

A good head makes the school just as a poor one can break it. A good head is one who is more concerned about the welfare of his wards than trying to impress you with the handsomeness and history of his school premises.

ENGLISH AS SHE IS SPOKE

The teaching of English is a matter on which many hold strong views. Schools have a clear responsibility to teach Standard English but teachers have a difficult problem. They cannot denigrate non-standard regional dialects which rules out elocution lessons to produce, if not uniformity, at least clear, well-enunciated English. There has been much groundswell feeling for Britain's regional accents, a return to salt-of-the-earth accents and slang that are now a feature of the hitherto sacrosanct BBC. The argument that language is dynamic must stand and what is important is the meaning conveyed, rather than what is the (arguable) norm. In this sense, it's an invaluable education to pick up on regional accents and even hone one's ability to practise them.

If you have the ability to switch from Standard English to whatever ethnic or regional form (e.g. Italian lilt or cockney) without the attendant derisory mockery, then it's a plus. Adapting this facility to a slightly different set of phonetics would seem a breeze.

Learning English in Britain

Coming to Britain to learn English can be fun. But it can also be miserable, lonely and expensive if your English is rudimentary. In the past ten years, many mainland Chinese young people have flocked here to study English but a fair number fall prey to London's seedy attractions and end up on the streets as hookers and drug pushers either because they have become disenchanted with their motherland or are simply young and gullible or have not grasped the basics of the language enough to want to continue to advanced levels..

Probably the best way to learn any language is total immersion—that is, make friends with the locals and take it from there. Living here makes it imperative that you not only need to be sufficiently proficient in the language but to understand the argot, colloquialism and quirky usage. Schools only teach the fundamental, the rest is up to the individual to absorb, apply and ultimately become totally conversant with the semantics of the language.

English language teaching is a huge money-making industry in Britain, especially London, so be aware that there are plenty of shady organisations. Just because it has an official sounding name and is a bona fide college does not mean you will get your money's worth. Go by personal recommendation or check with the official listings published by the organisation listed below. There are literally thousands of English language schools throughout Britain with different facilities, for instance, residential, English for executives, adult vacation courses, junior vacation courses, etc.

Learning English

Contact English UK for any information regarding studying English in Britain

56, Buckingham Gate, London SW1E 6 AG

Tel: (020) 7802-9200

Website: http://www.englishuk.com

MANAGING YOUR MONEY

Probably the most reverberating and with the furthest-reaching effect, right through your pocket, is the shock encountered when converting any currency into sterling.

My constant moan in the early years in England was the unbelievable price of everything, especially after I converted every single penny I spent. If you have a credo to live by anywhere in England, it must be this: don't convert, or go home. Unless it's in your favour.

In your first few months, you are apt to convert every penny you spend, especially on consumer goods and moan about the relative cost of everything. One lesson I learnt was not to insist on having things I used to have in Singapore. Everything imported is a premium product, especially if it has to travel thousands of miles. Imported fruits like Japanese pears, mangoes, mangosteens and even the humble star fruit can cost up to £ 1.50 each! A cup of coffee—this is a nation of tea drinkers and coffee is expensive—in a cafe might set you back £ 1.50 or more.

So you learn to live as the Brits do. Milk, flour, eggs and bread are cheap. So forget your traditional *nasi lemak* breakfast except for the occasional treat and opt for typical English fare which is relatively cheap and easy to throw together. It's all mental assimilation and you'll come to grips with the cost of living here in time. Below are some prices that you can expect in Britain.

Average & Posh

Average prices for familiar things:

Char kway teow (a poor version of) — £ 6.00

Airport to Central London taxi fare — £ 52.00

Ice cream cone — £ 1.50

20 Cigarettes — £ 5.20

Wine — £ 4.00

Bus fares (flat fares) — £ 1.20

Posh nosh and others:

100g Perigord Foie Gras — £ 25

50g Malossol Caviar — £ 45

1800 cc Nissan (brand new) — £ 17,000–£ 22,000

Louis Vuitton suitcase — £ 3,000.00

Personal Allowances

The income level for the 10 per cent tax band is £ 2,020.00, with the 22 per cent now at £ 31,400. The higher rate of tax remains at 40 per cent.

Pension Schemes

The maximum earnings figure is capped at £ 102,000.

Capital Gains Tax

The annual exemption limit is increased to £ 8,200 for individuals and £ 4,100 for trustees from 6 April 2004. The exempt threshold stands at £ 263,000.

Corporation Tax

The full rate for 2004–2005 remains at 30 per cent and 19 per cent for profits between £ 50,001–300,000. There is marginal relief between £ 10,000 and £ 50,000 and between £ 50,001 and £ 300,000.

Child Tax Credit

This remains unchanged at £ 442 given to families who have one or more children under the age of 16 living with them but it will be scaled down where the person claiming it is liable to tax at a higher rate.

Stamp Duty Land Tax

Purchase Price	Rate of tax
£ 60,000	0 per cent
£ 60,001–£ 250,000	1 per cent
£ 250,001–£ 500,000	3 per cent
£ 500,000 or over	4 per cent

For non-residential property, the 0 per cent rate applies to purchases of up to £ 150,000. A 1 per cent rate is payable for transactions of £ 150,001–250,000; thereafter, rates are the same as per residential property.

Opening a Bank Account

This is a simple matter and does not entail much searching as Britain has banks on every high street; high profile ones are Barclays, HSBC, Abbey National, Alliance & Leicester, NatWest (National Westminster) and Lloyds. Chances are there is a branch near where you live or work.

London has as many international and commercial banks as any other major city, and other British cities will have branches of at least Scottish, French, German and other major European banks. Given that you use banks during working hours, it is sensible to open an account where you can get to quickly. More and more banks are now opening on Saturday between 9:30 am and 12:00 noon.

For a current or cheque account, you need a permanent fixed address, which you can prove either with a bill of sale or driving license, and a letter from your employer or another bank which endorses your financial credibility. For a deposit account, you don't need any guarantor or fixed address. Every bank has an information section where leaflets of every type

Opening a Bank Account

There are many types of accounts with varying types of interests and regulations:
- Savings accounts with no lower limit or upper limit.
- Current account—where your income or salary is remitted and if it is more than £ 1000, the interest could be as high as 5 per cent. Otherwise, it is around 0.5 per cent.
- High interest accounts—there are many types and your banker will advise you.
- Investment portfolios—these are mainly medium to long-term speculative types that may or may not yield dividends depending on market factors.

To open a bank account you would need any one of the following:
- Any household bill dating back at least several months.
- Letter from your employer.

Because of increasing scams and frauds, most ATMs are now fitted with security devices. Never draw cash from a machine in a lonely spot, or late at night. Most ATMs levy a maximum of £ 300 per day withdrawal as an additional safety measure.

of banking service are available. Where once cheques were the norm, today's banking is either online or dependent on cheque cards with the minimum of fuss and writing. Virtually every bank has an ATM (automatic telling machine) just outside its premises and as many independent ones in town centres and shopping centres. Most ATMs are free but at time of press, there is debate about charging a nominal fee for every withdrawal. This is likely to provoke much public furore.

Building Societies

The original concept of building societies, as the name fully implies, was to help people buy their own homes. Over the years practically every one has moved even closer to becoming full-fledged banks where you can save, deposit, withdraw—in fact utilise pretty similar services that banks offer. Building societies now not only issue cheque books but also a pass book or cheque card which allow you to pay money into your account or to draw money out. Major societies have branch offices all over Britain and it's a simple matter to withdraw money.

Most also feature ATMS like banks and open normal banking hours, which is from 9:00 am–5:00 pm on weekdays and 9:30 am–12:00 noon on Saturdays for some branches. When it comes to buying a house, you can leave it entirely to your building society to arrange the financing. My building society arranged everything when I bought and sold my first flat and later my present house. When you first approach a building society to arrange a mortgage, you might find some will insist on a minimum residential period of two years before they lend you any money. I went to one leading society recommended by a friend, but they turned me down flat. It wasn't enough that I had a sizable bank draft waiting to be deposited. Their minimum residence period rule was inviolate. I subsequently went to one that I have been using ever since.

There are at least two dozen operating at any one time and so high profile you cannot miss them in every town centre. Shop around and go for one with a good track record or on recommendation. Operate a banking account by all means for day-to-day transactions, but keep your extra pennies in a building society to often earn better interest.

DIY

With cost of labour and non-existent weekend service, the acronym DIY makes for a hardboard jungle few can live without. Quite simply, Do-It-Yourself is far from a weekend activity for hobbyists. It saves you a lot of money, never mind that the shelf you just fixed is less than perfectly horizontal. You can stand back and admire your prowess and be smug about not paying twice as much for a ready-made item even if your home is littered with DIY semi- and total disasters. One knock-together shelving unit I bought even came with a boldly printed instruction to 'first calm yourself and totally absorb the instructions' before fitting tongue to groove.

On weekends, DIY stores all over Britain–and some are the size of a football field–resemble ant-filled colonies with families, young couples and serious-looking hobbyists piling their trolleys with wash basins, paint, wrenches, coils of wire and everything you cannot do without in a home. Like domestic entrails. In the vast hangars of MFI, IKEA, Homebase, Wickes, and others are all you can buy to build a complete home from.

For most, it's a serious and practical matter of putting up fittings, repainting brick work, paving the garden path and the dozen and one things that need fixing in the home. It's almost impossible to get someone to do a one-off job, like wiring for your doorbell. Even if you can, the labour charges would drive you straight to the nearest store.

I once rang for a plumber to fix my washing machine which had clogged up. He came, reached into the underbelly of the machine, pulled out a soggy sock and pronounced my appliance in perfect working order again. It cost me £ 28 call-out fee plus an hour's (or part thereof) labour fee of £ 8. Had I bothered to tinker around I could have done the same

at no cost. It happened a second time and I was wise, and richer by £ 36. At today's rates, a similar repair job will set you back about twice this.

Of course the *Yellow Pages* list any number of emergency services on 24-hour call. In practice, you rarely get anyone after 5:00 pm or on weekends. When your roof leaks after a violent hurricane, it will likely have to stay leaking till the following Monday. And then it might cost you some £ 80 for someone to lay on a bit of bitumen which you can self-help for perhaps one tenth the cost.

Few of us are naturally inclined towards messy plumbing and electrical wiring jobs, but, unless you are flush with cash, DIY is at least a saviour. You learn, with an ever-growing shed of tools, to fix this and that as they wear and tear. One major contributing factor in many homes is the shoddiness of fixtures to begin with. Before homes are put on the market, the vendor will hastily and cheaply get things ship-shape the better to seduce buyers with. More than likely, the owner would have gone out on a DIY binge and your would-be home is a glistening, gleaming and beeswaxes chocolate box—on the surface. Be wary of what you buy for many a thingamajig from DIY places look pretty but are far from durable.

Of course there are quality products but the mass market is generally of a uniform mediocrity. You could go to a bathroom specialist and fork out £ 1000 for a Victorian enamel affair with clawed feet or you could get a PVC one at Homebase for £ 150. The difference being the former comes with professional installation and the latter? Well, DIY. Or at least a moonlighting plumber who, likely as not, will site it so that when you sit down in it, the floorboards creak.

When I got tired of my scruffy garden, I rang a professional garden-landscaper for an appraisal to redesign the unkempt patch. He wanted £ 800 not including cost of materials. All it needed was returfing and raising a few flowerbeds with brick work. When I finally found the courage to DIY, it cost me all of £ 80 including materials. Alright, the turf looks like a mole's battleground and the raised beds are less than perfectly aligned. In time, the hedgerows and ground cover plants will hide the multitude of sins but it was an enormous savings albeit for a garden that will definitely not win a Better Homes competition. It did represent five weekends of back-breaking labour hoisting 25 lb bags of cement and making endless trips to ferry 120 bricks from MFI to car to home to garden.

If you are setting up home, be advised to invest in a set of basic tools to hammer, drill, plane and otherwise batten down carpets and banisters that tend to wrinkle and creak if not done professionally to begin with. An electric power drill is indispensable as most homes have brick walls that resist even unbending masonry nails.

With Britain's varying climate, every home has to withstand the stress that extremes of heat and cold can cause. A door isn't just a door if it's an old one. You need something called a draught

I once needed to paint the outside of my house and called in a few quotes. None was less than £ 300 and one stunned me with a £ 500 tag. I bought a couple of cans of paint, brushes and borrowed a tall step-ladder from a neighbour. I did the job with the help of a friend who didn't suffer from vertigo in four days and at a total cost of £ 50!

excluder, strips of synthetic around the frame to cut out chilly blasts. Even a half an inch crack can chill your front hall within minutes. Sealants around the bath tub often dry up, pop out and water seeps down the side to collect until damp rot sets in. Steam from hot water can do the most dastardly things in your bathroom. That beautiful regency striped washable wallpaper begins to peel if your DIY wasn't up to scratch. Mirrors scum over, lime scales every faucet because much of Britain's water is hard, and carpets need to be steam-cleaned every so often.

It will probably take a few months or even a year before you recover from the shock of frequent domestic fraying. Make DIY a top priority. You won't be sorry, out of pocket or neurotic trying to get service for jobs you can learn to do yourself. I never realised how indolent I was until settling here. I do now because it cost me half a week's wages just to rectify a fault in my washing machine. When your machine stops for no reason, think sock or be socked with an outrageous fee of anything up to £ 30 just for a call-out fee.

Quite apart from the practical and money-saving considerations, DIY is absorbing, fun and therapeutic. You get a bashed thumb or two in the bargain, but as my knock-down shelf instructions read: 'Calm yourself first' and you soon get the hang of it. There are things you never knew you had to do until you see your neighbour doing them. Like applying creosote to your garden picket fence. Creosote? It's a weather-proofing liquid that you coat wood with so it resists rot and all the punishments of weather.

For every household appliance, no matter how humble, from a £ 20 toaster to a £ 300 super espresso machine, make sure you take out a reasonable maintenance packet beyond the normal one year that manufacturers give. Better yet, ask for a five-year package that comes with a discount and costs a fraction of what you might have to pay when something goes wrong.

And DIY is not just buying packs that come together with instructions. It means keeping a close check on wear and tear that does not become blights in a house. Think of the problem when you decide to leave and have to sell it. Surveyors examine every house with a fine tooth comb and, unless it's in 'good nick', you'll find it may take months or even years before you can find a buyer.

In winter, water pipes can freeze solid if they are not properly insulated or 'lagged', or if your central heating system is not maintained properly. This is a professional twice-a-year job but you should check that the heating cycle does not allow circulating water to freeze during a cold snap. It got so cold one year that the fountains in Hyde Park froze in mid-spray!

If at the onset your tool kit is less than efficient, get neighbourly help. Most British homes have basic tools—even little old ladies know how to repair a leaky faucet. It can take a lot of money to shock you out of a state of helplessness. It's money down the drain, but much less if you think DIY.

MEASUREMENTS

Although Britain has been metric for over a decade, and its EC partners all operate on a metric system, the old imperial system is strangely persistent. You will thus notice all supermarket and grocery produce has both metric and imperial quantities—as do all cookery books. While a few modern thinking boroughs begin to implement local footpath notices with distances in kilometres, all road signs are still in miles, as are all published maps. No amount of legislation will prevent the British from drinking a pint of beer or the daily milkman from delivering his pints of milk. Children in school are taught to measure in metric millimetres and centimetres, fabric is sold in metric lengths, but planks and widths of wood remain in feet and inches.

HEALTH

The National Health Service came into being on 5 July 1948 under the National Health Service Act of 1946, covering England and Wales and under separate legislation, Scotland and Northern Ireland. The NHS is now administered by the Secretary of State for Health in England, the National Assembly for Wales, the Scottish Executive and the Secretary of State for Northern Ireland.

The NHS provides comprehensive health services based on the principle that treatment should be provided according to clinical need rather than ability to pay, and should be free at the point of delivery. Everyone under 60 years of age is, however, required to pay a prescription charge.

In April 1996, the District Health Authorities and Family Health Service Authorities merged to form 100 unified Health Authorities (HA's) in England. In April 2002, 28 new health authorities were formed from the existing HA's. These new health authorities were renamed Strategic Health Authorities (SHA's) and charged with creating a strategic framework for managing the performance of Primary Care3 Trusts.

These Primary Care Trusts (PCT's) became operational in April 2000 and in 2002, NHS Regional Offices ceased to function with the role was taken over by these PCT's. In April 2004, a total of 304 PCT's covered all areas of England.

PCT's is the care provided by people you normally see when you first have a health problem. It might be a visit to a doctor or dentist, an optician for an eye test, or just a trip to a pharmacist to buy cough mixture. NHS Walk-in Centres, and the phone line service NHS Direct, are also part of primary care. All of these services are managed for you by your local PCT. Your PCT will work with local authorities and other agencies that provide health and social care locally to make sure that your local community's needs are being met.

PCTs are at the centre of the NHS and will get 75 per cent of the NHS budget. As they are local organisations, they are in the best position to understand the needs of their community, so they can make sure that the organisations providing health and social care services are working effectively. For example, your PCT must make sure there are enough services for people within their area and that these services are accessible. They must also make sure that all other health services are provided, including hospitals, dentists, opticians, mental health services, NHS Walk-In Centres, NHS Direct, patient transport (including Accident & Emergency), population screening, pharmacies and opticians.

They are also responsible for getting health and social care systems working together to the benefit of patients. While the NHS is funded mainly through public taxation, in recent years National Insurance contributions, patient charges and other sources have been used to supplement the costs. For about £ 30 a month, you can buy health insurance that covers treatments not provided by the NHS, such as acupuncture, homeopathy and other alternative cures.

Foundation Trusts

The first ten NHS foundation trusts were established in April 2004 with a further ten established in July of the same year. NHS foundation trusts are NHS hospitals, they are part of the NHS but have their own accountability and governance systems, which function outside of the Department of Health's framework, giving them greater freedom to run their own affairs. (*Refer to the* Resource Guide *on pages 302–304 for details for all SHA's, PCT's and other NHS organisations in England.*)

Like any national welfare system, the NHS has its shortcomings but in terms of the latest advances in medicine, Britain often leads the field. Don't forget this is a country of cradle-to-grave welfare and the strain on resources is usually stretched to the limit.

Hospitals

All NHS hospitals are run and managed by Acute Trusts which make sure that hospitals provide high quality care, spend their money efficiently and also decide on strategy for how the hospital will develop to improve services.

Seeing a Doctor

So much depends on who your doctor is, the area you live in—ratio of doctors to population—and the nature of your illness. Coming from any country where state health services are efficient and private medical treatment relatively inexpensive, Britain's NHS can often seem lacking.

When you first settle in, find a doctor near your home and register every member of the household. Once registered, you generally see the same doctor if he or she is available. Most surgeries have two or more doctors in attendance.

Surgery hours (the common term for clinics' operating hours) are usually between 10:00 am and 12:00 noon, and 5:00 and 6:00 pm, Monday to Friday. Usually the clinic is closed one day every week. Every visit has to be by appointment and doctors don't take kindly to treating minor ailments like coughs and colds. Some clinics now offer a same day appointment if you call between 8:15 and 8:45 am.

Self-medication is the norm for these sniffles, with chemist chains all over the country. The largest nationwide one is Boots with a branch in practically every major town, and hundreds of independent pharmacists scattered throughout the country. You visit a doctor for more severe symptoms or when they persist despite self-medication. Between surgery hours, it's difficult to get a doctor and all you can do is to leave a message on the answering service. Only in an emergency will your doctor see you on weekends.

Many doctors do their rounds in hospitals inbetween their surgery hours and are not at your beck and call. In an extreme emergency, ring the hospital near you, but admittance will

You do not need a doctor's prescription for medicines to treat common ailments such as colds and coughs. The local chemist will advise you on what to take for simple ailments.

depend on the severity of the ailment and how busy they are. Admittance to an NHS hospital is almost always via a doctor's referral. Hospitals are usually busy, so be prepared to wait until a doctor can see you unless you're in very bad shape. Hospitals in the major cities are generally understaffed and bed space is on a priority basis.

All treatment is free under national health and you pay for the prescription if you're over 18. Both treatment and prescription are free for under 16s and up to 18, if you are in full-time study. It is totally free for all over 60. Depending on the prescription, medicines are generally under £ 5.

Clinics do not dispense medicine—all prescriptions have to be taken to the nearest chemist. The system is fairly rigid and you simply have to abide by it. Not all doctors will give you a thorough examination, some just sit and listen to your symptoms and prescribe accordingly. Remember some doctors in heavily populated boroughs may have as many as several thousand patients under their care and they simply do not have the time for protracted individual examination, unless your symptoms demand it.

Don't expect lickety-split service. For instance, I had a check up in October 2004 for mild deafness and was found to be in need of a hearing aid. I was informed that it would take about six months to get my hearing aid. In some cases, you could wait even longer for the sheer number of elderly people with the same problem.

Generally your doctor will listen to your chest and check your blood pressure. You get all of five minutes if you're lucky. This is not painting a dismal picture of the medical services. The majority of patients suffer from ailments that really can be treated with patent medicines from the local chemist. Every chemist has one or several fully qualified pharmacists who will give you all the help you need, short of an examination. You soon realise it's much more convenient to self-medicate, though you may pay marginally more without a prescription, unless you are sure you need antibiotics, which are only available by prescription.

The biggest problem with the National Health Service is surgery. Unless it's a dire emergency, you may have to wait months, even years, to have a minor surgery done. Like removing tonsils. This is compounded by a shortage of government doctors. The reasons are two-fold. Salaries are low and hours are long. You often read stories of housemen in NHS hospitals doing straight 90-hour shifts with scarcely any break.

Others may choose to go into private practice, which earns them much more money, and they work more regular hours. As for house calls during off surgery hours, at night and on weekends under national health, you may as well forget it. Unless you're old, infirm and have had a bad accident, and your doctor is concerned enough to see you straightaway. Otherwise calling for an ambulance is the best option.

Private medicine is very expensive and not necessarily more efficient. It all depends on your relationship with your family doctor, whether he takes calls or is permanently unavailable after hours.

Health Insurance

There are all kinds of private medical insurance policies you can buy if you should worry about urgent treatment for chronic ailments like heart problems and old age symptoms. Many today also cover alternative treatments like acupuncture, reflexology and other traditional medical practices. Shop around and choose the policy that suits your needs and pocket.

Hospital visiting hours are generally flexible, but the ratio of staff to patients is chronically imbalanced. British hospitals do not pamper patients, and nurses, also chronically overworked, can get stroppy if you are excessively demanding. But once under hospital care, you get proper medical treatment.

Depending on the hospital, there is often a walk-in service provided for such as blood tests. Check with your local hospital to see if they offer this and if they do, it is very convenient as you do not need to make appointments. Simply walk in but expect to wait for anything up to an hour to be seen.

The pharmaceutical business in Britain is a huge enterprise because most people self-medicate and avoid seeing the doctor unless it is absolutely necessary. More often than not, dragging yourself out of bed to make an appointment and then having to wait interminably can make you more ill. Send someone out to the chemist giving the pharmacist your symptoms and you generally get better without all the hassle.

Getting an appointment to see a specialist is another long-winded affair. Most specialists will not make a telephone appointment. They need a letter from your GP and then it may take weeks before they can slot you in. In a country where you are likely to live a few miles from the nearest doctor, clinic or hospital, keeping a medicine chest of basic drugs is the most sensible remedial action. You could die of frustration just getting an appointment. If you think you have something contagious, don't just march into your doctor's clinic without telephoning. Many doctors use their own home as their clinic and may have children around.

Dental Treatment

There are an estimated 18,000 dentists in England that provide NHS dental services and also have private patients. They are responsible to the Primary Care Trusts in whose areas they provide services. Patients pay 80 per cent of the cost and since April 2003, the maximum charge for any treatment is £ 372. The following qualify for free treatment: people under 18, full-time students, pregnant women, women who have had a child in the last 12 months, people on income support, fully disabled people on tax credit by up to £ 70 and people named on a HC2 Certificate issued by the Health Benefits Division. A booklet on HC2 is available from all main post offices and local social security offices. For a list of family dental clinics, telephone: (016) 4232-0000.

Dental treatment is basically the same as medical treatment, but less of a hassle as dental surgeons do not have as many patients as GPs. Students also qualify for braces should they need them.

Opticians

National Health covers only for under 18s and even then with a limited range of frames which are all pretty awful and uniformly unattractive. Private prescriptions for glasses are expensive and an average pair costs upwards of £ 50—and as much as £ 300 for designer frames. Shop around as the choice of frames is cosmetic anyway.

Illnesses

Hay Fever

This is a peculiar problem that hits millions every year on the onset of summer. It is caused by the level of pollen in the air and, when you get it badly, your eyes itch and stream and you feel flu-ish for weeks. Like the common cold, it defies medication although there are patent anti-hay fever treatments available at most chemists. Weather reports in summer give pollen counts everyday so that you know how to at least avoid coming into contact with it by staying indoors.

Winter Chills

Adapting to the cold is one of the most common complaints among foreigners from warmer climates. With the first blast of wintry wind, your resistance to colds is lowered considerably and even a little draught from under the door can cause sniffles. There are dozens of cold cures available but it depends on the severity. Massive doses of vitamin C are the best prevention I find.

Cold Rashes

The first time I had these I thought I had shingles. You get uncontrollable itches all over as the skin becomes very dry due to the cold and the best cure is to soak in a hot bath with some medicated bath salts.

Arthritis

Peculiar to cold climates, this is a debilitating disease that often cripples people badly. It generally affects people in their 60s but is not uncommon among younger people. Treatment is difficult and often ineffective. Improper heating in the home compounds this.

TRANSPORTATION
Cars

Unlike living in sprawling suburbs of big countries like Australia or America where public transport does not provide a comprehensive network, living in Britain does not really necessitate owning a car. It is a great pleasure, though, to be able to drive out into the country every weekend at a moment's notice. Car prices are generally affordable.

A decent 1600 cc car, brand new, will set you back about £ 12,000. The prices go right down for second-hand ones, depending on how old. Because of strict regulations, most second-hand cars have to be good condition and save you a walloping amount in capital loss when you decide to sell.

You could even get a 1000 cc, four or five-year-old car for as little as £ 1000, but the cost of overhauling it could be prohibitive. Many tourists buy such a jalopy, drive all over Europe for several months and abandon it in the knowledge that they've had their money's worth!

Most people buy on instalment and pay over one, two or three years. It's not the cost of a car, but maintenance that gets expensive. Normal service after your first free one, if it's a new car, costs an average of £ 125. Comprehensive

Unless you work in the centre of London, driving is a pleasure in Britain. Cars are not too expensive and the road network is very comprehensive.

insurance works out between £ 250 per year to anything up to £ 3,000 depending on your age. The younger a driver is, the higher the insurance. Road tax is another £ 150 or so. Petrol is getting more expensive by the minute and hovers around £1 per litre.

A full tank for about £ 30 can get you from London to Cambridge and back with some to spare. Compare this with train tickets for five people at £ 20 return and you realise the economy of a car. Every time you renew your road tax, your car has to pass the roadworthy Ministry of Transport (MOT) test. It could be six months or a year, depending on when you renew and for how long.

If your car is roadworthy, the other essential is your spare tyre. It could be miles between stations and having a flat in the middle of nowhere, at night, without a spare is a nightmare. The cardinal rule in Britain is to check all systems and tools before setting out on a long trip. Motorway signs tell you what services are available and how far away; so keep a sharp lookout. In inclement weather, your heater and windscreen wipers must be in mint condition or it could spell trouble.

Accidents

Depending on the severity, always pull up on the hard shoulder, and either telephone for help if you can or flag down passing motorists. DON'T simply stop in mid-traffic to argue it out with the car you are involved with. Simply take each other's details and make a report.

Car Washing

Don't think that washing your car is a cinch. During all but the warmest months, your fingers could get frostbite from the cold water. Far better to spend £ 2.50 in a car wash once every few weeks or when your car gets dirty. It is quite important to keep your car clean during snowy weather, when local boroughs put grit on the roads to prevent skidding and to melt snow. This can, with time, start to corrode car bodywork. You don't have the problem of excessive heat here but getting into a car in winter can be just as painful. If you happen to have a garage, it makes all the difference in

In Your Car

As a checklist, the following should always be in your boot all year round:
- Warm blanket
- Battery water
- Anti-freeze
- De-icing spray or scraper
- Jump-start lead (hope to hail a passing car)
- Basic first-aid box
- Torchlight
- A good road map of the country
- Small change for public phones
- Driving license (always carry this with you)
- Your AA membership card and telephone key. AA emergency phones are dotted along most motorways. The RAC (Royal Automobile Club) is another motoring service club with much the same facilities.

the wintry mornings without the half-hour ritual of warming up both engine and interior. Most petrol kiosks and motoring shops sell woolly seat covers for extra warmth and it's worth getting a set if your original is basic upholstery.

Anti-Theft

Last but not least, invest in an anti-theft alarm. Like in any urbanised country, car thieves are always looking out for careless owners.

Coaches

One of the cheapest and most common forms of travel in Britain is also one of the slowest. There are hundreds of coach companies that do day and overnight trips for minimal cost. Many have full facilities like toilets, video and even hostess service for long hauls. Check with the local British Tourist Association (BTA) office for addresses or look through the *Yellow Pages*. Coaches often get you to places that trains don't and are ideal for long trips if you don't drive.

Buses

Perhaps more than any other symbol of Britishness, the red double-decker bus has come to represent the nation in the most unlikely forms. Together with the phone box, bobby's helmet, the Union Jack and pillar-box, this trundling vehicle has been metamorphosed and shrunk into china saving boxes, chocolate cartons, table mats and dozens of other Britannia collectibles.

The cheapest form of travel, if not the fastest, the British bus has been subjected to many changes in the past decade. First there were cheery conductors (clippies) who knew passengers by their first names and went out of the way to help the old and feeble. Many have been phased out and replaced by one-man-operated vehicles where the driver collects the fares at the door. Not all the public are happy with this system and there are several

Britain is probably the best country for fielding user-friendly buses. People in wheelchairs, Zimmer frames or are simply feeble will find that almost every bus has ramp facilities and special-needs corners to park prams, wheelchairs etc.

Buses are cheap and easy to take, although they are not very punctual.
London's red double-decker is one of the symbols of Britain.

reasons. There is an inevitable delay at every stop and the driver could be brusque and indifferent to the needs of old people who have trouble getting on and off.

Routes are constantly changing because of much motorway and flyover construction which confuses the majority of elderly passengers. Weekend services are frequently disrupted or stopped altogether with industrial disputes over pay and working hours. Many old people who only leave their homes on Sundays to go to church find this a great disappointment. In London, many bus services are now privatised and whether this is an improvement on state-run ones is debatable.

Where it counts, the British bus system provides an essential service in areas where there are no trains, few taxis and (in Greater London) where the tube does not reach. Fares start at around £ 1 for short journeys, and in provincial districts, it is even cheaper.

When you see a 'Request Stop' sign, it means exactly this. Put your hand out, otherwise the bus might pass you by. Most services run at 15-minute intervals though the timetable is often not adhered to. Night buses are a boon in cities where tubes and trains stop running after midnight. A check with the local transport office will tell you what these are.

Road Signs

Sign-posting, if not always succinct to the visitor, is nonetheless clear and easy to follow. By far the most speedy means of getting anywhere in Britain by car are the motorways, marked with the prefix letter M. The M1 is a major motorway, the A1 a secondary road—in fact, a dual carriageway for almost its entire length, turning into a motorway, called ingeniously A1(M) in stretches—and the B323 a winding rural road. Arm yourself with a good map of Britain, map out your route beforehand and there are virtually no places in the country you cannot get to.

Do observe motorway driving rules. Take the left lane if you are going at a leisurely pace, the middle lane at an average speed of 96 kmph (60 mph) and the right lane for overtaking. Speed limits vary from area to area but motorway limits are 112 kmph (70 mph), though most drivers seem to be clipping ahead at something like 160 kmph (100 mph). As of going to print, Britain has not gone metric on the road.

It's not just flouting the law and being fined heavily, but the dangers in speeding are ever present. In winter and during bad weather, skidding at even 64 kmph (100 mph) can cause horrendous pile-ups and even death. At twice this speed and involving juggernauts, the consequences can be devastating. Such is the human failing that a clear stretch of straight road means an all-out burst of speed. Beware the oil patch ahead before it's too late. Beware too the camera traps as they are all too pervasive.

Services are generally well strung out along most motorways and there will be signs telling how far it is to the next service station. There are as yet no services on the M11. If for any reason you have to pull up on the

Despite the network, holiday time can be horrible on the motorways for even these multi-lane ribbons can be choked with traffic that often creeps to a virtual standstill. Add to this the other elements of inclement weather, irresponsible driving, bottleneck tunnels and half the country going on holiday at the same time, and you get a nightmare picture of urban strangulation by automobile.

side, make sure it's on the 'hard shoulder', a patch designated for such a purpose on the very left hand side. You can only stop for reasons of mechanical breakdown—just having a rest or a quick 'hedge-hop' could land you a hefty fine. Otherwise it can be dangerous with cars whizzing inches past you.

Once off the motorway, roads leading into the towns narrow down; here beware of the one-way systems for which British towns are notorious. You often go round in circles trying to find some place that you can actually see ahead of you. Stop and ask for directions as most locals will untangle you. There is no short cut to learning Britain's road system—it takes regular driving and knowing the shocks to come that you learn to navigate.

Emergency phones can be found along all motorways and they can be operated only by an AA membership key or if you ring the police for help. Never drive for long distances without making sure your car is in good nick, you have a spare tyre, proper tools and an extra blanket or two in cold weather in case of breakdown. It may sound like an evacuation exercise, but better be safe than sorry.

WEATHER

A topic and an unpredictability that never cease to enthral, the British weather is a subject held forth with equal fervour in the most sumptuous of salons and by down-and-outs on their patch of pavement. The British talk about it so much because there is so much to talk about. 'Will it rain?' brings on great discourse about the comparative reliability of raincoats and umbrellas. It is a major query that has direct bearing on the well-being of every individual. Impending rain means a dive into the deeper recesses of your wardrobe for suitable rainwear, boots and whatever else is necessary to battle this wet element. Not being prepared means you're exposed to sudden change in weather that can be irksome when you're somewhere miles from the nearest shelter.

Because warm, dry sunny days are often a rare premium in these isles, the sun's benign smile on the land brings out the best in people. Caught without a trusted 'brolly' when the British rain comes down in continuous, cold, chilly drizzle, even the most sanguine temperament is taxed. People's mood swings are to an extent dependent on the weather, so you are less likely to find a stranger in forthcoming mood if it's damp and dreadful.

Be advised never to leave the house without first checking the weather forecast, especially during the colder months of the year which are generally between October and March. You may end up with pneumonia if you are caught unawares. British weather can be infuriatingly unpredictable, uncomfortable, endlessly grey, glorious and magnificent depending on nature's whims and your own disposition. Yes, there can be pristine beauty in a cold, grey day if you have the soul of an artist, a robust constitution and a positive attitude.

Official dates aside, as they don't mean anything, the four seasons are roughly divided thus, global warming notwithstanding:

- Spring: late March to May
- Summer: June to August/September
- Autumn: September to November
- Winter: December to February

Early spring, despite a beauty that has inspired the greatest poets to extol the splendiferous sight of banks of daffodils nodding their buttery-yellow heads in the sparkling air, can be nippy. Be advised to have a sweater with you, in case a pre-autumn gust cuts through your ribs. It's a time when Britain's splendid flora comes to life, when people take on a joie de vivre which is quite heartening to watch. When the darling buds of May waft their glorious scents and the sky is an incandescent blue, the spirits soar. Daffodils, crocus and tulips herald this season of flowers, but please do not pick any that grow in public places. The temperature hovers anywhere between 12°C–18°C (54°F–64°F).

Summer is hazy, lazy Sunday afternoons; half naked people in the park soaking up what are invariably fleeting rays of the beloved sun. I have never seen people worship the sun so much, to the exclusion of even work. In the heat of a baking summer day, office workers would drag their lunchtime, doff their outer clothes and spread themselves on the grass in a park, on a verge, anywhere that catches the rays of warmth and blithely ignore the passing of time.

> Summer is a time for glorious fruit harvests, for many farms open to the public to pick their own fruit for a pittance. There is nothing quite like picking sun-ripened apples, pears and plums then. Farm owners find it more remunerative to let you pick your own rather than pay workers to do so.

It can get hot, like in 2004, reputed to be the hottest in 70 years. It went up to around 36°C (the high 90s°F) and in some places, even higher. In France, this was the cause of many fatalities among the aged and infirm in hospitals where air-conditioning was inadequate or non-existent. It was a stressful time for all but thank goodness, it lasted only a few weeks.

Summer also means endless crowds because all the schools break for the longest holidays of the year—up to 12 weeks—and every resort, spa, tourist attraction is bursting at the seams. Book your holidays well in advance (six months preferably) to enjoy your break without the hassle of uncertain accommodation.

If you're staying put, this is the time to do battle with the creepy crawlies. Britain is not known to have them in abundance but come a warmer than normal summer, flies, gnats and ants pop up. For most of the year they seem to disappear somewhere. Generally dress lightly, shorts being practical gear when out driving on weekends. This, however, is not a favourite form of wear among the British who would choose lightweight trousers—

only trendy young people will sport them. Remember that it can cool down considerably in the evening.

From April onwards, the days are long and it stays bright until 10 pm in July. Temperatures average 18°C–26°C (64°F–79°F). Summer weather is never predictable, and some years are full of rain, others can be cold. Never travel far without a sweater and either a waterproof raincoat or an umbrella—better to be safe than sorry. In northern Scotland in summer, even when the sun shines, you can feel a chill in the wind, and a thick sweater is essential.

Autumn is a beautiful time if you live in the country. The colours of trees range from tawny gold to russet and glowing auburn, and the late evening sun casts a stunning glow on every blade and leaf. The air is clear, sparkling though chilly, and does not quite have the bite of winter. The shops will have brought out their corduroys and wools by early September and be advised to have a coat with you at all times. Most flowers begin to die then but the rainbow colours are replaced by the autumn hues that inspired such great artists as Constable and Gainsborough to put their magic on canvas. Temperatures begin to dip to as low as 12°C (54°F) and the evenings begin to draw in. If you are lucky enough to have a really good summer, central heating would have been turned off by May and need not come on again till mid-September.

Winter really begins to bite in January, though December can be cold—if not cold enough to have a White Christmas. Much as it is a lovely idyll, this is rare and in 22 years I have had the pleasure of falling snow at Christmas only twice. And then it was briefly, not enough to build snowmen and have snowball fights. The flakes start to come down in January and February, and the sight of one's first snowfall is pure wonder.

Like clouds of cotton wool, the snowflakes make you want to run out and catch them in your hands and look up at this scene of winter wonderland. Until your third winter. When the magic palls a little and you begin to swear at the slush of the first melt, when everything turns to mush. And somehow, even the prettiest swirling snow shower loses its charm! French windows condense with the dripping chill and it can be quite a job mopping up. Extreme cold plays havoc with the machinations of a household—pipes freeze, metal window and door frames stick and the smallest crack lets in icy draughts that congeal the hottest stew in minutes.

If you do not have central heating, make sure every room has an electric or gas heater. Your heating bills will more than double and taking a bath or shower is an exercise in aerobatic dexterity. Emerging from a hot shower, you can get chilled if you don't climb fast enough into a bathrobe. Heated bath rails for towels are a comfort.

Sometimes it seems you can't wear enough layers to keep you warm. The best option is to have a really warm coat instead of wearing multiple layers when outdoors. A cotton or wool vest next to the skin is good insulation. Having to wear coat, scarf, hat and gloves can be cumbersome and it's best to acclimatize quickly by braving the elements in small doses. It took me about a year but by my third winter I could do without a scarf on all but the coldest days.

During your first year you are likely to go mad and buy things like ankle warmers, muffs, chunky sweaters and boots. As your body adjusts you'll find most of these quite unnecessary except as a fashion statement. The thing is to buy a sensible wardrobe that sees you through nine months of the year. You can make expensive mistakes like splashing on a costly leather jacket that is really no better than a sensible wool jacket at half the price.

Before winter sets in, check all your systems. It can be distinctly uncomfortable when your old boiler breaks down in mid-winter and repairmen cannot get to you immediately—like on weekends. It pays to service all heating and

Winter can be a time of great content, drinking hot chocolate by a roaring (gas!) fire and huddling into a thick robe to watch television. Few houses other than those in the country and farms have live fires as solid fuel is hard to come by. Britain's famous fogs in the last century were caused largely by coal fires and laws were passed to outlaw open hearths in all but the most rural of places. The toxic peasouper fogs went by the middle of this century. You still get the occasional fog but nothing like the yellow scourge that spawned so many Sherlock Holmes stories.

insulating systems regularly. Some weather tips you should remember are:

- Always have one or two standby heaters as central hearing systems can break down any time, especially in winter when it is used a lot.
- Never leave home without an umbrella—a brolly as the British call it. The sun may be shining one minute but the rain may also come when you least expect it.
- Always have an extended warranty for heating appliances, the longer the better and cheaper as repairs in Britain can be expensive.

The past several years have seen the usually predictable British climatic four seasons behave erratically. Green issue people blame it on the rape of the ozone layer but whatever the reason, there have been strange turns. One summer stretched into autumn and winter never really took hold. Another winter was so bad it crippled the country and hurricanes and gales, not usually a part of the temperate climate, lashed down with unfamiliar ferocity. The weathermen's consensus is that British weather has become unpredictable and world weather appears to be warming up.

Weather Reports

There are more than enough reasons for the nation to be overly concerned with the weather. And when they are caught unprepared, the weathermen are the ones who get the blame. For example, when the Met office for some inexplicable reason did not or could not predict a hurricane, they met with a people's wrath equal to that of the howling elements.

There are weather reports on radio and TV frequently everyday, usually following the news that give fairly detailed breakdowns of where's dry, wet, sunny, dull, hot or cold, and normal temperatures. Some weather reports also cover European forecasts for the benefit of travellers. This is relevant if you make frequent trips especially by sea or air. Bad weather often means flight cancellations, and sailings, though not as badly affected, can be extremely uncomfortable in squally weather. Newspapers have weather reports on a less detailed basis but are a reliable indication of what to expect.

TELECOMMUNICATIONS

There are many companies offering you phone lines ever since the business was privatised a decade ago. It is getting increasingly sophisticated and such as ADSL (Assymetric Digital Subscriber Line) is technology for transmitting digital information at a high bandwidth on existing phone lines to homes and businesses. It also enables you to access the Internet many times faster than with conventional phone lines. Unfortunately, access to broadband is limited and its introduction to Britain slower than in most other developed countries.

The two main providers are British Telecom (BT) and NTL and even the Post Office has got into the act by offering the same service. There are several independent companies offering cheap rate calls but not the rental services, such as Tele2 that averages 2.5 p per minute for international calls. As for mobile phones, the major players are Vodaphone, T-Mobile, Orange and Hutchison.

Practically every house has phone lines already installed, whether you buy a brand new house or an old one. You only need to phone the provider of your choice to activate services and this takes only a few days. There is no limit to the number of extensions you want, but you have to pay rental for each one.

Phone Etiquette

With reference to mobile being so varied across the world, it is just as well to clarify a few things. In America, they are called cell phones, as in cellular. In Britain and the EU they are simply called mobiles. In colloquial parlance, they are referred to as hand phones. But they all mean one and the same thing.

In cinemas, trains, restaurants and other places that mobile phones may interfere with their working routine, they are not permitted. Trains, for instance, have certain carriages where mobile phones are not allowed. So do clinics, hospitals and places of worship.

THE BRITISH MEAL

'Do you eat 'spotted dick' or treat it with antibiotics?
Or do you sit on 'bubble and squeak' as a jokey toy?
You eat them both as the British have great affection
for bread pudding and sausages and mash—
as the aforementioned are these national dishes.'
—Terry's journal, July 1984

BRITISH FOOD

On the whole, British food, as you would find it in the motorway service stations, pubs, cafes and chain restaurants along every high street, runs the gamut between mildly interesting and plain boring. Meat, poultry, fish, peas, carrots and chips are the order of the day unless you have a budget that stretches to more upmarket establishments. Then again, the only difference might be the plate in which your carrots and peas come. Since there are relatively few restaurants offering traditional dyed-in-the-wool British fare—when the British eat out, they prefer continental food—you have to contend with the aforementioned fast fare.

Oriental and continental cuisines have far more to offer in terms of savoury choices and even a fast-food pizza is still more palatable than a dry cold Bacon Lettuce and Tomato (BLT) sandwich. If you are not too picky, there are a number of places in every town, city and usually along the high street that sell one or the other of the American or continental fast food products.

London retains its reputation as one of the world's great gourmet capitals with every conceivable type of cuisine—from Afghan to Russian—and every other kind in between. Points worth noting are

British food, be it Scottish haggis, Welsh rarebit or English stew, is alive and well only if you seek it hard and far afield enough. You will also find the British rather apologetic about their food. It will take you a while to understand that not everyone is passionate about food, the British among the very least. Drink, yes.

the increasing number of establishments that ban smoking, tipping is standard practice (the norm is 10 per cent) and last orders are usually 10:30 pm. Sadly, London is not a late-night place compared to other international cities.

The top supermarket chains in Britain are massive, with hundreds of outlets in every town, city and even village. They are Sainsbury's, Morrisons, Tesco, Marks & Spencer, Asda, Waitrose, Somerfield, Iceland and Safeway. All are generally open seven days a week, most until 10:00 pm and a few for 24 hours from Monday to Saturday. Sunday opening hours are fixed between 10:00 am–4:00 pm according to trading laws.

Supermarkets are also a tasty answer to the lack of ethnic dishes. Most outlets now stock a basic range of Chinese, Indian, continental and some South-east Asian products. The rest is up to your cooking skills and ingenuity. In addition, supermarkets are stocking more and more ready-to-eat dishes, especially Italian, Indian and Chinese, and even a few Thai and Indonesian ones.

Generally, all over Britain, there is a supermarket near where you live that stocks enough basics for anyone to whip up home-cooked fare at a fraction of the cost of eating out. £ 35 will get four people a very basic meal in a restaurant. The same amount buys enough groceries to feed a family of four for three to four days. Also, what used to be esoteric is now commonly available as long as your tastes do not extend to gourmet rarities. Even then, you can find these in the London area—shark's fin, ginseng, caviar that costs as much as a week's wages for one silver-forkful—if you are prepared to pay the price.

The food scene in Britain has seen a tremendous change in the last decade. Mainstream supermarkets which did not even stock tinned pineapple on the premise that they were 'foreign' now even feature as esoterics as galangal, lemon grass, *choy sum* etc. It will be some time yet before you can see durians, mangosteens, rambutans, *belacan* and *cincalok* in Sainsbury and I dream and hope for that day to come soon.

Short-term residents and students will either have limited or no facilities to cook, even if they do have some culinary skills. For flat-sharers, the discovery of a British kitchen is short-lived euphoria. Even if you stay long enough to warrant stocking up on utensils basic to your cooking. Most are poky with just about enough room to swing a cat, or the equipment is so basic that eating out seems a better option. Longer-term residents, less concerned about finding a cheap inner city bedsit, will find that British houses and even large apartments do have large enough kitchens.

Be adventurous and make forays into the local food scene much as even the British themselves admit to a bland, stodgy cuisine. There is good English food, not necessarily of the savoury genre, to be found in some places. Traditional cream tea for instance, with hot scones, home-made jam and thick clotted cream is as British as can be. Enjoy it for its intrinsic worth even if you suspect the jam comes from a supermarket bottle.

No longer can you find carvery chains that used to typify British food. This has largely been replaced by more continental establishments that serve what can only be termed Modern European. But there is still traditional British fare at a price. You'd want to try out places like Fortnum and Mason in Piccadilly, The Savoy Grill in the eponymous hotel in the Strand and many outlets that do decent roasts, salads and Tex-Mex stuff.

With the advent of chain merchandising on the premise of value for money and catering to the conservative masses, the food scene invariably suffers. Throughout the British Isles, you will come upon eateries like Little Chef and the Happy Eater among others, located at just the place when your hunger pains begin to gnaw and there's nothing else for miles around.

With such a captive market, they don't need to apologise for being the antithesis of cordon bleu cookery. But then they are catering for Joe Public who is more used to potatoes and meat. You might have to psyche

In essence, the mainstream British taste is fairly conservative and chain eateries cater to this by and large. Do not expect to see anything more exciting than pasta or chicken tikka masala in a drive-in place along the motorways. Even the airport canteens offer traditional fast food menus with every thought for bottom line profits and none for ethnic taste buds. It's a veritable trail of burgers, pizzas, pasta and sandwiches.

yourself before breaking journey for a meal at one of these places.

Tired salads, dry burgers, microwaved-to-death pastries nonetheless are better than nothing when you're 162 km (100 miles) from the nearest hot dog kiosk. Unless you opt for safe American or Italian fast food. They are much more widespread in the provincial towns than in the big cities which have at least a few ethnic eateries.

The shock comes when you go a little more upmarket to French cuisine. A simple meal of soup, main meat course and a sweet can set you back £ 50 per head or more at a restaurant proper. They cater mainly to local residents who like an occasional night out replete with silver service, supercilious waiters and pricey wines. Curiously, much as the British say they hate the French, dining out Gallic style is very much a social priority. It gives them the chance to show off a nouveau oenophilist knowledge, bury their own meat and two veg for a while and generally soak up the elegance of being treated like sophisticated gourmets. Of course, restaurateurs riding on these pretensions charge a premium for their European culinary refinement. In fact, high profile chefs like Raymond Blanc, Gordon Ramsay and Jamie Oliver are treated like royalty and charge similar regal prices for the privilege of dining at their establishments. And they are usually booked solid for months.

Pub Food

Pub food is good value and easily available. As well as the traditional ploughman's lunch of bread, cheese, cold meat and pickles, many pubs—particularly those in the countryside—offer a range of hot dishes as well as salads and desserts. It is well worth purchasing a guide to good pubs and their food if you are touring the country, as a visit to a pleasant pub, serving well-kept real ale and a hearty meal, can really be a highpoint of your sightseeing. Do be careful not to expect too much at all pubs: traditionally they are drinking places, and many still keep to this role. Others will stop serving lunch at 2:00 pm sharp on Sundays and may not serve any food on Sunday evenings.

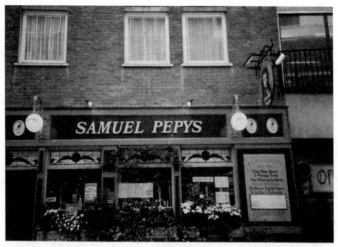

Pubs offer cheap and hearty food, a variety of beers and ales, and a great atmosphere. Literature is not left out either, as shown by this pub sporting the name of famous 18th century diarist Samuel Pepys.

You are allowed to take children into a pub to eat food with the landlord's permission: they should obviously not consume alcohol. Again, up-to-date guides to British pubs will list those which are children-friendly and those where you can be assured of peace from children's screams.

The British Fry Up Breakfast

Were it not for the proliferation of American-style fast food joints, this British tradition would still hold sway among those who relish the fundamental British fry-up (usually breakfast) of sausages, baked beans, eggs, chips, black pudding, tomatoes, bacon, fried bread and toast. Born of the transport workers' need for cheap, hearty fare, and later spreading to the high street corner, cafes (pronounced 'caff') are distinguishable for being unprepossessing, with formica-topped tables, the ubiquitous bottle of HP sauce, cheerful service and cheap prices. It used

Some upmarket places in London now offer rather swish breakfasts that can cost up to £ 25 per meal. Check out Claridges where breakfast can be had amidst Art Deco splendour and even champagne. Simpsons-in-the Strand in Piccadilly offers a Great British Breakfast for £ 16. Or really go upmarket at London Hilton's Window on the World in Park Lane, where on a clear day you can look down on Buckingham Palace. Her Majesty is definitely not amused at this intrusion.

to be the traditional breakfast across the country but became a whipping boy after the health penny dropped. Nonetheless, there is a comeback despite its greasy promise and when you are in London, there are many places that serve it as early as 8:00 am. Check out *Time Out's* website.

Home-Cooked Food

When invited to a British home for a meal, expect simple fare, usually meticulously or elegantly served. The British are not into buffets or an elaborate menu when entertaining. A typical meal for most families on weekends—the only time real cooking is done—is a roast, masses of potatoes and a vegetable or two, usually peas and carrots. There is also a growing trend for modern, fusion European type of food especially among many upwardly mobile people. The supermarkets have latched on to this demand and now feature special sections where you will find such as pasta in myriad shapes, polenta, ready-packed rocket salads and fruit cocktails, microwave Indian, Greek, Italian and Chinese meals and small selections of sushi. There is sea change going on and British tastes buds are getting more sophisticated each day.

IT'S BEEN KILLED TWICE ALREADY. ONCE ON THE FARM AND AGAIN IN THE COOKING

Feasts Not So Unlimited

On the other hand, you'd be lucky to get more than cold meat and salad at a British function, and many British 'drinks parties' or 'cocktail parties' are precisely that, with perhaps peanuts or other nibbles to help wash down whatever you are drinking. In fact, food is low priority at most functions apart from private dinner parties when perhaps a particular host is a foodie and you can get an interesting meal. Or it came from professional caterers who can make a salmon look like a Rembrandt still life.

Otherwise the standard fare is soup, meat, salad, pies, chips and bread. You get much the same at English restaurants but served with panache, and at a price. There is however a lot of media coverage of good British food that the Victorians enjoyed. When this will translate into commercially available repasts is hard to say. But if you try cooking them at home, it might at least be therapeutic enough to diffuse the shock of missing the familiar.

Traditional British Food

Sadly, traditional British food, like mash, pie and jellied eel, are rare and getting rarer. Even that seaside delight of whelks and assorted crustacea served with vinegar and salt is fast disappearing in the face of the fast food explosion. Such seaside resorts like Brighton (the pier has been beautifully refurbished), Bournemouth, Margate and Blackpool, in fact wherever there is a pier, used to feature this traditional British seafood stall.

Today, you have to look hard for it and then the whelks come in plastic tubs. As for fish and chips wrapped in old copies of *The Times*—forget it. I have not had one good fish and chip meal in ten years and even when sent to the so-called best places in and outside London, always came back with the same dismally tired chips and battered to death skate, cod or halibut.

Fish and chips may be the simplest idea but so many places get it wrong. Did you know that 16 varieties of potatoes can be used for the chips and the way the chef cuts them makes all the difference? Some of the best fish and chip places are run by Jewish proprietors who seem to know the secret of the batter.

Traditional English food is fast disappearing. What is advertised as 'Traditional English Fayre' is alas a far cry from the genuine thing.

I once asked a friend to take me to a place known for its eel and mash pie (a Victorian culinary gem). Tongue drooling, we made for the place somewhere in Enfield and found to our horror a large sign advertising the impending opening of yet another pizza place! He was flummoxed as to where else one could go for such historical servings. Such is the influx of American fast food that the best of British has been shell-shocked out of existence. Some things, sadly, the British have not been able to preserve.

ETHNIC FOOD

On the whole, the food scene in Britain is pretty cosmopolitan outside the posh nosh offered by five-star hotels. But then when you convert a £ 45 per head meal of hot soup, meat and gateau, the shock can send you right back to your kitchen. One really upmarket French place charges £ 180 per head for soup, fish, meat and dessert!

But be advised that what you read on the menu isn't always what you may expect. The interpretation of any foreign food can be far off course. Reconstituted dry rice noodles given two stirs in a wok do not a noodle dish make. Nor what passes for spaghetti bolognese, unless it is a reputable Italian establishment. The point is most are geared to what the British are familiar with—not too rich, not too spicy, in other words, anglicised beyond the pale. Some restaurant chefs will do the fine tuning, but it comes with a hefty price tag.

The shocks will dissipate when you learn to cook and buy in bulk where you can find your favourite vegetables and spices. But then you might eventually get to like British food. Which will send the British into shock. But underlining this, any British will warm to you if you genuinely show your appreciation for their culinary tradition, which is the whole point about assimilating and alleviating culture shock.

Mexican

Another buzz word in Britain is hot Mexican food. Well, Tex-Mex at least. The sum total of this cuisine is hot salsa—a fiery sauce made with chopped tomatoes and chillies. And with melted cheese, it goes on everything, from tortillas to enchiladas.

Indian

From the sub-continent comes the ubiquitous tandoori that you can take or leave. North Indian food is now so familiar in Britain that you will find a restaurant in virtually every small town throughout the country, even in the most tucked away villages. Most are small affairs that wisely stay open after pub closing hours, catering for those beer-induced hungers. Which probably explains why a meal of curry and beer has been voted Britain's top takeaway.

Some restaurants—you'll soon discover these—have a penchant for preparing every dish in the same sauce and usually swimming in oil. It's a matter of time before you discover the good ones and those best avoided. Happily, with so much competition from the other ethnic establishments, even the most complacent restaurateurs are pulling themselves up by the apron strings. Media food critics can be positively vitriolic when a restaurant they review tries to pull one over consumer's eyes and taste buds.

Chinese

It would come as a great surprise to many British to hear that there are many different types of Chinese food. The most common type in Britain is the high street takeaway restaurant, serving a pseudo Cantonese style of bland flavoured fried rice, sweet-and-sour pork, chicken with cashew nuts and beef with black bean sauce.

Some Chinese takeaways, with a beady eye on bottom line profits, have tuned in to the British love for fish and chips and mushy peas. So, they combine these with spring rolls and prawn crackers that have collectively become classic takeaway fare. Restaurants in London's Chinatown and elsewhere in bigger cities do serve a wide variety of dishes at prices that won't break the bank, and with varying degrees of excellence. Chinatowns of any sizeable nature are only in Birmingham, Manchester and London and where you will find hundreds of restaurants all offering much the same fare.

Chinese Food

When I ran my own South-east Asian restaurant 15 years ago, I was astonished at one particular customer request of ordering dishes by numbers. Apparently, in years gone by, most Chinese places featured standard menus (printed in Taiwan) of dishes numbered 1–200. Therefore, punters believed number 58 was beef and black bean sauce throughout the realm of Chinese food! The fact that my place was South-east Asian went by the wayside as there was then little understanding of Asian cuisine semantics outside Chinese.

Mediterranean/Middle Eastern

Greek (actually Cypriot), Lebanese and other Middle Eastern offerings are pretty much basic meat and rice meals without spices. One of the most familiar sights along high streets in towns and cities is the *donner* kebab restaurant. Cheap and plentiful, they are always available when you need to satisfy your hunger pangs, though the quality varies enormously. In the more upmarket places in major cities, Middle Eastern fare has become much more sophisticated, served with flair and seducing ever more taste buds with couscous, pilaf dishes, *dolmades* (stuffed vine leaves), *kleftiko* (stewed lamb with herbs) and the like.

South-east Asian

South-east Asian food was introduced to Britain some time in the early 1970s and although in London it quickly became a buzzword, it is still not much understood. Generally, the chattering masses cannot place Indonesia, Malaysia or Singapore on the food map and tend to feel everything must be Chinese. Today, in some of the provinces, there is usually a good Malaysian or Singapore restaurant. For want of a more precise description, most restaurants serving Southeast Asian food are called Malaysian because the genre was a pioneer. The menus are usually a hodgepodge of Indonesian, Chinese and Thai.

Japanese

When once you'd be hard put to find a Japanese restaurant that did not charge an arm and a leg, you now are spoilt for choice in many British cities. Sushi bars and medium-priced places have proliferated in the last six years or so and all fairly affordable if you avoid the choice viands like tuna belly and orange roe. A growing phenomenon and once considered very outré, sushi bars are the rage in London, Birmingham, Cambridge, Oxford et al. Expect to spend about £ 20 per head for an average meal without sake or wine.

Thai

If there is a buzzword in today's British eating scene, it is Thai. Just about every high street and small town—even in traditional British pubs—features some kind of Thai eatery. At last count, there are almost 500 Thai restaurants throughout the UK—compared to less than a dozen 20 years ago. It seems Britain has fallen in love with lemongrass, *tom yam* and green curry and there seems to be a Thai restaurant opening every week somewhere in Britain.

The fact is in every street in every town, even in country pubs, Thai cuisine has become very high profile.

Thai cooking has also leapt into the international arena and European and other Western chefs are feverishly experimenting with ginger, lime leaves and lemongrass that seem to be the basis for many Pacific rim and fusion dishes throughout the Western world.

Understandably, Thai cuisine did not arrive in Britain on the backs of dreadful takeaway fare and established itself from day one as an uncompromising and authentic taste. Even conservative mainstream supermarkets now offer small ready packed herbs containing galangal, chillies, lemongrass, shallots and lime leaves. This was unheard of barely five years ago.

THE ETHNIC SHOPPER

Oriental City is the first ever South-east Asian supermarket and shopping mall in Colindale in North West London and offers a wide range of fresh vegetables, herbs and other exotic ingredients from Thailand, Korea, Malaysia and Singapore. Here you can find frozen paratha, fish balls, Thai curry pastes—in short, a delicious slice of the East. The food court echoes those of Singapore and Malaysia featuring more than a dozen stalls selling Chinese, Korean, Vietnamese, Indonesian, Thai, Japanese, Singapore and Malaysian dishes. Tuck into fairly genuine chicken rice, *char kway teow*, *tom yam*, *nasi lemak*, paratha etc. The place also boasts several upmarket Chinese restaurants including a conveyer belt sushi place. It is open seven days a week from 10:00 am–9:00 pm, Monday to Saturday and 12:00 noon–6:00 pm on Sundays. (Tube stop: Colindale, Northern Line, about 10 minutes away.)

For everything Chinese, Soho has supermarkets like Loon Fung, Loon Moon, Golden Gate and See Woo leading the field in Asian merchandise. They stock every conceivable Chinese food and fresh vegetables hitherto unknown in Britain.

There is a chain of Chinese supermarkets including cash and carry departments under the name of Wing Yip with centres in London, Croydon, Manchester and Birmingham. They stock a large range of Chinese, Thai, South-east Asian and Japanese products. The main London store is at 395 Edgware Road, London NW2, open seven days a week from 9:30 am–7:00 pm and from 11:30 am–5:00 pm on Sundays.

In places where there are sizeable ethnic communities, you will find smaller ethnic supermarkets selling a range of Chinese, Thai, Indonesian and Indian produce. These may not be extensive but adequate if you really miss your coconut milk and *ikan bilis*. Even durians, that were once reviled, are now popping up all year round. All said, ethnic ingredients are much more available today across Britain then they were a decade ago.

EATING OUT
Restaurant Hours
Restaurant hours are fairly consistent throughout Britain. Most open at 12:00 noon–3:00 pm and again between 7:00 pm–11:00 pm. In the larger cities, they stay open all day from 12:00 noon– 11:00 pm. Touristy towns might have late night hours until midnight or even 1:00 am. Sunday opening is geared mainly to places that attract large numbers of visitors. Otherwise, most establishments operate a six-day week to avoid running into overtime wages and equipment fatigue.

Service
Sevice is wide ranging, from toffee-nosed French-style replete with floor-sweeping aprons and thinly-veiled distaste for unsuitably-dressed customers to rowdy Italian family-type and plain rude Chinese. Whatever you do, don't plonk yourself at the first empty table. It is an unwritten law that you wait to be seated by the waiter or waitress at a table he or she designates. Any vehement choice for a particular table is likely to be met with a cold eye and a sharp tongue. The place might look half-empty but every house has its own system of seating, not to mention a waiter's particular whim.

At places mindful of professional service, you will be given a menu and a wine list for some 5 minutes to study. At others, you might be ignored for 10 minutes before being attended to. Be patient—they're just busy, not indifferent. Expect to wait an average of 10 minutes for your starters to arrive. Restaurants tend to cancel tables if customers turn up more than 45 minutes late.

If you have a predilection for extras, ask for them when the order is being taken. Plain water is never served unless you ask for it. Nothing is for free in this country and most places will ask if you mean mineral or spa water which costs about £ 1 per glass. You are likely to get withering looks if you ask for six glasses of plain water because there's nothing in it for the waiter.

A restaurant that seats 60 people will have no more than two or three waiting staff. Excessive demands will only be met by curt reaction or outright insolence. Few restaurants in Britain have a retinue of staff hovering to serve every little whim. For this kind of service at high-class places, expect to pay upwards of £ 40 per head. Top professional service comes with a hefty price tag. It is a known fact that highly-skilled waiting staff earn up to £ 400 a week—net.

Ethnic restaurants are more laid back in service and, being smaller—average seating 35 people—manage better with one waiter than large establishments with six. Smaller establishments also depend more on tips than those backed by a conglomerate or chain.

Tips

10 per cent is the norm, though a recent law prohibits this from being printed on a bill, and it has to be totally discretionary. But, as an entrenched habit, tipping is a common practice. Waiting staff are not about to have the carpet pulled from under them and generous tips mean less skating on financial thin ice. Say weekly takings are £ 5000 in a four-waiter place. 10 per cent or £ 500 divided by four means a tax-free £ 125 on top of the basic £ 50. On the other hand, don't tip if service is most unsatisfactory. Or tip more if you have been particularly well-served. Tourists and back-packers are not the most popular customers as they are notorious for not leaving enough tips or any at all.

One good tip: become a waiter to earn extra cash. All you need is common sense, steady hands and sturdy feet. It's also probably the profession with the highest turnover, so there are always jobs a-begging.

Eating Modes

Thankfully, few continental restaurants intimidate with a battery of knives, forks and spoons, even for an elegant meal. The basic is a butter knife, meat and fish knives, a soup spoon and a dessert spoon. The usual pattern is to work from the outside in, but most establishments now lay cutlery depending on what you order. Since most waiters will pour your first glass of wine, there is less reason for nervousness when dining posh.

Most Asians used to street hawker food find eating on the run—or rather, on the stroll—a natural habit. The British recoil at this simply because they do not have a hawker heritage and are self-conscious about eating in public. Fast food is eaten on the premises and those seen eating outdoors are usually visitors or young people with no such hang-ups. I know British friends who would not even eat a fruit unless they are indoors.

THE NATIONAL CUPPA

The Japanese may have elevated the drinking of tea to an art form. The British regard it with no less reverence, if differently. Next to the weather, tea is probably the most favourite subject of conversation. Nowhere else would you see such passion for a beverage. It is almost a national panacea for all ills and assorted chills; the watery British sun rises and sets on tea—Earl Grey, Lapsang Soochong, Orange Pekoe and whatever else the plantations in faraway India and China may yield.

A true Brit would be loath to greet the day without a steaming 'cuppa', an affectionate colloquialism and the pulse of British life. Everyone drinks a few cups a day. Indeed, 'having a cuppa' is a national advertising tagline on buses, hoardings, television and radio. The statistics say that Britain downs some 120 million cups of tea every day—the most in the world.

It brings a smile to the face of an old age pensioner the way caviar and lobster would not. It uplifts and soothes, whatever the leaf, served in fine bone china or in cracked tin cup. Real tea-drinkers will swear by age-old rituals. The water must be

Tea, in short, is not merely a hot beverage to warm oneself. It is as British as the Union Jack, to be indulged in with the utmost sobriety and reverence or jovial bonhomie, in humble homes or grand salons. Even the tea lady, once a ubiquitous feature in offices, has become something of a symbol of endearment.

boiling hot, first to rinse the pot and then to brew the tea. Even though tea merchants have put them in practical bags, purists will insist on brewing their cuppa from loose leaves.

Today, most tea retailing companies resort to this tradition as a unique selling point. One brand went even further—using a bunch of chimpanzees to caricature the tradition and embracing the jollity of blue-rinsed ladies and salt-of-the-earth British gentlemen chatting over their brew. Does it sell the stuff? By the millions, even in bags. It is the British wry sense of humour at work and, far from taking offence at being so likened, the public lap it up by the pot.

When invited to a British home, the first thing you're likely to be offered is a cup of tea. When you accept it, it will pull you close to the bosom of the people. Which is what living here is all about.

In factories all over Britain, 'elevenses' are a sacrosanct part of the working day. It means that, come 11:00 am, everyone,

A pensioner couple enjoying a cup of tea in a garden centre.

barring the go-getting workaholic, breaks for tea. It may be a can of coke or a sneaked glass of wine, but the reference is always to 'tea break'. Even the looming presence of a coffee machine does not detract from a beloved custom.

The Miracle Cure

It never ceases to amuse when you see a situation such as the following. A man has just been knocked down by a motorcycle but is not seriously hurt. The lady in the house near where the accident happened opens her door and says: "Oh dear are you all right? Come in and let me make you a nice cup of tea and you'll be fine." Like I said, tea is somehow perceived as panacea for all ills!

Even when organisations like British Rail are lambasted for indifferent food, the key issue is invariably tea. BBC disc-jockeys, in self-effacing mood, make fun of their canteen tea. In one programme the prize for a quiz is, guess what? BBC tea bags. And the obsession goes down the line. Workmen at construction sites all over the country will down tools in unison for a communal pot of the brew. Members of Parliament will put aside matters of state for a 15-minute tea break.

Even if you are not a tea-drinker, you will find yourself drawn to this charming tradition. Coming in from battling the cold wind, a hot cup of tea courses through your system like a gush of warmth.

PUNCTUALITY

It wouldn't be fair to assume a picture of national unease but the British tend to be less bothered about being clockwork punctual than, say, the Swiss. Generally, they dislike rushing and pell-mell activity that characterises faster-living societies. Outside the cities, people thrive on a much slower-paced lifestyle that not all foreigners fully understand or tolerate at first.

It is not in the British psyche to squeeze 25 hours out of 24, barring the workaholics. As a foreigner, you will encounter this first—from the airport to the railway station to the hotel reception. Why is everyone so slow? But you get used to this. As for lateness in appointments, there are attendant reasons, given the variability of travel and weather conditions. In London especially and other urban sprawls, public transport schedules and perpetual city centre congestion make mincemeat of appointment times.

When someone agrees to meet you at 10:00 am from perhaps 80 km (50 miles) away you can expect him to be delayed anywhere between half an hour and 2 hours. The great ribbon tarmacs criss-crossing Britain are a dream to drive on when nothing untoward happens. It takes but one minor accident to cause a traffic jam and resultant tailback stretching for miles. And once on the motorway, you can do nothing except creep, jerk and crawl until the next junction or roundabout where, with any luck, you might find an alternative route.

Social events tend to be the most affected by unpunctuality. British people are averse to being like clockwork when having fun. It's not rudeness if people turn up later than specified,

but simply a laid-back attitude towards leisure pursuits. It's not a matter of life and death to be punctual. However some people take this to extremes and do not show up at all without any explanation. They are usually service people like plumbers or repairmen. And they do not always give a plausible reason.

You just have to get used to the largely inexplicable tardiness of repairmen. This is not a national lacklustre attitude, to be fair. There are often extenuating circumstances that, unfortunately, you will not know about until you've torn your hair out by the clump. Traffic jams, delays in previous jobs, etc. They do not treat the customer like he's the be-all and end-all, simply because there's more work than they can cope with. Hence the cost of repairing anything.

You soon learn to be a master at whiling away time at the post office, bank, clinic, railway station, etc. Maybe that's why the British are mad about crossword puzzles. They really help in quelling exasperation. A little philosophy also helps. Being stuck in a 32 km (20 miles) traffic jam or waiting hours for a repairman, it's good pause for reflection. It certainly makes for less stress.

Don't forget too that the size of the population means you simply have to wait in line—be it repairing a faulty phone or a washing machine. Few after sales services will commit themselves to a fixed time. At best, it will be am or pm. At worst, it'll be 'sometime in the week'.

Public transport is much more guilty of tardiness than the individual. All bus stops have time schedules that are often a laugh because they might just as well not be there. Where buses are supposed to run at 15-minute intervals, they more often than not appear at half hour intervals especially in the provincial towns. Few British seem to really mind, moan though they do, but with an almost resigned sigh.

'Summer is time for everyone and his aunt to
have their 'hols'. So you join the seething masses in a
race for a change of air and environment during this
frenzied exodus that usually involves extricating
yourself from a 10-mile tailback on the motorway.'
—Terry's journal, June 1984

HOLIDAYS

The annual holiday (never 'vacation', that is a resoundingly American term) in Britain is something of a sacred cow on a scale that never fails to send shock waves across the British Isles come summer and bank holiday weekends. These are gazetted national off days and always on Mondays. Travel companies must advertise their delicious offerings (some hidden truths read like horror stories) more fiercely in Britain than anywhere else. When people take their holidays, weekend jaunts or day-return trips en masse, roads, rail, sea and air routes naturally clog up and it can be a nightmare. The newspapers are full of such stories at peak season.

Other menaces are travel company shysters and dodgy organisations. Headlines scream on about families booked on package trips that promise all and deliver precious little. What's more, many families save for months—even years— booking equally far ahead only to find their two weeks in a European 'paradise' an exercise in wretched frustration. If this paints a ghastly picture, it's perfectly true, year after year. With millions of pounds in the offing for travel companies, there will naturally be cowboy

Thank goodness for consumer watchdog programmes on television that alert one to these confidence tricks. It is not unknown for people to be booked on a holiday to Spain that promises luxury hotels, stunning sea views etc, and only to find that the hotel is still a hole in the ground and the sea is five miles inland. These are extreme cases but they do happen. So always check before you pack.

outfits without the slightest conscience about fleecing innocent clients.

Common is the story where such fly-by-nights set up shop, take their money and run, leaving their victims with no-go packages. It must have been with wry mirth that one company advertised on their hoarding: 'You've tried the cowboys, now try the Indians.' They were Indian travel agents.

Overbooking is a common cause followed closely by timetables that eat into precious time, not leaving enough for travellers to recoil from their travails. These journeys into the unknown can befall almost anyone constrained with budgets that disallow booking the more upmarket tours.

Travel Smart

To buffer yourself against the possible shocks and scams, choose your holiday package carefully:

- Book your holiday months ahead. The Brits do—not just weeks, sometimes even a year ahead.
- Never take holiday brochures (especially continental packages to the British-swamped countries of Spain and Greece) at face value. Check for cheap loopholes. Cut price usually means cut everything else—from bug-ridden beds to foul food.
- Boats, trains and planes are chock-a-block at the best of times given the great British penchant for holidays, and delays of up to two days are not uncommon.
- Read the daily press for horror stories. They don't mince words about appalling accommodation and other travesties. One Spanish hotel advertising 'glorious views of the Mediterranean' actually looked out on a hole in the ground where part of the hotel was still being built.
- Travel insurance is a resounding must. Theft and other misadventures are less likely to send you on a tailspin if you can get compensation.

There are literally hundreds of small companies offering 'two weeks of paradise in Costa del Sol'. Every Sunday the papers are packed with holiday deals that offer ridiculous prices, like £ 5 to Milan. Many are bona fide within the special promotions category, but just as many are rife with catches or simply a scam.

Driving Holidays in Britain

Marvellous though British roads are, they can be car-strangled and grid-locked during peak travel months and bank holiday weekends. Some drivers mockingly cite the national anthem for British motorways holidays as 'The Car Strangled Spanner' in a send-up of the American military march 'Star Spangled Banner'. Tailbacks on the motorway are so common I usually avoid them when we drive out on long weekends. Take the smaller country roads that are not only less of a hassle, but also offers picturesque views. Motorways, even when clear, are ribbons of absolute boredom.

Don't leave accommodation to chance at such times. Even the tattiest bed-and-breakfast places are full in summer. Get hold of any number of brochures and leaflets from any British

Tourist Authority office (every town of tourist interest has one) and book ahead. Most will honour a phone booking.

Pack your own food if your journey is to take more than several hours. Motorway service stations—places to top up car and stomach—are notoriously iffy on food. So too are many roadside chains, though you may chance upon a good, unpretentious transport cafe where lorry drivers can rely on decent meals at very reasonable prices. Otherwise, expect meat and vegetables with lumpy gravy. Or an endless hamburger trail.

Car hire is relatively cheap in Britain and costs a fraction of train travel if you are in a group that can squeeze into a saloon. Say five people would pay something like £ 20 per head (petrol and car hire) to drive from London to the Lake District and all over for a weekend, not counting accommodation. And make sure your MOT is up to date. MOT simply means Ministry of Transport but in specific reference to the roadworthiness of your car. Any car more than three years old has to have an MOT test before the certificate of roadworthiness can be granted.

It doesn't apply to new cars, but when you get your road tax renewal notice, you have to get an MOT done before you can renew it. If your vehicle is basically sound, it should have no problem passing the test which vehicular mechanics will do at garages. This latter reference does not only apply to where you keep your car—it's the general description of car maintenance shops. And MOT costs vary depending on the state of your vehicle.

Passports

As of January 1983, under the British Nationality Act of 1981, UK passports are issued to British citizens, subjects, Dependent Territories citizens, overseas citizens, protected persons and nationals (overseas).

You are eligible for a UK passport by birth in the UK or British Colony, naturalisation in the UK or a British Colony, registration as a citizen of the UK and Colonies or legitimate descent from a father to whom one of the above applies.

Visas

Very few visitors to Britain need visas for a six-month visit. Check with the relevant embassy in your own country. For all visa and passport enquiries, contact: Home Office, 50 Queen Anne's Gate, London SW1H 9AT [tel: (087) 0000-1565].

OUTDOOR ACTIVITIES
Traditions

The reference here applies not only to those of a religious or historical nature but also those pursuits held dear to the bosom of the British. As a people, they set total store by the familiar and the security of tried and tested leisure activities. These embrace a wide spectrum from the almost-obligatory two weeks holiday a year to sport. In between, there are any number of traditions still adhered to by villages and small towns.

Parks

Entertainment isn't always the obvious variety. Britain's public parks and private gardens are among the most magnificent in the world and are either for free or for a small charge to cover maintenance. There are hundreds of beautiful green lungs all over the country that provide much pleasure if your taste is to commune with nature. Every county and

city has some kind of park, whether just open ground for romping in or beautifully landscaped gardens for stunning presentation. Feeding ducks in London's Regent's Park is as therapeutic as it is educational as the birds come from many different countries.

Soaking up the sun

Most foreigners, especially the Chinese and Indians, are rather diffident about sprawling on public parks when the sun shines. Perhaps they have had enough sun or are too shy to do what many British do. On glorious summer days, you will see dozens of people in swimwear simply soaking up the warmth in their backyards. Initially, I was bemused by so much sun-worshipping but in time, after years of chill, I began to appreciate this rare commodity in Britain. After all, you can only go bare-chested in public a few months a year. And you won't get arrested as long as you don't bask in the altogether.

The British love a bask in the sun.

Window Shopping

Window displays are an art form, especially in big city stores, which should not be missed. At Christmas, the major department stores usually have animated window displays that are veritable stage shows. I've seen full tableaux of Snow White, Cinderella and other Grimm fairy tales that put to shame some live shows. These marvels of electronic engineering and creativity make shopping a joy in Britain during the festive season.

NIGHTLIFE

Alas, Britain is not generally a late-night country. Some big cities have clubs that stay open till 2:00 or 3:00 am. The licensing laws are strict even in London where there are jazz clubs that cater for dawn-watchers. Transport is the major problem unless you drive, for taxis after midnight can be hideously expensive. Most places shut down by 1:00 am.

Pubs

An abbreviation of 'public house' with usually the host, a publican of rather sociable nature. Pubs are more than just places to drink. Each is a watering hole for devoted patrons, a bolt hole to unwind in or catch up on the latest local gossip. Many are listed as historical buildings owned by brewery chains with their names not too discreetly affixed under the pub's quaint hoarding. Throughout the country, you are likely to see dozens of establishments called the Crown, King's Arms, The George, The Victoria, Fox and Hound, Duke of York, or Horse and Plough. There are something like 80,000 pubs throughout the British Isles.

Many pubs date back to the 16th and 17th centuries but most are Victorian or Edwardian when they were private homes where the owner sold ale at his doorstep. Before the era of steam trains and cars, many such buildings became coaching

Although pubs are basically inns where beers and ales are dispensed, they mean much more than mere watering holes. Patrons who frequent their 'local' regard it as a welcoming oasis in their lives. Others may specialise in the type of clientele i.e. gay, executive, Jewish, Asian, elderly et al. In a way, each caters to a parched or special need and the ambience in each place is very special because of this.

inns–halfway houses for travellers to change horses and bed down after a meal and drink. But it was during the Victorian era that pubs flourished, with proprietors going over the top with etched glass panels, acres of marble, gleaming mahogany, flocked wallpaper and an ambience reflective of grand houses. Many have been lovingly restored and any that smack of modernity, chrome and steel should be given a wide berth.

Whatever the weather, however woeful the workday has been, pubs are usually packed wall-to-wall in the evening, and especially on a Saturday night, with people intent on downing as many pints as they can before last orders. Relaxed drinking hours now mean people can drink right through the day and until midnight in some places, though 11:00 pm is the usual closing time. A recent suggestion for 24-hour pubs provoked the usual vociferous public reactions from both sides of the fence. The matter is yet to be resolved with legislation. And when they say 11:00 pm, it literally means the shutters come down with an uncompromising clang on the dot though you may go on drinking what you have ordered before this closing bell.

Age of Consent

As for the age of consent, the law says you may not enter a pub if you are under 14 unless accompanied by an adult. And you may not buy alcohol if you are under 18. But the law is rarely applied. Many pubs admit whole families, toddlers and all, and rarely ask for proof of age. This is permitted by law if you are all eating.

If you are nervous about entering a pub, let alone propping yourself nonchalantly at the bar to order a beer or even an orange juice, don't be. In time, you will find it to be the kind of place where the British warm up much faster than anywhere else. The same person who greets you like a long lost friend is apt to give you the cold shoulder on a train or tube.

For a few pounds, a pub is hard to beat for a drink, social banter and getting to meet the locals. Racism rarely shows up in a pub. One can conjecture that ambience conducive to relaxed senses brings out the best in human nature. When you are in a pub, it is customary to buy a 'round' of drinks for the group of people you are with. If there are more than five or six of you, someone may offer to split the cost. You in turn will be bought a drink when others buy 'rounds'. It would seem odd, even rude, to buy yourself a drink if you are with friends or colleagues, or having started a conversation with a fellow drinker.

Pub Stage

When once the dartboard provided an outlet for aggression and friendly competition, the plush snooker table is now an imposing fixture in the larger establishments. Others, not so privileged with space for such a clumpy piece of sports equipment, offer the 1990s version of entertainment—loud music. And it can be extremely loud music in places where the clientele is young and accustomed to eardrum-bursting hard rock.

Some places offer more refined entertainment like a resident pianist or even a full-scale musical band trying to out stage the West End with their production numbers on a postage-stamp sized stage. With 80,000 pubs, there must be one to suit every need no matter how esoteric. Purists moan that all this defeats the purpose of a pub's function, which is to provide good brew and conversation. With changing mores and a younger pub-going population, any publican with his eye on profit will be shrewd to supply whatever is in demand.

Even more enlightening (perhaps a horrific development for serious drinkers), is that many pubs now have a section serving non-alcoholic drinks. I visited no less than half a dozen in the London area and there were as many (usually lunchtime) patrons who quite happily quaff the stuff. Young professionals take their job seriously enough not to exhale alcohol breath at an executive meeting.

Pub clientele today is largely a mixed bag where an old-age pensioner is likely to find his favourite chair occupied by a yuppie type drinking orange juice. Conversation is as likely to be peppered with the latest stock market prices as whose aunt Nellie has gout. The point is, whether you drink or not, a pub is the one place that provides a good springboard and live stage to assimilate and observe the British way of life at its most grass roots level.

An aberration for serious drinkers, the alcohol free bar is nonetheless gaining more popularity with younger professionals who enjoy the cosy ambience of a pub without the after effects of alcohol.

Wine Bars

Compared to the age of pubs, wine bars are really fledgling establishments that have now sprouted apace with the yuppie generation and are now taking their place among the serious restaurants. Just what is a wine bar? It serves wine, spirits and food—though not on a restaurant scale. In a word, a wine bar is a place to display your knowledge of wine (a relatively recent adoption among the British via their continental cousins), nibble at a quiche or sit down to an exotic Mexican, Spanish, Thai, Malaysian or Indian meal.

A rather strange assortment of gustatory pleasures but much loved by the hard-working, up-and-coming executive. It wouldn't be fair to label a wine bar as a yuppie place because it isn't. Because of the smallness of most, the atmosphere is very 'matey' and food fast, if not silver service, and an inexpensive way to spend a convivial evening. It is a different matter from going out to a restaurant because in a wine bar, you don't have to eat if you don't want to. Nurse a glass of house white the whole night through and the proprietor will not turn a hair. Try to do the same at a restaurant, and you will be shown the door before you can say, "Beaujolais". Herein perhaps lies its popularity given the British penchant for the grog; all the better if it has a French name because it reflects a European sophistication.

There are relatively few wine bars compared to pubs and they are located mainly in the bigger towns and cities where offices abound. They offer a wide selection of wines and soft drinks, with ambience geared to small sit-down groupings. Some wine bar tables are so small that they can practically be covered by a tray! Still, patrons mind little the elbow jostling, even regarding it as chic to crouch on minuscule stools in their designer gear. The clientele is generally more sophisticated and cosmopolitan.

Prices are marginally lower than restaurants: you should expect to pay an average of £ 8 for a bottle of house wine, which you can also buy by the glass, and anything from £ 40 to £ 100 for good champagne. Food ranges from the indifferent to good ethnic offerings like satay, samosas, Thai bites and dim sum.

THE VERY PROPER ENGLISH TEA

Whatever else is going by the wayside, the traditional English cream tea is alive and doing very well from Cambridge to Clacton-on-Sea. Virtually every town with anything to offer visitors by way of history or natural scenic beauty boasts of at least one tea shop. For something like £ 4 (depending on how touristy the place is), you get a pot of tea, hot scones, homemade jam and thick cream. It is a real pick-me-up at around 4:00 pm (they serve them all hours too) and one can steep oneself in history. At the upmarket places in Central London like the Ritz, the price can go up to £ 34 for the same spread!

Most places will have made some effort to document the history of the place, whether it's Tudor architecture, for instance, or has had a visit by some other literary luminary, or simply that it is several hundred years old. Pretty tablecloths, dried flower arrangements and delicate bone china are de rigueur as are side offerings of potted jams and honey to take home. As a weekend jaunt, tearooms are lovely to soak up British history and culture, all the better if you strike up conversation with a very proper English gentlewoman who just happens to have lived in the area all her life and knows about all local lore. If it's anything that will break the traditional British reserve, it's to have a healthy curiosity for their history, murky or otherwise.

Ancient abodes seem ideally suited for this lovely tradition, where you are not rushed off your feet by insolent waiters. Tearoom proprietors, especially in the country, are charming, warm, and will make you feel welcome. There are hundreds of these places throughout Britain where history goes back four or five hundred years. Many still retain their original woodwork, fireplaces and atmosphere that are as much an attraction as the brew. For under £ 10 you get a real slice of British history that no fast food place can ever hope to provide.

DOING THE COUNTRY

Driving around the country is a tradition that practically every mobile British person, single or weighed down with kids

The tearoom is a regular feature of any town or village. A hot pot of tea, delicious freshly baked scones, jam and cream: a perfect dream of pastoral gentility.

and grandparents, indulges in. And one which every visitor should take every opportunity to enjoy. It's a wonderful break from weekday tedium, gets clean air into your lungs for the price of a full tank of petrol split among four, five or six, and brings great discoveries the tourist brochures don't tell you about.

The British Isles are literally stuffed with country places you can get to within an hour or so from wherever you happen to be. Sheep-laden trails, trout farms, pick-your-own fruit farms and guesthouses with delightfully warm proprietors are everywhere. Every county has pretty, gorgeous or at least interesting countryside to offer. It would not be fair to name any particular one as scenic beauty is in the eyes of the beholder.

One of the joys of driving through the country is stumbling upon charming little villages where the pace of life is slower than in the cities.

Do not expect, however, a wide choice of eating places with at most a pub, teashop or hamburger stall. Hot dog stands can be found along many roads and dual carriageways but the shock comes in waxy sausages, dreadful tea and greasy onions. You're better off buying a punnet of strawberries or whatever fruit is in season.

Pastoral Idyll

On a warm summer's day, when the sun is shining and the temperature hovers around 22°C, ambling along a country lane to the twittering chorus of fleeting starlings, the raucous 'caw caw' of black crows and the occasional somnolent 'moo' of a cow, is the stuff of pastoral idyll. This is one of the most beautiful times in the British calendar of natural pursuits.

Bed and Breakfast

The British tradition of offering bed and breakfast for a nominal price of £ 25 to £ 45 per night (this varies depending on season, type of place, etc.) is the visitor's best friend. Outside large towns and cities, hotels are a rarity. Country folk who turn their homes into B&B places are a far cry from formal hotel staff. They're warm, friendly and go to great lengths to make your stay comfortable whether for one night or ten.

Don't expect the plush amenities of a hotel though. Your room will be basic, cosy, clean and probably full of personal artefacts. Quite likely, the owner's son has had to give up his room for the family's extra income. Often, you will join the family for dinner, at a nominal cost, of course. But it is the breakfast that warms most visitors and there is usually a choice of continental or full English—the latter being a substantial menu of toast, bacon, eggs, sausages, tomatoes and all the tea you can drink. Most B&B places can accommodate several families and you will have the pleasure of company for this traditional meal. Lately, as a gesture to cosmopolitan mores, many places have begun to serve a range of cereals, juices, fruit, cheeses and cold meats.

It is advisable to book your B&B accommodation well in advance whatever the time of year just to be on the safe side. The British countryside can appear to be isolated if you are stuck with no accommodation and scouting for one on speculation can be daunting especially in inclement weather, and if you do not have your own transport.

There is nothing more glorious than enjoying this repast while looking out onto a pastoral scene. There are literally hundreds of these places in every province and at least several in small villages. Apart from in high summer, they are not usually full, but half the fun is in stumbling upon a charming picture-post-card farmhouse with a beckoning sign on B&B vacancies.

SPORTS
Football

The British passion for football transcends mere enthusiasm for the sporting life. Since its invention some 125 years ago (by the British of course) football has become a national preoccupation, a cult movement almost provoking feelings within the public breast that range from mere ra-ra support to fierce fanaticism. And along the ugly periphery, loathsome loutish behaviour that has unfairly tarnished the game. In

the past decade, a few boorish fans more intent on creating mayhem than cheering spirit have been receiving more headline press coverage than goal-scoring prowess.

The game has remained much the same as it was since its invention. It is a game of skill based on the player's handling of the ball with his feet or head and is steeped in the tradition of sportsmanship. However, if the players display sportsmanship on the field, the same cannot be said for some of their supporters. British football in the past few years has been plagued by the problem of violence off the pitch. And British football fans have acquired a reputation for loutish behaviour overseas, as their misbehaviour has spilled over the rest of Europe during international matches.

Violence at football matches is a sticky problem of national proportions. Crowd control measures, enforced club membership and police cordons will not always ensure the prevention of volatile behaviour that can lead to disaster. But the Football Association assures that the game itself remains sacred to the British and unsullied by emotional upheavals around it. There will always be the lout bent on creating chaos, be it a football match or rock concert. It simply means any large gathering of people must need adequate policing as much for likely hooliganism as for smooth flow. The riot syndrome is a volatile one, usually mindless, and it manifests itself when human instincts are reduced to herd levels. It is, however, not a frequent occurrence. It is comparatively rare to experience or even notice any trouble at most football games, and you should attend one to experience this element of British culture, even if you do not support a particular team.

The football season is between August and May each year with games played every Saturday at 3:00 pm and on Tuesday or Wednesday at 7:30 pm. In England and Wales, a major change occurred in 1992 when a new FA Premier League was started, comprising 22 clubs. The remaining 70 full-time professional clubs play in the three main leagues. In Scotland there are 38 clubs, in Northern Ireland, 16 semi-professional clubs play in the Irish Football League. During the season, over 2000 English League matches are played and tickets range from £ 5 to £ 25 depending on the division.

For the ardent football fan, there are specialised shops which sell everything he needs to show his support for his favourite club.

Football Matches

It's not easy for the casual spectator to get tickets for a good game. Tickets for top league (Premiership) games are all but impossible to come be, making it hard to see teams like Manchester United, Arsenal and Chelsea. Tickets for London clubs in all three Nationwide League divisions are cheaper and easier to obtain. For more information check out the FA website: http://www.thefa.com

As for amateur football, there are 42,000 clubs in England alone, so if you hanker to kick a ball around, there is always a pitch near you. Every county in Britain has a regional football association.

Cricket

There seems to be no middle ground for feelings about this sport from the British public. Either they believe it should be buried deep in the ground or will go to great lengths following the teams around. But not without a selection of novels, carafes of wine, fruit, a rug and pillows to snooze on. It does go on a bit and what does one do during those endless tests? Yet at every cricket season, there is madness everywhere with aficionados taking French leave from work to cheer the home team and traffic grinding to a halt outside Lord's cricket pitch in Northwest London. Or the Oval in Surrey.

Whether you actually like the game or not is not the issue. The media cover the games in great detail, as well as the behaviour (on and off the pitch) of the major players. Popular sentiment for the game is so high that some players have attained star status. The cricket season runs from April to September when the British weather is at its most friendly.

- **Lord's Cricket Ground**
  St John's Wood, London NW8, 8QN
  Tel: (020) 7342-1066
  Website: http://www.lords.org
  Ticket prices from £ 10–£ 50
  Tube: St John's Wood

- **Kennington Oval**
  Kennington, London SE11 5 SS
  Tel: (020) 7582-6660
  Website: http://www.surreycricket.com
  Ticket prices from £ 5–£ 50
  Tube: Oval

Polo

This is known as a king's sport or for those with money to burn, and the elite as it costs an arm and a leg to own and maintain polo ponies. This premier (read expensive!) sport gets coverage more so because Prince Charles likes his weekly chukkas than the game per se. And of course the prospect of rubbing shoulders (or rather horse's shanks) with the rich and famous. Definitely not within reach of the hoi polloi—it'll cost you plenty not just to maintain the paraphernalia, but also the social cachet indulged by polo circles—but the best way to become a celebrity.

Both Princes William and Harry are adept at this sport but they do not have to worry about the money of course. Like their father, they do not have to give their kingdom for a horse especially as the family owns a string of them. Of course, the press will wait and watch for every royal tumble or blue language. Prince Philip used to turn the air purple with his language when he was playing. Alas, age has caught up with him and the old princely bones can now only indulge in horse and carriage racing. A very genteel sport—except for the poor sweating horses.

Swimming

Unless you're seriously into lapping for Olympic honours, this sport is not the most comfortable for those unaccustomed to temperatures below 15°C (70°F). There are several indoor (heated but not very warm!) swimming pools in every major city and town charging a small fee for the facilities. Avoid the holiday months of April, August and September when most pools are thick with students. Come autumn (November onwards), unless you're a masochist, swimming is a distinctly chilly experience. In very warm summers, the coastal resorts in the south like Brighton, Bournemouth and Eastbourne offer sea swimming. But even with temperatures around 30°C (the high 80s F), be prepared for the sea to be still chilblain-inducing. For more information, look in your local directory or the *Yellow Pages*.

Cycling

Outside the cities, Britain is a cyclist's paradise. Probably the healthiest, cheapest and most fulfilling form of transport. For a low outlay of £ 50 for an average bicycle (they can cost up to £ 500 for souped-up models with 12 gears), the country is your pedalling oyster. It is the best way to see Britain if you have the time and calf muscles. British Rail allows you to board with your bicycle, but not the London Underground. It is also wise to wear a safety sash fluorescent green or orange in colour when riding at night, especially along rural areas where street lighting is inconsistent or non-existent.

Make sure you have a very strong lock for when you park and chain your bicycle to some secure railing or post. In public parks, look out for signs that prohibit cycling, especially on manicured lawns or flowerbeds. On city roads, there are designated cycle paths, so use them for your own safety. It is not an uncommon sight to see men in suits and well-dressed women cycling to work, or at least part of the way. During transport strikes—which can happen any time—your bicycle is invaluable, never mind that you're a judge or banker. The British are unfazed by such irksome hiccups and simply 'get on with it'.

Cyclist Alert!

Herne Hill Velodrome

Burbage Road, Herne Hill, London SE24 9HE

Tel: (020) 7737-4647

Website: http://www.hernehillvelodrome.org.uk

Train station: British Rail Herne Hill and North Dulwich

Costs: £ 8 with bike hire and £ 5.50 with own bike

Jogging

There are relatively few designated jogging tracks in Britain for the simple reason that there is a whole country (outside the highly congested city areas) available for this sport. Public parks are your best venues where the air is bracing and you do not run the risk of being knocked down by juggernauts and other motorised vehicles. Given that it's cold ten months a year, wear warm jogging gear and proper shoes. If you like jogging in company, contact your local sports association or council which will put you in touch with the right people.

A Note of Caution:
It is not prudent to jog alone in out of the way places at night. If you have to, keep within well-lit areas and wear fluorescent sashes. All public parks are closed at sundown. Never jog on motorways or on ice-bound roads.

Once a year, in summer, the London Marathon brings out the zany, eccentric, charitable, passionate and plain nutty jogger to participate in the most colourful and humorous race of all. People in gorilla costumes (even in extreme heat), ballet-tutus, nappies—every conceivable and inconceivable getup—join the fun. The serious joggers will have left them miles behind within minutes but these merry marathoners get the best press inevitably. Behind most of the zaniness lies a good cause as thousands of pounds are raised every year for charity.

Walking

The British do not regard walking as a mere ambulatory means of getting from one point to another. Most people from hot climates find walking a chore and take a little getting used to when they have to move thus in Britain. But the climate is entirely conducive to walking and a distance of four or five miles is a whisker's twitch to serious walkers. On average, commuters chalk up a mile or two each day walking from home to train, tube or bus station and back. Not to mention the distances you have to cover changing stations and negotiating escalators and walkways. It is healthy and rarely uncomfortable unless you're physically feeble. Once you get past the notion that a mile is a mile anywhere, walking in Britain is exhilarating and enlightening. You can discover much more about history, tucked away places of interest and gems of historical interest.

Almost all of Britain's suburban and rural areas are ideal for serious walking. But be armed with maps, basic medical kit and other life-sustaining items, should you like walking in real country like Cumbria, Scotland, Wales and other craggy highlands. Sensible, comfortable and stout shoes are de rigueur especially in the cold months. Proper hiking boots should be purchased for serious fell walking, and you should always take waterproof clothing when hill walking in areas such as the Peak District, Yorkshire Dales, Snowdonia and Scotland. Check with local authorities where walkers generally go to and what dangers there are in isolated places.

Walking is a national sport for many and highly recommended for those disinclined to other more vigorous sport. Avoid doing this alone for obvious reasons. And always have some nourishment with you: water, thermos and biscuits, should you lose your way. There are relatively few places in Britain where a public phone or farmhouse is not within a few miles' reach.

Tennis

Anyone, it seems, is for tennis during Wimbledon month. Is it all sport you ask? Not on your nelly. It's as much about lace knickers, strawberries and cream and picnic hampers from Harrods. It seems being actually there is less fun than pouring through the tabloids each Wimbledon day to find out who's screaming foul language at whom, who's wearing what and the comparative prices of strawberries at supermarkets. All in dead seriousness. Tennis? Wouldn't be the same without the fruit.

Seats for Centre and Number Courts are so precious they have to be applied for by ballot a year ahead, although if you queue on the day itself, you might just get into the outer courts.

Did you know that the game originated in the Middle East? Yet, it seems so British with all its genteel accompaniments. Each Wimbledon event is preceded by the Stella Artois tournament where the men's circuit warms up for the main event in June.

Anyone for tennis?
All England Lawn Tennis Club
PO Box 98, Church Road, Wimbledon, London SW19 5 AE
Tel: (020) 8944-1066
Website: http://www.wimbledon.com
Tube: Southfields

Henley Royal Regatta

For four days in early July every year, Britain's premier rowers take to the Thames in a regal boat regatta that dates back 170 years. The first Oxford and Cambridge boat race took place at Henley-on-Thames in 1829. Ten years later it was formalised as an annual festival and in 1855 received the royal stamp when Prince Albert became its patron.

It is a boat race like no other in Britain, or any international boating event for that matter. Participants row upstream because the currents disallow stands to be erected at the finish of a race. It is strictly an amateur affair despite the

Whether you're a boating enthusiast or not, Henley-on-Thames is a lovely spot for a summer's day picnic or simply for soaking in the delicious riverside ambience. Turning up in regulation gear, perhaps with a hamper of fruit, wine and pies, will ease you into the spirit of a very British tradition. Check out *Time Out's* July issue for details.

royal suffix, but the anomaly does not prevent thousands of enthusiasts from turning up each year. And for all this, there is no permanent grandstand or even facilities for spectators.

It's one of those terribly British events steeped in tradition with no rules that correspond to any international ones. Yet, there are Henley regattas in Canada, Australia and America, such is its anglophile appeal among the aficionados. Henley is not jeans and T-shirt. White trousers, striped blazers and rowing caps are de rigueur; an amusing sight to see people of all ages and physical types strutting about looking like sixth form boys. Most have never held an oar in their lives! Like Royal Ascot, ambience is all. It matters little what your nautical inclinations are.

Royal Ascot

Britain's royal family are nuts about horses—the irreverent refer to them as the 'horsy set'—and one of their favourite events is the Royal Ascot. Which is really another betting event graced by royalty. Of course the Queen and her family own some of the most splendid stables but the monarch does not bet. The others are free to do so, and they do.

The first race meeting at Ascot Heath in Berkshire was in 1711 and Queen Anne was said to have been present. For the next 50 years, the event seemed to have been forgotten and it was in 1760 that the Duke of Cumberland got it going again. Subsequent members of the royal family added to the sense of prestige and, by the time King George IV came to the throne, attending Ascot had all the trappings of a regal procession.

Today, the Queen and her family travel by car from Windsor Castle and then transfer to her magnificent horse-drawn open landau with a full escort of scarlet-coated outriders. They proceed down the Straight Mile at the start of each afternoon's racing. They make for the Royal Box before which stretches the Queen's Lawn that no commoner can set foot on. Invitation to the Royal Box is by invitation only by the monarch herself. But if you should be so lucky, you might get into the Royal Ascot enclosure where the minor royals, assorted hangers-on and glitterati mingle. Some 3,000 people in Britain vie for this privilege every year.

When once an impeccable lineage and a spectacular wardrobe were essential, this stomping ground is now for the likes of assorted pop stars, nouveaux riches and the odd gatecrasher or two. It is a showcase of the regal, eccentric and serious horse breeders. Milliners come out in technicolour and outrageous glory to outdo each other with their confections, most of which make the front pages of the daily tabloids. Sometimes, Ascot seems to more about funny hats than racing.

Health Clubs & Spas

It seems everyone is into health clubs and many have mushroomed over the past two decades. The leaders are LA Fitness, Fitness First and David Lloyd and even the local council in many boroughs offers cut-price versions with basic amenities in community health clubs. What amenities you get depend on how much you pay and at the top of the range clubs, it can be very plush with indoor swimming pools, steam rooms, Jacuzzis, beauty spas, cafeteria etc. Membership fees vary enormously ranging from £ 1000 per annum at the more upmarket places and down to £ 250 for smaller, independent clubs. Whatever, in most cities throughout the UK there will be a health club and keep-fit centre usually in the town centre. The leading chains like LA Fitness for instance have as many as 40 branches throughout Britain including Scotland and Northern Ireland.

Spas have a somewhat different connotation and they are places you go to for a day or a week to chill out, as the saying goes. These spas do not focus on the pain-for-gain fitness regimes but rather a more holistic approach with massages, Turkish baths, yoga and other body and mind pampering services. They can be very expensive in the swish places like Champneys, a world-renowned spa in Hertfordshire and Ashby-de-la-Zouk in the north of England.

CUSTOMS AND CELEBRATIONS

City dwellers the world over are inclined to be blasé about age-old customs and the British urbanite is no different. But those in rural Britain are less dismissive of traditional lore that makes a welcome change to their daily routine; a refreshing anchor even for hard-boiled city people, in a rapidly changing world. For one thing these traditions are not as transient as the latest hip hop. For another, most British people have their roots in a rural and agricultural past.

Many traditions have links with what were regarded by the Church as 'heathen' practices. They were pagan rites that became inextricably entwined with Christian festivals. Christmas, in all its present joyousness, came from a mixture of Roman pagan cults and the heathen Germanic mid-winter feast of 'Yule'. In Roman times the week preceding Christmas was a 'Saturnalia' of debauchery.

Many traditions evolved from superstition, and despite rationality and Christianity, the British still consider certain things taboo. They may enter into the spirit of things for sheer novelty and fun but would not dismiss some superstitions lightly. Not all British traditions have ancient roots though. Certain festivals were nurtured from Victorian times onwards but all have been perpetuated by that most pervasive of media—television. Paradoxically, this housebound passive pastime is seen as a potential destroyer of traditions expressed via communal outdoor activity.

At least for a foreigner who may not have the opportunity to observe, much less participate in, a folksy tradition unfolding on television in glorious colour in his living room helps him to understand the British better. Passive it may be, but still an absorbing way to enrich one's knowledge of a foreign culture. It makes for much better understanding of the people, all the better when you do not have an opportunity to participate in a particular ritual.

Christmas

25th December is the date of the Roman Winter Solstice with the celebration dating back to the 4th century after Christianity became the state religion of Rome. By then it

Calendar of Public Holidays

1 January	New Year's Day
March/April	Good Friday
March/April	Easter Monday
Early May	Early May Bank Holiday
End May	Spring Bank Holiday
August	Summer Bank Holiday
25 December	Christmas Day
26 December	Boxing Day

had adopted aspects of popular pagan cults, like debauchery and drinking to bacchanalian excess. In the 10th century Christmas adapted many customs from the German heathen practices of Yule and by the 11th century all the elements were synthesized into a recognisable Christ's Mass.

Sword dancing, wassailing and Yule logs were heathen practices condemned by the Protestant Reformation. In Scotland, puritanical Calvinists suppressed all public Christmas celebrations and till this day the New Year is celebrated with more fervour than Christmas. It was in 1840 that Prince Albert and Charles Dickens pioneered the great sentimentality, traditionalism and the Christmas spirit embodied in the classic literary work *A Christmas Carol*. Who has read this heart-tugging story and not been moved by the pathos of it all? Thus the Victorian Christmas set the stage for present day celebration.

Today, Christmas in Britain appears to be one big, brash commercial affair that begins as early as September when the stores put up their bunting and stock their shelves with Christmassy items. Main shopping precincts begin to trade up by October and in early December, some places are impossible to traverse for human traffic. In London's Oxford Street, police have to be called in just to move pedestrians on as every sidewalk is wall-to-wall people.

Christmas Cards

The Victorian age also witnessed the start of Christmas cards, the first being the work of one Henry Cole in 1846. In Britain today, more than a billion cards are printed and sent out all over the world, giving the post office a nightmare from August onwards. You'd be wise to send your cards no later than the second week of December if you expect them to arrive in time.

Presents

The giving of presents dates from mid-Victorian times when it was the custom to give them to servants and children. Until then presents were given out on New Year's Day and Twelfth Night. Much of this has diffused and people give presents on Christmas Day itself or just beforehand. The stores are a veritable Aladdin's cave of gift items from October onwards, with gift vouchers now an accepted part of the tradition.

Christmas Decorations

Some people deem it unlucky to put decorations up, especially evergreens, before Christmas Eve. They have links with midwinter rites pre-dating Christianity, and are therefore pagan. Holly, ivy and mistletoe are believed to be magical plants bearing fruit during the season when everything else is dead. The berries of the holly are believed to ward off witchcraft as they represent Christ's blood and its spines his crown of thorns. Ivy symbolises immortality but mistletoe is dismissed by churches as a pagan heritage. Its survival is largely attributed to the home practice of hanging a branch above a doorway so people can kiss anyone passing under it without fear.

Most revered is the Christmas tree popularised by Prince Albert in 1840 and which became the much-loved centrepiece of Christmas celebrations in every British home, commercial premises, etc. What with the plastic age we live in, artificial trees inevitably make the scene but most British will try to buy a really nice, fresh uprooted conifer for their living room.

Come Christmas Day, most of Britain is like a cemetery as almost everyone is indoors enjoying their traditional meal, in church or generally sleeping off hangovers. There is no public transport on this day and it is strange driving along city centres as most are eerily quiet and devoid of humanity. On New Year's Day, all public transport in London is free.

But by the Twelfth Night, every vestige of the evergreen centrepiece must be removed—indeed every trace of Christmas bunting—or the household will be blighted with bad luck.

New Year's Eve and New Year's Day

New Year celebrations explode in vast public gatherings in Edinburgh, Glasgow and London on the eve. Every noise-making paraphernalia you can think of joins in a tremendous cacophony as thousands link arms to sing 'Auld Lang Syne', everyone is boozed to the gills and the church bells peal in ear-splitting unison. The London Trafalgar Square celebrations are most famous. Something like a million people are crushed together with quite a few casualties at the end of the day after. If you dare to brave this human quagmire, ushering in the New Year in Britain is an unforgettable event.

There are many superstitions attached to New Year's Day in northern England and Scotland. It is believed that nothing must be removed from the house and people refuse to lend anything to neighbours until 2nd January. It is the firmly held belief that the New Year must begin happily, luckily and after a clean break with the past. Hence the practice of resolutions which, today, is generally the result of the season's over-indulgence and lasts only till its aftermath!

In Scotland, if the first person who sets foot in someone's house is tall and dark, he is believed to bring good luck. In Yorkshire and Lincolnshire, fair men are the harbingers of good fortune. But if you have flat feet, are lame, cross-eyed or have eyebrows that meet in the middle, don't on any account step into someone's home on New Year's Day. Of course only the superstitious will take all this seriously, but as a foreigner, it is always more prudent to be aware of likely gaffes. If you want to be invited back.

Easter

The most revered of all Christian festivals, it celebrates the resurrection of Christ from the dead, on the first Sunday following the 21st of March after the full moon. Because of lunar variability, Easter can be anywhere between 22 March and 25 April. All devout Roman Catholics and Anglicans attend church and receive Holy Communion.

Many traditions dating back to ancient times are still observed at Easter, but mainly in rural areas. Most others are apt to use the four-day holiday to get away from it all—including church! In fact the Friday before Easter is one mad scramble throughout the country when people try to get away to their favourite resorts, spas or country cottages. Road, rail, sea and air routes are usually choked!

As for the Easter egg, which is an ancient symbol of new life and spring awakening that became attached to the festival, its 20th century role seems to be quite removed from reflecting the resurrection. Traditionally given away for good luck after being ceremonially blessed, Easter eggs today are chiefly remarkable for supporting the chocolate industry. Creamed, coated, beribboned and otherwise jazzed up to make cute, elegant or zany presents, they reflect little of the religious significance. Manufacturers and confectionery

Celebrating Easter in a big way.

shops are less bothered with their raison d'être than that they bring in the cash.

April Fool's Day

I have never seen a people go to such great lengths in national leg-pulling! The British penchant for 'send ups' is in top gear on this day and the media, especially, pull out all the stops. One year a national daily ran the story of a master plan to move Trafalgar Square several hundred yards from its present site. Hundreds of people turned up to watch the titanic engineering feat! Of course the whole thing was a monumental hoax.

This licensed mischief, believed to be derived from the irreverent Roman Saturnalia, flourishes from boundless ingenuity of perpetrators all over the country. There is a curious rule that binds the mirth-making. At noon, all jokes must cease or the hoax rebounds on the jester. Watch out for the cleverest ones in the national press.

A BBC television programme devoted much time and effort to put one over the public. In dead seriousness, the presenter came on to say an unearthly creature had been discovered on the misty slopes of the Himalayas by archeologists. This 'Lirpa Loof' had a blue body, funny ears and excreted purple turds! The discovery was then caged in London Zoo and the cameras were there to record public curiosity and befuddlement. And the BBC never explained their cheeky hoax.

Halloween

The 31st of October is All Souls' Day, when in olden days witches were believed to meet and plot together. Today American style 'tricks or treat' visits of small children, often wearing masks or fancy dress, are becoming more frequent in large towns. In order to avoid anything nasty from happening, keep a bag of sweets or some small change handy if you are home on 31 October.

The State Opening of Parliament

Even within the small square of a television set, the State Opening of Parliament in October or November is a not-to-be-missed spectacle. British Parliament is more than 700 years old and in this time has developed complex and grand customs and ceremonies second only to the monarchy in opulence.

On the evening before the opening, cellars of the Palace of Westminster are ceremonially searched by Yeomen of the Guard with light from candle lanterns. It is believed to date back to 1605 when a similar search uncovered the infamous Gunpowder Plot perpetrated by Guy Fawkes.

Two processions then set out from Buckingham Palace, each with a mounted escort of Household Cavalry. One carries the crown in its own gilded coach, guarded by the Royal Watermen. The second procession comprises the Queen and her family. At 11:00 am, the monarch, now with her crown and in her parliament raiment, leads the way to the House of Lords to assume her throne. Her messenger, known as Black Rod, then summons the members of the House of Commons. He knocks three times with his black rod and then conveys his message. Historically, since 1641, no member of royalty has entered this lower chamber in person, symbolising the disastrous attempt by Charles I to arrest the Five Members. The monarch then reads her speech which, in reality, is an announcement of the government's political programme.

There are many curious customs but none more so than that governing tobacco. No MP may smoke during Parliament but they may take snuff. This is contained in the House of Commons Snuff Box, made of wood taken from the chamber destroyed by bombs in 1941. It is kept by the Principal Door-keeper. Members also have the right to stop all traffic while crossing the road to the House. At the end of each ordinary session of Parliament, members cry out "Who goes home?", echoing the days when members banded together under armed guard each night before setting off home.

Guy Fawkes Day

On 5 November 1605, a plot to blow up the Houses of Parliament was discovered and its perpetrators apprehended and hanged. Ever since, it has been a great tradition to celebrate Guy Fawkes Day and the continuation of parliamentary government by building and then burning a huge bonfire. Models of effigies of Guy Fawkes, called 'guys', are made beforehand and burned on the bonfires, generally with a fireworks display which echoes the exploding of gunpowder.

Many boroughs give a public bonfire and fireworks display, either on 5 November or on the nearest Saturday, using money from local rates to entertain their residents and also hoping to limit the annual accident rate as individuals injure themselves with fireworks and fire brigades throughout the country are stretched to full capacity.

You will often see small children collecting money for fireworks with a ragged 'guy', outside London tube stations, in shopping precincts and near supermarkets. They will call 'Penny for the Guy'—but will sneer if you give less than ten or 20 pence.

Changing of the Guard

At 11:00 am each day, in summer and alternate days in winter, bearers of the Queen's Regimental Colour from St James Palace march down the Mall to join the Buckingham Palace detachment. This symbolises the changing of the old and new—St James is the oldest established royal residence—and at 11:30 am, the ceremony begins. The retiring guard hands over the palace keys and the new sentries take their posts with military stamping and slow music. It is a brilliant visual experience reflecting the pomp and pageantry of royal lifestyle, with the guards in bearskin helmets and scarlet coats. The public take delight in trying to make the sentries twitch or move a muscle. They are trained not to do so and nothing, not even a nosy camera inches from their nostrils, will produce a quiver.

FAIRS

One of the most English of all traditions, fairs spring up at the drop of a hat. Annually, there are something like 8000, some little village affairs and others spread over a whole county. Whatever their traditional history, fairs are for the most part an excuse for merry-making, eating and, of course, drinking.

Until the 19th century the majority of fairs were commercial exercises—markets for goods, farm produce and animals. Then, only large towns had shops in the modern sense and a fair meant a shopping spree for people living in remote places. They could stock up on meat and other staples while having a nice day out.

The Thai Food Festival in Battersea Park each summer year draws thousands of people enamoured of the cuisine that is the fastest growing one within the ethnic spectrum in Britain. Each festival features dozens of Thai food, entertainment and craft stalls and is a must-visit.

Every village, town, borough and even a housing estate holds some sort of fair at least once a year, especially in summer. Some are no more than a collection of stalls selling anything from samosas to homemade jams while others will feature very loud bands. Each becomes a platform for local residents to gather, make acquaintances and spread community spirit. It is at these functions that you find the traditional British reserve melting.

In the past two decades, there has been an emergence of food festivals throughout the year. These range from massive affairs like the International Food Exhibition in Birmingham

Country fairs retain a touch of medieval pageantry. In the past, they played an essential role in trade and socialisation.

in March, to smaller ethnic ones like Thai and Indian food shows scattered throughout Britain.

Boot Sales

This is a curious phenomenon that has grown spectacularly in the past two decades. Originally a junk sale from the boot of a car (hence the name), this has mushroomed into massive events. In most cities, towns and villages, most warm weekends will see hundreds of traders, opportunists and others sell all manner of bric-a-brac spread out on ground sheets in car parks and fields. Some are so large you need a whole day to traverse them. And you can by anything from a used battery to a bathtub—anything goes at boot sales! Local papers advertise all the details.

ENTERTAINMENT
Theatre

London is the sparkling gem in the diadem of Britain's theatrical heritage, but small towns throughout the country are not exactly entertainment wastelands either. Local playhouses abound and amateur productions by hobbycraft thespians provide good entertainment. Come Christmas, the heritage of pantomime hilarity is given full mirth with any number of professional productions, some featuring international names usually in the role of the peripatetic 'Dames'.

> Many actors would give anything to get into a hooped dress, furbelows and war paint just to get the family screaming with laughter. It is probably the best known of British entertainment genres, a national tradition in fact. Amateur or professional, they give 100 per cent entertainment value even if the props leave much to be desired.

Most British actors would not consider themselves successful until they have appeared on some West End stage. It's regarded as the sternest testing ground for talent, though the money they earn is a fraction of what television and films offer. Nonetheless, many would gladly give up mega salaries just for a small role in a top West End hit.

And if you're good enough to be accepted by the Royal Shakespeare Company, the world is literally your stage. The best names in show business have at one time or another appeared with the RSC.

The desire to 'tread the boards' must be a great buzz for Jason Donovan to want to appear in the stunning stage production of *Chitty Chitty Bang Bang*. Such mega American stars as Jason Scott Lee, Dustin Hoffman, Kathleen Turner, David Hasselhoff and Nathan Lane have all given a few weeks of their expensive time to star on the London stage for a fraction of what they can earn in big budget films. For someone who makes millions a film, being paid £ 1000 a week is small change but the kudos is immeasurable.

Britain produces more actors than its theatres can offer roles to. At any given time, some 90 per cent of them are unemployed or between roles. What do jobbing actors do while waiting for that great role? They work at anything they can get—waiters, salesmen, buskers—and the waiting for most of them can take years.

As a theatrical cornucopia, London's West End is outstanding for both choice and the vicissitudes of getting tickets! It draws audiences from all over the world by the planeload, especially from America. It was crisis time some years ago when American tourists decided to give England a miss after many Middle East political upheavals threatened their travel safety. Theatre companies reeled in shock at the drastic drop in business. Locals rejoiced at the ease of getting tickets.

Under normal circumstances, one has to book months ahead for a hit show, even given that there are no less than three dozen different shows going on at the same time each night. The most practical solution is to plan your theatre night as far ahead as possible, to avoid disappointment. There are ticket agents dotted all over London, in department stores and within the ranks of shifty touts lurking outside every theatre. But be warned that you might pay up to several times the actual value. And it is illegal.

Prices can vary greatly depending on your astute forward planning, ignorance or sheer desperation. Expect to pay at least £ 20 for a second line show and as much as £ 50 for a hit. Generally, agents charge a small booking fee. Booking direct on the phone with your credit card also entails a fee between £ 1 and £ 4. Queuing up at the box office avoids this, but the chances are you won't get the seats you want because, as luck would have it, the person in front of you just bought the last ticket.

If you're going alone, a good bet is to wait outside the theatre half an hour before showtime and pounce on cancellations. There is a half price booth for theatre tickets at Leicester Square, but the trouble is the endless queues. One cardinal rule about theatre going, whether in London or in the provinces, is, don't be late. Firstly, it's annoying to others already seated and secondly, you might be stopped from going in until the next interval!

Most evening shows start at 8:00 pm, so allow yourselves plenty of time to travel, especially if you're going a fair distance. Matinees, usually on one weekday and Saturday, start between 2:00 and 3:00 pm. Cameras and other photographic equipment are not allowed in all theatres. Neither is smoking. Interval time is usually 15 minutes, enough for a quick puff if you must, perhaps a drink at the bar or some ice cream.

In London's West End almost all theatres are within walking distance of each other. In Edinburgh, Glasgow and

There is no dearth of entertainment in Britain, particularly in London's West End where all the big stars dream to perform.

other major cities, there are good theatres if not as many as in London. In Wimbledon, Hampstead and Hammersmith, there are theatres of no mean repute. For one thing, many West End bound productions try their act out in these out-of-the-way places first. But far from being 'rehearsal venues' they are bona fide theatres that often put on first-rate productions that don't get the same media hype. Because of the sheer volume of visitors, West End theatres have a captive audience all year round. Some productions bomb out after a short run, but by and large they run and run.

The Theatre Heritage

Britain's theatre heritage goes back hundreds of years—to the time of Shakespeare when theatres in the round were common public entertainment. Actors played on an open stage with audiences sitting or standing all around. One such theatre, the Globe, was recently excavated in London and believed to date back to the 15th century. Many leading lights of the theatre lobbied for the remains of the Globe to be preserved and built up again in the face of threatened development. Kevin Spacey, the Oscar wining American actor threw his whole weight and money behind this legendary theatre and is currently its prime mover in putting on top dramas.

Such is the lure of the acting trade that many will gladly starve and work at jobs that do not bind them down just in case the phone rings and a role is up for grabs. Dancers do the same grinding rounds of auditions in the hope that the next one will be it. Most come with impeccable credentials: graduates of such well-known drama schools as the Royal Academy of Dramatic Arts, Italia Conti School, Central School of Speech and Drama and others too numerous to mention. Professional standards

First-time theatre-goers might find many of Britain's theatres quaintly grand and ornate, and not always conducive to perfect viewing. For instance, either end of front row seats, while costing premium prices, can cause severe cricks of the neck because of the angle at which you watch. Others have a pillar blocking half your view and yet more are situated in 'dead' corners where views are limited. Always check with the ticket office which these are and avoid them like the plague.

are among the highest in the world, but the profession is one of the most precarious.

Television productions, especially soap operas, have been saviours for many talented people who might get a series or two, or a walk-on part. Exposure is the name of the game and nothing is more than forgettable than not being in the public eye. Stories of 'discoveries' are legend where some young talent is plucked from obscurity and thrust into the global sphere through a major film. It is the stuff of thespian dreams. But theatrical life is far from stardust. Those in the profession moan about the constant grind of doing six shows a week plus one or two matinées. Their lives revolve around their work, with little time for leisure during a production's run, which may be anything from two weeks to years.

For anyone visiting or living in Britain, soaking up the theatre is a priority (if fairly costly) that must not be missed. It is sheer joy to see a first-class production, great music, acting and glitzy entertainment that is worth all of £ 40 for two hours. Unlike one-dimensional cinema, live theatre gives one an incredible buzz with its rapport and technical brilliance in many productions.

Today's top shows sun the gamut of the entertainment spectrum, from the sassy, sexy *Chicago*, Jerry Springer the *Opera*, Mel Brooks hilarious *The Producers* starring the effervescent Nathan Lane, *Mary Poppins* and the classic Andrew Lloyd Webber productions of *Phantom of the Opera* (in its second decade) and *The Woman in White*. Whatever you think of Webber's music, he still remains a doyen of theatre, both in Britain and America. Another iconic drama is Agatha Christie's *Mousetrap* that has continuously being presented for an incredible 53 years to sell-out audiences every night!

As a cultural offering, British theatre offers a unique insight into the life and mores of the British people. Restoration, contemporary straight plays, comedies, musicals, operettas and avant-garde theatre echo much about historical, social and political Britain in the most entertaining way. It beats reading musty tomes in a library! One of the best ways to understand the quirky British sense of humour is to see a

There is no lack of realism in British theatre—not least the ones that dare to stage what others fear will fall foul of the censor. One of the most provocative productions I saw in the 1970s was the musical *Hair*. Total nudity was its springboard but done with such finesse and superb choreography that few could take offence.

comedy. The first-rate ones give rare insights into what tickles the British funny bone with a wealth of slick one-liners, wry humour and brilliant wit.

Musicals are a showcase of talent with some of the best dancing you can see anywhere in the world. Classical productions breathe life into great literary works by such luminaries as Chekhov, Shakespeare, Coward and Feydeau.

Technical production can leave you breathless with its sheer wizardry. In *Chitty Chitty Bang Bang*, the vintage car is actually flying over the audience at one point and has to be seen to be believed. The *Cirque du Soleil* is quite simply mind-boggling at the Royal Albert Hall.

Soaking up British theatre rubs off in many ways on one. One cannot fail to be moved by the level of professionalism, talent and production techniques that trigger off positive responses, especially for drama, music and stage production students. The cultural richness aside, British theatre is like an enormous open university where you learn the true meaning of discipline, dedication, artistic passion and the finest points of language.

Concerts

In public areas like London's Covent Garden, tube stations and outside theatres, buskers provide amusement, often of polished calibre. Indeed, many are would-be professionals hoping for that big break or are between gigs and hone their talents for whatever they can get. Once hounded by police, they now can apply for performing licenses to entertain in underground tube stations. Flautists, violinists, even harpists make the underground their stage everyday, if they're not drowned out by a saxophonist and his ghetto-blaster accompaniment. Baroque, hip hop, steel band or a-cappella—they're all for free, or a donation.

There is the lovely British tradition of summer seasons— usually musical variety shows with top billing—at Britain's

A street steel band, all part of the vibrant entertainment culture in Britain.

resorts. Many make it an annual pilgrimage to entertain at places like Blackpool, Brighton, and Edinburgh and wherever the British spend their summer holidays. These are generally cheap but excellent value, if a little provincial with their jokes. They don't cater to an international clientele as such and, like the annual Christmas pantomime, are British to the core.

Serious music fans can have their fill of concerts throughout Britain, but especially at London's Barbican where top names are regularly featured all year round. Unlike West End stage shows which are usually booked solid months ahead, those for orchestral and solo performances are generally easy to get and cost about £ 15 for a good seat. Top bands at venues like Wembley play to packed houses and tickets have to be booked well in advance if you want to catch the likes of Beyonce and other superstars.

There is the annual Edinburgh Festival with a programme to cater for every taste and Glasgow is known as Scotland's cultural city with regular offerings of quality performances from Shakespeare to Robbie Williams. Anyone living or even visiting Britain would be doing himself an injustice by not taking advantage of such a plethora of entertainment.

This is a country where there is little justification to say one is bored for want of cash to seek entertainment, because money is often not the price—it just takes a little effort. A scan through the daily papers will tell you there is something going on somewhere, for free or within most people's budgets. The entertainment media is an extremely well-oiled machine with any number of specialist publications hitting the stands daily and weekly. Friday papers are usually rife with information on who's doing what, where.

One of the nicest and cheapest ways to spend a summer afternoon is to attend an open-air concert in one of the parks that dot Britain. It's usually free and the only costs are perhaps drinks and ice cream for several hours of splendid music by professional bands. In Hampstead's Kenwood, summer concerts are reflective of the Hollywood Bowl and listening to the stirring strains of Sousa's military marches and Strauss' waltzes under the stars is spine tingling.

Even the ethnic communities have organised their own video clubs, cinemas and other live shows to cater to Bangladeshi, Chinese or Afro-Caribbean tastes. One is spoilt for choice really and apart from public holidays, there's usually something to entertain everyone from six to 90 every day of the year. Museums, zoos and art galleries hold regular specials, especially during school holiday periods when children are catered for.

TELEVISION

Like the British press, television is subject to regulations by the Office of Communications (OFCOM) that also has responsibilities for other media like radio, telecommunications and wireless communications services. The commission exists to further the interests of consumers by; balancing choice and competition with the duty to foster plurality, protect viewers and listeners and promote cultural diversity and ensuring full and fair competition between communication providers.

The number of people in Britain who choose to ignore television is so small they never count in statistical studies.

Given the influence of this most invasive of mass media, surveys concern themselves with how many sets each household has and how many hours people spend watching the idiot box as it is curiously called by some.

The accusatory fingers are out every so often that children are hopelessly addicted to TV. The latest survey shows that one in every four British children has his own TV set, and is glued to it for 13 hours a week, which works out to a solid two hours every evening. A cause for parental worry with many wringing their hands in despair that there is little control over what the kids watch, ruining their imagination in the process, never mind that homework takes a poor second place.

This is especially so when they go beyond the 9:00 pm watershed for adult programmes that show explicit sex, violence and other undesirable facets of low life. Others worry that television is a harbinger of family life breakdown. Socialists and mass media analysts' efforts to alert the public to television's pervasive dangers seem so much waffling. Once there was just the BBC and ITV, but now satellite, digital and cable TV have joined the circuit and homes all over Britain can tune to literally hundreds of channels 24-7.

It is estimated that BBC 1 and 2 have the lion's share of audiences at some 37.6 per cent, ITV at 11.3 per cent, Channel 4 at 9.6 per cent, Channel 5 some 6.4 per cent and satellite, digital and cable at a combined 18.6 per cent. And each service spends millions enticing the public to watch, as they promise ever more package news, entertainment and sport in British living rooms. The oft-repeated public outcry is that the line between education/information and negative influence is thin enough as it is without the world becoming the viewer's oyster.

BBC1 and BBC2 are non-commercial terrestrial services depending on annual license fees and government subsidy. The company also has the digital services for BBC One, BBC Two, BBC Three, BBC Four, BBC Knowledge, BBC News 24 and BBC Parliament, all of which are also funded by the license fee.

Watchdogs, watersheds and censorship aside, British television does indeed pervade, distract, entertain and alarm, depending on your moral views, self-discipline and, in the case of parents, vetting powers.

The ITV Network comprises 15 independent regional television licensees and one licensee providing the national breakfast time service. In addition to the terrestrial channel ITV 1, ITV also has ITV2, ITV News and CiTV. Channel 4 and S4C (4th channel in Wales) each with distinctive character. Channel 5 began broadcasting in 1997 and now reaches some 40 million viewers.

British Sky Broadcasting is a direct broadcast satellite service operating in the UK and Ireland. Launched in 1989 originally as a four-channel service owned by a Luxembourg-based consortium, it merged with British Satellite Broadcasting in 1990 to form British Sky Broadcasting.

Sky Digital, launched in 1998, offers over 300 channels, pay-per-view services and interactive entertainment, including e-mail, on-screen shopping and voting. BSkyB has some 16 million viewers in seven million homes and also runs Sky News, Sky One and Sky Sports.

Many channels are now 24-7 and vie ceaselessly for viewers with snap, crackle and pop 'breakfast television' that can range from the inane to the arty. Contents are a hodgepodge of current affairs, world news and pop gossip that aim to capture the attention of millions of people rushing off to work before 9 am. The ratings war becomes the yardstick for the rise or fall of such programming and the efforts to sustain viewers often reach ridiculous heights.

Provincial stations like Anglia (east of England), Border (Border countries and Isle of Man), Central (east, west and south Midlands), Channel (Channel Islands), Grampian (north of Scotland), Granada (north-west England), Meridian (south and south-east England), London (London region), Ulster (Northern Ireland) and Yorkshire (Yorkshire) have somewhat different schedules but pool their news coverage.

It takes an average of a year before hit films like *Titanic*, *Matrix*, *Chicago* and *Troy* come on satellite TV. When you consider it costs about £ 8 to see a film in cinemas, it's worth the wait, never mind what they say about epics being better on the big screen. Plus the fact that the whole family can watch it for free.

All papers print daily and weekly viewing schedules for every station. It is as impossible to use a blanket description for British television as it is to pigeonhole public tastes. You could use every adjective in the book and still not encompass what appears on the little box. At best, accolades and brickbats are only a reflection of individual taste.

Commercials

Revile them, love them; no more, no less annoying than any other commercial station with an average of four 'ads' each break and three breaks in a half-hour programme. British commercials are in a class of their own, often more entertaining than the programme they interrupt and many commercial 'stars' are cult figures in their own right. A beautiful woman may be seen selling perfume one minute and the next, she's appearing in some situation comedy on another channel. Many actors and actresses between jobs grab at the lucrative contracts offered by manufacturers, which often catapult them to stardom that bit movie parts do not.

There are no commercials on the two BBC channels though there has been constant talk about the Beeb going commercial. So far, the world's most famous broadcasting name is resisting the lure of multi-million pound revenue with the argument that quality will be compromised if they sell their souls to consumerism.

Today, you see the likes of Nicole Kidman for Chanel, Patrick Swayze for Orange phone, Andie Mcdowell for L'Oreal and so on. By the same token, many other top stars are seen endorsing products and become identified so strongly with their product that the roles they play in straight dramas become so much less credible.

Cigarette advertising is totally banned, and underwear and alcohol are strictly controlled by a code of time and suitability. The impression one gets is an overwhelming barrage of household products, almost always with a wry twist of humour in the message. This is a distinctive British feature. Hard-sell commercials are far outweighed by those that feature the inimitable British touch for humour. Whatever the product or service, the treatment is inevitably humorous and memorable. Britain, in fact, is regarded by the rest of the advertising world as the think tank of creativity.

Watching commercials is a marvellous way of boning up on British consumer goods without leaving the house. In a few months, you'll learn the comparative merits of one lager against another, which bread is healthier, what your dog likes to eat (how they know I'll never know!), when and where to buy spring lamb, which car is tested by robots and driven by humans (it won an award), etc. In this sense, it is a matchless education for a foreigner getting to grips with the British lifestyle.

After all, you don't want to use just any detergent—it's got to be the one that makes your whites cleaner than white. I say, do not disappear to make a cup of tea when the commercials are on. If nothing else, it's gloriously funny to see a car being transformed into a dancing robot to hip hop music!

Documentaries

When the British produce good documentaries, they rarely have a peer. In the area of wildlife and ecology, the BBC has a stable of first-rate programmes that have not paled even after repeat showings over decades. Perhaps the most distinguished of all documentary creators is Sir David Attenborough who has chronicled an immense range of subjects from bird's nest gathering in Borneo to the sex life of desert ants. A past master of wildlife minutiae, his programmes have rarely been off the air for the past 30 years, each one more beguiling, educational and entertaining than the previous one.

Other documentaries of the artistic, historical and entertainment genre are generally very watchable. In the field of art, British television provides an absorbing and often scintillating insight that museums can never hope to do. The weekly *Antiques Roadshow* attempts to play the role of dream merchant in identifying bric-a-brac brought along by hopeful owners. Viewers join in the

On its heels is another programme called *Flog It!* that is all about people wanting to sell their attic daubing in the hope one might turn out to be a Van Gogh!

excitement of a possible discovery that a dusty objet d'art might turn up to be a rare treasure worth a small fortune! The queue is unending and the programme looks like it will run and run.

Watching it makes you want to rummage through your old chest in the hope of finding that your ginger jar is really a Ming vase. History and theatrical arts do not get enough airtime, alas; they are deemed elitist entertainment hardly likely to match the viewership of such staple fare as *Poirot*, *Eastenders* and *The Weakest Link*. Which explains why most serious documentaries are aired late at night, past prime time. Ratings, you see, are the barometer of populist taste and programmes of any intellect tend to be slotted in when the masses are in bed. No survey has yet been made to find out if eggheads go to bed later.

Situation Comedies (Sitcoms) and Soap Operas

Now, these are bywords of television addiction. It seems every time TV producers run out of creative juices, they fall back on the sitcom and drag out yet another 30 minutes of life's situations that can be hilariously funny, boring or baffling. Yet, each can be an invaluable insight into British lifestyles: days of yore, upper crust, pastoral or cockney working class. British humour, whether in sitcoms, soaps or feature films, tend to rely on the verbal assault rather than the slapstick high jinks popular in some American programmes.

The soap operas (some have gone on for years, like *Coronation Street*) reflecting contemporary lifestyles, replete with unintelligible accents (to the foreigner at least), can be viewed in an educational light. Even if at first you do not understand what is going on. Heavy on the argot, colloquialism, British domestic crises or rural pastiches, some are eminently watchable once you overcome the culture shock barrier. It is life, warts and all, as British producers are chary of too much artificiality.

Then you have the other genre of sex and sensationalism. Witness the popularity of *Absolutely Fabulous*. It is half an hour of pure mayhem generated by the shenanigans of two women working in the fashion world that pulls no punches in taking the mickey out of the brittle world of glamour. It's fun, it's irrelevant and it is lapped up by global audiences. At the moment, riding the waves of sitcom popularity are *Sex and the City*, *Gimme Gimme Gimme* and others of a similar sexy genre.

Costume dramas and historical epics are more expensive to produce and, if they bomb, a lot of money goes down at the same time as the ratings. The few soaps that pop up occasionally are generally tempered with salt-of-the-earth characters as if to inject reality into fantasy. These are no way near the American soaps that would have us believe every woman goes to bed with full make-up on!

The classics, yes. A British actor would give his eye teeth to appear on stage in a Shakespeare play for a pittance rather than earn a small fortune making a cameo in *Friends*. It seems this top rated American sitcom pays its top stars a cool US$ 1 million per episode—silly money really. At least those who respect their craft and can afford not to bite the Hollywood gilded carrot. As one British actress was heard to say, "Why, you never see people in American soaps ever going to the bathroom!" Real funny is how one can sum up British comedy.

British comedy may not be everyone's cup of tea or even understood. The few attempts by British TV companies to transport this genre across the pond to the American audiences have failed. They just do not get it. When you watch programmes like *Fawlty Towers* featuring the madcap antics of John Cleese, or *One Foot in the Grave* about a perpetually grumpy old man, Victor Meldrew, it might take you a while to appreciate the wry sense of humour. But when you do, like I did, you are hooked. Which explains why these and other similar comedies keep getting repeat airtime over decades.

No consensus of opinions, much less an individual, can be arbiter of what constitutes education on TV, in as much as viewers are captive and range from the age of awareness to that when myopia hasn't quite robbed a person of sight. But we are not talking about education per se, rather the knowledge which can be gleaned from every programme by a foreigner trying to understand what makes the British tick. Given that the British can be unfathomably quirky, even to other British, the job of television programming is downright difficult.

Quality and entertainment value are therefore secondary, if you regard television as audio-visual reference. Soap operas that reflect contemporary lifestyles, historical documentaries turning back the pages of time, comedies that reflect particular British humour, programmes on art, music and dance, and cops and robbers replete with gore and gratuitous violence are educational, if viewed in this light.

It's as much how you view as what you view that can provide important data to help ease you into the mainstream that will not give cause for bewilderment. British producers of straight contemporary drama have a penchant for realism, down to the earthy facets of suburban routine, even in a slick, glossy production. In this way, British television differs vastly from its American cousin that rarely ever shows people in other than unreal glamorous settings. British critics are apt to scoff at American imports of which there are quite a few, to name the key ones, *Friends*, *Joey*, *Becker*, *Ally McBeal*, *Charmed* etc.

A British bobby, after duty, will go home for his tea. An American cop slides into his Porsche and drives off to his hilltop mansion. How does he afford it on a policeman's pay? Should television sell escapism or should it be straight from the hip? Whatever your view, it must be appreciated that too much gloss can stick as too much realism provides little relief from life's tedium. Fortunately, British TV sits somewhere in between these extremes. What is refreshing is the fact that British TV and its stars are easy to relate to, making one feel that fame and fortune are that much more attainable. This proclivity for showing life, warts and all, can only give hope to millions that, one day, they can be up there too. Perhaps it is the very tenet of television realism that rubs off on its actors, altogether not a bad thing.

Feature Films

The lack of good, current feature films is a bone of contention among many British viewers. While I tend to agree with this, the question of subjectivity again rises to the fore. The BBC tends to drag out old films which it may well believe to be classics and therefore good for the people. Someone paying

£ 70 a year license fees may want a steady diet of James Bond and Indiana Jones blockbusters. Then again, those old chestnuts from the *Carry On* stable are still popular (they were made in the 1960s believe it or not and most of the stars are either old-age pensioners or dead!) with the general public and get prime time over such overpriced and overdone epics like Star Trek I, II, III, IV.

On average, with the number of channels on offer, you get a choice of at least 12 feature films 24 hours a day. Come Christmas, the channels pull out all the stops and hit you with an avalanche of movies, some traditional regulars like *White Christmas*, *Scrooge* and *A Christmas Carol* and others of epic adventure. From 23 December to 2 January, every home with a TV set is like the local cinema gone mad. I find it difficult to decide whether to go out or stay in because there are no less than a dozen films and as many extravaganzas and musical specials to sit through every single day, round the clock and throughout the season. TV wins out invariably over going out.

Everything is shut tight for three days over Christmas and wakes up sleepily only after the New Year. Your TV set becomes a real friend. It is also when DVD shops clean up. Be armed with at least two dozen blank tapes just to tape the Christmas offerings for your own repeats.

Travel Shows

Annual holidays being big business, television naturally sets itself up as a consumer watchdog and you get regular series telling you about the where, when, what and how. In fact, travel programmes spare no expense in production with entire crew and presenters hopping from hot spot to hot spot, giving viewers the real low-down on value for money. Most are entertaining and informative while a few seem like too much indulgence on the producer's part. It's all very well to titillate the travel taste buds with exotic delights of a Caribbean paradise and quite another to overcome the problems and budgetary juggling to get there. However, the trend now is to offer not only enticing bites of exotic locations but online or telephone booking facilities.

Live Shows

These are usually inane quiz shows that tax no more than one's ability to add up the cost of products in a supermarket trolley. One series, *The Price is Right*, was a weekly free-for-all where the audience had to guess the cost of items. If they got them right, they won the products. It didn't matter that critics panned it as mindless; week after week, it had millions riveted to their sets.

Then there are the traditional Royal Command performances live from Her Majesty's Theatre, variety shows, panel games, talk shows and symposiums that can range from sober discussions on nuclear physics to chaotic political fracas. There is an endless queue for tickets to these live shows, but you can write in to the BBC or ITV and expect to wait for months.

One variety show that annually causes critics to unsheath their claws is the *Eurovision Song Contest*. For some inexplicable reason, though millions love it, entertainment writers seem to derive sadistic pleasure in tearing it apart!

News

British news dissemination is first class. Little that happens of national import gets past the news hounds. Tragedies, high drama, crime and some frivolous pursuits—in short, news that the public wants—get airtime and up-to-the-minute presentation literally round the clock with some channels and from 6:00 am from others. British TV newscasters are virtual stars in their own right and earn whacking salaries for their skills. £ 1 million a year is not unknown among the top journalists, for journalists they really are, not simply readers. What you see is 20 minutes of condensed news produced by a large team, writing and pruning the vast amount of information that inundate the TV studios every hour of every day.

More and more world news is being shown, dispelling the belief that British television is insular and provincial. However, local news still constitutes the main bulk of news bulletins for the British are more interested in knowing about what is happening in their own country. The main bulletins are at 6:00 am, 1:00 pm, 6:30 pm and 10:00 pm on BBC 1, and 12:30 pm and 10:30 pm on ITV1, 10:30 pm Newsnight on BBC 2, on Channel 4 at 12:00 noon and 7:00 pm on Channel at 12:00 noon and 3:30 pm. Radio and TV schedules feature full details.

Presentation is slick, short, sharp and concisely relevant and with naturalness reminiscent of American style presentation. British TV newsreaders take most things in their stride, faux pas and all, without going into a panic. Once, the BBC news studio was invaded by a lesbian protestor who somehow chained herself to the newsreader's seat! The reader, Sue Lawley, simply glanced at the invader and carried on calmly with an off the cuff remark that "we seem to be invaded."

Sports

Every weekend and all weekend, TV covers every possible sport that is enjoyed by the masses or a few. Most Saturday and part of Sunday afternoons are devoted to sports of one kind or another.

Ethnic Programmes
Satellite, Digital and Cable television now feature many ethnic channels at the click of a switch. Sky TV offers a plethora of free and pay-per-view channels like Sony TV Asia, Star News, Star Plus in Hindi and Urdu, PCNE in English and Mandarin covering China, Muslim TV for religious broadcasts, Bangla TV and even limited coverage of Al Jazeera.

Religious Programmes
Sunday evenings give ample coverage to religious—predominantly Christian—programmes, songs of praise and evening worship type mainly.

OTHERS
Radio
Far from being overshadowed by television, British radio is alive, well and very listenable. Domestic radio services are broadcast over three wavebands–FM (or VHF), medium wave and long wave. A number of radio stations are now digital on 217.5 to 230 MHz.

With more than 40 stations to tune in to, you're spoilt for choice. From contemporary pop music on BBC1, popular music and entertainment and comedy on BBC2, classical music on BBC 3, news, documentaries, drama and talk shows on BBC4, news and sports live on BBC5 to outrageous independent—even pirate—stations, programmes and broadcasting styles run the gamut from high-brow to plain rudeness. BBC 6 and BBC 7 are digital only with BBC Asian Radio catering specifically for British Asian Indians. The BBC also runs local stations in every major town and city from Berkshire to York and there's the august BBC World Service that broadcasts in an astonishing 43 languages to a global audience of 150 million.

As an information service, radio is vital to millions of commuters dependent on up-to-the-minute travel and weather reports. In a country where sudden turns of the weather and nasty traffic snarl-ups can make mincemeat of journey plans, British radio is an essential lifeline. For entertainment, it offers tremendous value even over television, with so many stations to tune in to. In the wilds of nowhere, a transistor set triumphs over the idiot box.

Virtually every television personality received his early training in radio and many prefer to stay in radio despite the visual glamour of the small screen. Radio disc jockeys attain as much cult status as their TV cousins do, often getting paid as much. The top voices can earn up to £ 100,000 a year. One former radio star, Terry Wogan, who went on to front his own chat show three times a week on TV, and now back on radio is regarded as a broadcasting icon.

Newspapers

Most importantly, there is no state control or censorship of the British press, although it is subject to laws on publication and the Press Complaints Commission was set up in 1991 by the industry as a means of self-regulation. It replaced the rather archaic Press Council that had been operation since 1953. The PCC's functions are basically to consider, adjudicate, conciliate, and resolve complaints of unfair treatment by the press, and to ensure that the press maintains the highest professional standards, with respect for freedom of expression, the public's right to know and the right of the press to operate free from improper pressure.

For anyone enamoured of the printed word, Britain is a wordsmith's paradise. Whatever your tastes, whether you are an egghead or voyeur, highbrow or inclined to sex and sensationalism, there's a broadsheet or tabloid for you. Your first encounter with Britain's popular press—often given the ignominious slag-off as 'gutter press'—is likely to be startling to say the least. At first glance the *Sunday Sport* might seem to be all about football scores and cricket overs. Perhaps a few pages; the rest are devoted to coverage of events quite out of this world.

'Woman gives birth to alien!'

'Elvis spotted shopping in Burbank!'

The headlines scream, enticing you to pour over the features therein that are the antithesis of responsible journalism. Pictorial coverage has nothing to do with good or bad taste, simply overt sensationalism. Nothing is sacrosanct, not even the physically handicapped. It's not a newspaper—it's a window on the weird, unbelievable, a veritable sci-fi serving that purports to make sense of the ridiculous.

Or if other people's sex lives and assorted skeletons in cupboards make your Sunday reading, you'd devour the *News of the World* with relish. Everyone in the public eye is fair game, be it getting out of a car in mini-skirt or canoodling in a nightclub. Nothing and nobody is sacrosanct—not even the spectre of libel suits—to this rag mag. Its reportage has landed the paper in the law courts but it goes on selling by the millions. No celebrity in Britain is safe from this paper if he is less than discreet or prudent. Or if the truth is less than interesting, thinly veiled aspersions of sexual perversion and everything deviant make up the copy.

Of course these papers outsell such respectable journalistic flagships as *The Times*, *The Guardian* and *The Independent*. It depends on whether you want a lascivious bite out of the gossip grapevine or to ponder over serious political dissertations. Sunday reading in Britain can take all of your day, even if your tastes are singularly pristine; a whole weekend if prurient and eclectic. Each Sunday paper is thick enough to make a door wedge, plus the assorted colour magazines and supplements. They seek to inform, provoke, entertain, titillate and tantalize. And they do, to the exclusion of all other activities.

There seems to be curious social divide determined by what you read in Britain. Call it snobbery, call it pretension but some people take great care not to be seen reading such as *The Sun* in the belief that it tells on their intellectualism and social standing. Well, a few have been known to cover their preferred rag mag reading with a copy of *The Times*, that when they reach home, will be consigned to the bin.

Some get right under your skin. *The Independent's* hoarding advertisements snidely question your individualism: 'Are you independent enough to share our views?' Others sell on the basis of pull-no-punches reportage. One says there are no

Newsstands all over Britain present a cosmopolitan array of newspapers and magazines in English and other European languages.

sacred cows within its pages. The problem arises when a *Sun* (the one with the page three nude) reader does not know the meaning of this symbolic animal. Is it a farming journal then? The paper you read, of course, reflects your level of intellect. It doesn't matter if you buy *The Financial Times* to wrap cheap fish and chips with it—reading it on the tube gives you a certain cachet.

Like the latest screamingly expensive mobile phone, serious broadsheets imbues a certain aura for those who read them—and preferably in public. Conversely, it can get disconcerting when half a dozen pairs of eyes are boring into you while yours burn into the naked body of the page three girl. This is the raison d'être for some of the tabloid papers. Once you've had your fill of naked bosoms, the rest of the paper is made up of juicy bits of news hardly likely to shake the world. A few page three girls have gone on to make fortunes from their physical endowments. Such is media exposure. If you want to know about people—pop stars and glitterati to be more specific—read *The People*.

Somewhere between these two opposite poles are *The Mirror*, *Express*, *Today* and *Daily Mail* that are basically

serious tabloids but not serious enough to tax the brain
cells. World news and intellectual views do not necessarily
sell newspapers. A situation that has Britain's educationists
wringing their hands in despair. What can be going wrong
with a country that sells millions of a paper with little else
to offer apart from naked bosoms and mere thousands of a
heavyweight, thinking man's newssheet like *The Times*?

Opinions will vary on this disparity but the tycoons of
trashy media go on laughing all the way to the bank. And if
circulation appears to be dropping, why there are always the
giveaways, lotto games, bargain holidays, hard cold cash and
a hundred and one assorted freebies to help boost sales. And
they do, for there are always people who fall prey to such
check-book journalism schemes.

London's only evening newspaper, *The Standard*, is a
hodgepodge of both serious and frivolous. As a monopoly, the
captive market keeps it afloat. Others have tried and folded
because newspaper loyalty is an inexplicable poser in Britain.
As a nation of commuters and Sunday domestic plodders, a
10-minute skim on the tube, even a protracted read on the

train and weekend flipping over gossip and pictorial exposes win hands down over masses of grey text.

With some 13 daily and 13 Sunday national papers and several hundred local papers that are published weekly or twice weekly, and hundreds more provincial newspapers and dozens of other specialist and other general information publications, no taste is left out, however deviant. Every borough has its own newspaper, usually stuffed with advertisements for everything from aspirin to zoologists. These come free and are pushed through your mailbox whether you read them or not. I find them useful to flog my used stuff, or to get hold of a second-hand heater.

Most major newsagents in the big cities with cosmopolitan communities stock German, Italian, Spanish, French and Arabic national papers. Chinatown shops, even supermarkets in London, Birmingham, Manchester and other cities with any sizable Chinese population stock a number of Chinese language papers. And there is now a European paper as well.

Magazines

There must be more magazines on newsstands in Britain than dead leaves in autumn. The list is a veritable A-Z of leisure and purposeful reading, from *Aeroplane Monthly* to *Amateur Gardening*, *Birding World*, *Classic Cars* to *Yachting Monthly* and *Zest* ad infinitum.

The high profile ones like *Bella*, *Computer Weekly*, *Cosmopolitan*, *Elle UK*, *Hello*, *Homes and Gardens*, *GQ*, *Woman's Own*, *Readers Digest*, *Vogue* and the like have been selling for decades with scarcely any change in format. But the past two decades have seen hitherto rock-solid magazine publishing houses reaching for the Valium. Inflation, changing tastes, distribution costs and other factors can force a new magazine to go under within weeks of hitting the newsstands. And the established ones cannot afford to be complacent because of the fierce competition.

Hello!

Now this is one magazine that has caused a few waves, specializing in impossibly glossy spreads of celebrities' homes, weddings and all the glitz that accompany their lifestyles. Rumour has it that it is jinxed as no sooner has a marriage been given the '*Hello!* Treatment' then divorce proceedings are round the corner. Whatever, it has become iconic.

Magazines for blacks, for the handicapped, for the young, not-so-young, yuppie, executive, sports-mad, new woman, etc., entice with glossy covers. Most are within the £ 4 range and are very accessible. Every newsagent, makeshift stand outside train stations and supermarket sells them hot from the press. And there are book and magazine stores in every high street in every town throughout the UK.

DIY journals, home repairs, and homeopathy: all the answers to the minutiae of life's daily trials are spelled out in reassuring tones. Come Christmas, every other magazine will tell you how to stuff a turkey, plan your countdown to that grand family dinner and what to do with your chestnut shells. It's comforting to know that some publication somewhere will tell you how to make quince jam, unplug a clogged sink and mend your own dentures. Where service doesn't come cheap, if it comes at all, Britain's general interest and self-help magazines can be your lifeline to sanity.

ART

One of the greatest pleasures of life in Britain is the wealth of art available (largely free) to the public. And it's not just great masterpieces in galleries and museums—art is everywhere in a civilization that goes back more than a thousand years. The heritage remains in gloriously preserved state or in crumbling relics.

Though not in the same league as the Renaissance cities of Europe, Britain and its artistic heritage speak of a magnificent past full of heraldry and pomp. For art is not merely on tangible canvas but in the splendid auras created by great builders of cathedrals, churches and edifices of historical import, by artisans who created beauty and form in furniture, fabric and works of art.

Britain is seemingly stuffed with great houses and castles which in turn are stuffed with great works of art, furniture and the paraphernalia of grander than grand lifestyles. You could explore a new place everyday for a lifetime. In Scotland alone there are more than 4,000 castles. In every village, town, borough or city you will find art in endearing or pretentious forms. A village teashop might display a tapestry from the 17th century. That beautiful chair you sit on in a country pub might have come from a medieval castle. Art is not always in obvious forms. The art of the 15th century blacksmith would be manifest in the fine lines of a portcullis now adorning a country pub.

Galleries and museums are too numerous to name for there are literally thousands of them all over the country. Seek out art through architecture, in the glorious gothic temples to Christianity, Norman churches and Christopher Wren's magnificent domes and turrets. Stately homes themselves are works of art for such great designs are a thing of the past. Beautiful mouldings, plaster work and sculpture adorn the noble homes now entrusted to the state for upkeep as few private individuals would have the means to do so.

Of those still living in the grand style, the prospect of having tourists gawk at one's private quarters is a heavy, but necessary, price to pay. How else could one raise £1 million a year to maintain 100 rooms, priceless furniture and masterpieces?

A few pounds is a cheap price to pay for the privilege of enjoying such great art by Tintoretto, Rembrandt, Constable, Dali and other great artists. These are the private collections of great families. Others can be seen for free, for example in London's Tate, National and Portrait galleries. Whichever period, field or style of art you prefer, much abounds in this country for you to enjoy. Half an hour in front of a luscious Vermeer or two hours fathoming Dali's surrealistic genius—they're all available for the price of an ice cream cone, if at all.

Don't pass over the street artists who will paint your portrait for £ 10, as commercial trash. They are very talented and may be tomorrow's grand masters. Exhibitions are mounted every so often ranging from mildly pornographic photographs to Indian jewellery. Even department stores cash in on art as a promotional teaser and entire stores often run thematic displays of ethnic or European art forms. Be it in fabric design, furniture or porcelain, the artistic image is irresistible.

Art from Antiquity

When the Romans left Britain in the early 5th century, the country was plunged into the Dark Ages. However, archaeological finds indicate that the British enjoyed a high level of artistic sophistication even within their barbaric lifestyle. Abstract and symbolic examples of pagan art have been found in ancient buckles and clasps made of gold, glass and enamel from a 7th century ship burial at Sutton Hoo in Suffolk.

By the 11th century, a renaissance of art had come about after Christianity had banished much of the paganism.

After the Norman conquest of 1066, Anglo-Saxon art was greatly influenced by France. The conquerors brought with them a Romanesque style now evident in the awesome carved Apostles of Malmesbury Abbey in Wiltshire and in the 12th century reliefs of Chichester Cathedral. By the Middle Ages, the lifestyles of the nobility and Church began to influence art. Sumptuous cloths, devotional ivories and manuscripts were produced for the great courts of Europe but almost exclusively to the glory of God.

The concept of individual artistic genius only emerged at the end of the 16th century, much influenced by the European Renaissance that began in the 14th century in Italy. The best-known artist of this Tudor period was the Swiss-German artist Hans Holbein who devoted much of his skills to painting the flamboyant Henry VIII. Some of his best works are in London's National Gallery.

When the Stuart period came, British art flourished. Charles I brought over the talented Flemish Van Dyck, commissioned paintings from Rubens and the first Italianate buildings in England. The Banqueting Hall in Whitehall, London, designed by Inigo Jones, was to affect the whole course of English architecture.

The Restoration period was a time of prosperity, peace and the flourishing of art culminating in the establishment of the Royal Academy in 1768 with the aim of raising artistic status. Among its founder members were some of the greatest names of the world of art—Hogarth, Reynolds, Constable, Gainsborough and Chippendale who put his name and signature on some of the most magnificent examples of English furniture. By the late 18th century, the penchant for ornate rococo and Chinoiserie began to pale giving way to the 'neo-classicism' much advocated by the Scottish painter and architect, Robert Adam.

This was also the period Josiah Wedgwood raised ceramics to a prestigious status.

Today, Wedgwood has become a household name in elegance—a much sought-after collectible that graces homes around the world. You can't mistake the characteristic blue or green alabaster with white relief of classical figures on anything from amphorae to ashtrays.

With Queen Victoria's ascension to the throne in 1837, artists were freed of the tyranny of portraiture. In its place, piety, patriotism and melodrama were dominant moods with a strong strain of the sentimental.

Victorian artefacts became increasingly industrialised, reaching their apogee in the 1851 Great Exhibition at London's Crystal Palace. It was a proclamation to the world of the beauty and eclecticism of Victorian art, many examples of which are still to be found in former colonies. There was sharp reaction to this

The Norman influence can be seen in medieval art and architecture. Some Norman churches are still in good repair.

mechanization mania, a nostalgic yearning for the lost paradise of individual craftsmanship.

The greatest protagonist was William Morris whose designs have undergone a tremendous rebirth in the last century. His stunning work today adorns homes all over the world, on wallpaper, fabrics and other household accessories. Unfortunately, he could not stem the tide of inevitable marriage between design and machinery which came about in the 20th century.

In Britain and all over the world, visual arts were characterised by extremes and upheavals. The catchwords were abstraction, impressionism, cubism and all other -isms of a period of great artistic ferment. French Surrealists had their English counterparts; Francis Bacon, one of the leading names in figurative painting, distorted reality to express his view of humanity. His works in London's Tate Gallery are startling visages of contortionist nightmare.

Henry Moore, born in 1898, overwhelmed the art world with his monumental sculptures. In turn he influenced his students to exploit the texture and colour of steel plates, beams, girders and industrial techniques of welding and riveting.

Post-war Britain saw the need to boost morale and artists of all kinds combined to present an optimism of the nation in the Festival of Britain in 1951. Bacon was still producing sinister art, Moore's protégé Anthony Caro perpetuated his master's massive forms and other 'pop' artists began to come out of the woodwork. Richard Hamilton exploited mass media for his imagery and David Hockney represented a more traditional form of figurative painting.

Surrounded by so much beauty in art, you begin to understand the British loathing for contemporary structures of glass and steel. You begin to appreciate too the value attached to homes with historical character and ambience— as much to preserve their intrinsic value as the perpetuating of craftsmanship that is constantly being threatened by an avalanche of soulless high-tech materials.

As for the street artists mentioned, you'll find them usually near certain art galleries. On weekends in London, practically the entire Bayswater Road becomes a street gallery with paintings and other artistic endeavours hanging on the railings of Hyde Park. There are too many art schools to mention and where you enrol depends on the field you want to specialise in. Contact your Local Education Authority for information. Better known art schools in London are St Martins which also offers all forms of commercial art and Chelsea Art School. All galleries and museums have an information section which will give you general or specific information about the world of art.

Of the Pop Genre

From posters to hoardings, from body daubing to surreal sculpture, much that is quintessentially British art takes wild and wacky forms. No idea is too way out to receive public appreciation and artists fairly wallow in a liberalism that allows total expression. Whether it's sketching the glories of a British autumn or indulging in the caricaturing of celebrities, artistic bent is never short of conducive ambience and willing subjects. The entertainment section of most newspapers lists the daily events and exhibitions of the art world.

NIGHT HAUNTS

Britain is not generally a late-night country. Some big cities have clubs that stay open till 2 or 3 am but the London nightlife scene remains unrivalled despite strict licensing laws. There is every genre available in London—the big five being Hip Hop, House, Techno, Drum 'n' Base and Breaks as well as recent innovations UK Garage and Electroclash.

The scene is real 21st century with many clubs offering life music. The main areas to head for are Brixton where the extensive Caribbean and Black community have largely shaped the vibes, The West End (Soho) and the East End including Shoreditch, Hoxton and Clerkenwell. On Friday and Saturday nights these places are seething with sweating humanity.

Many of these venues are clandestine and the best way to investigate further is to keep your eyes peeled for street posters and flyers in shops. There are jazz clubs that cater for dawn-watchers but the nightclub scene does not thrive on a 24-hour cycle, or even into the small wee hours. The drink-licensing laws are Draconian and public transport conspire to send members of the public home before midnight. Still, for the past decade, there has been much change for the better. The closing times for the city's biggest venues like the Hippodrome often extend to 6:00 am.Check out such watering holes for night birds as:

- **Ministry of Sound**
  103 Gaunt Street, Walworth. London SE1
  Opening hours: Wed: 10:00 pm–3:00 am, Fri: 10:00 pm–5:00 am, Sat: 11:00 pm–8:00 am
  Admission: £ 12–£ 15
- **Madame Jo Jo's**
  8-10 Brewer Street, Soho, London W1F 0SP
  Tel: (020) 7734-3040
  Website: http://www.madamejojos.com
  Opening hours: 10:30 pm–3:00 am, Wed–Sat
  Admission: £ 5–£ 8.
  Tube: Leicester or Piccadilly Circus
  Cabaret sleaze, funk and hip hop to 1960s and 1970s music. Wonderful venue if you like high camp, loud music and wall-to-wall people.

SEX AND SLEAZE

No matter what the moral watchdogs do, Britain's sense of liberalism spills over onto the stage so often that it becomes difficult to judge what is justifiable and what is smut. Nudity, full frontal or partial, is always the issue here but the creative people usually have plenty of reasons to defend their stance. It can be difficult to decide what is bad influence and what is art even with the most liberal. Smashing up a guitar on stage may be hailed by the teenyboppers as right, but it can cause apoplexy in adults to think such violence is condoned.

Four letter words are allowed in some films and not in others, at some times and not others. The rules are a veritable quagmire and it boils down to personal dictates. Children under the stated age are not allowed to see films not rated for general entertainment but many cinema operators simply close one eye. Other cinemas cater exclusively to a taste for soft porn (especially in London) boldly endorsing the freedom of choice.

Cinema Classifications

- U – for universal viewing with no restrictions to age. Films in this category are not likely to offend sensibilities or ethnic cultures.

- PG – with parental guidance for those under 15 years of age. In practice, some cinemas simply ask the age of a young person who is accompanied and do not insist on proof if the parent states he or she is over 15. Films under this category may contain swear words, some gratuitous violence and subtle sex, but nothing explicit.

- 15 – this category bars anyone under 15 with or without parents as the film has explicit sex, violence and other elements deemed unsuitable and likely to adversely influence young persons.

- 18 – those under 18 are not allowed to view these films as they contain explicit sex scenes, gore and violence. You are likely to be asked for proof of age at cinemas showing films of this rating.

Television is probably the most watched in terms of moral values but what passes as acceptable for the British may not for another race. Neither should one judge British moral values by one's own standards. People from different cultures with different attitudes are not likely to see eye to eye about this issue. Keeping an open mind is the best stance to take. Don't get huffy if you see semi-nudity on TV—it's totally acceptable here, if in context, and does not mean decadence, at least not to the British. Nor should they regard you as prude for objecting to what you feel is beyond good taste. If nudity per se upsets you, don't watch. But don't be overly critical.

BRITISH TALK

CHAPTER 8

'In Yorkshire they say 'coom oop' and see me
sometime. In London, 'cor blimey' is explosive
Cockney exclamation. In arty Chelsea, a 'nice hice' is a
'nice house' through stiff upper lips. In Britain, you'll
hear more accents than in an UN conference.'
—Terry's journal, August 1984

THE ENGLISH LANGUAGE EVOLVED from a Babel of Celtic, Anglo-Saxon, Latin, Norse and Norman French dialects. The untrained ear to this linguistic mix would be hard put to tell the difference between a Scots accent and an Irish one, both involving convolutions of the tongue, rolling of the 'r's' etc. Being a largely monolingual country, Britain is at least comforting for anyone who reads and writes the language, no matter how rudimentary. How much English you should know in order to feel comfortable is a rather vague barometer. Suffice that you should be able to read road signs, bus, tube and train schedules which have the basic destination/times/frequency/routes information.

Obviously being able to speak basic English is a must; otherwise you are likely to feel isolated. It doesn't stop one from shopping at supermarkets and department stores as they are largely self-service and you simply pay what is rung up without any need for conversational exchange. Again, it all depends on your livelihood, where you work and who you need to relate to.

Many foreigners, Chinese, Iranian, Cosovan, Indian, etc, have got by for decades knowing barely six words of English. It makes the difference between feeling perpetually alien and at home. Few English find the need to learn a second language; a recent survey showed that 90 per cent of students drop French by the time they do their O-level exams at age 15 or 16, and they generally feel that

The fact that you are reading this means you already know the language but there may be family members coming with you who do not and who have to have at least a basic knowledge. To this end, they'd have to enrol in one of the hundreds of English language schools in Britain.

anyone who lives here has a duty to learn English. Which is a practical attitude as the whole structure of society is based on one language.

With the EU now a political and geographical reality, most language institutes are doing a thriving trade as much for Europeans to master English as for the English to master one or the other of the EC languages, and increasingly, Mandarin, Arabic and Japanese. Outside the specific need for a foreign language, say in the travel or European banking industry, the British are justifiably complacent about being monolingual. It is always useful to know more than one language but the fact is that, in England, simply knowing English is quite enough.

Nor do the English see the need to learn Chinese or Gujerati or Thai as second and third generation foreigners are totally at home with the local language after years of immersion in English schools where, at best, a few hours are devoted to a second language. As for the immigrant languages, British education authorities believe that it is best left to the individual parents.

ACCENTS FIRST

Accents can vary so much that you may wonder what languages you are hearing. Whichever gateway you choose to enter Britain, your ears will be immediately assaulted by the dozens of regional accents. This is more so in London than in any other port or city. And to make you even more confused, you will hear quite a few hybridised accents, the result of being wrapped around migrant tongues. Like a Punjabi speaking broad Scottish or a Vietnamese spouting a lilting Yorkshire dialect. Standard English is increasingly getting muffled amid the Babel; it is only audible among the better educated. Even street conversation sounds alien to the untrained ear not familiar with multiple nuances of a monolingual base.

Standard English pronunciation is not typical of any particular area of the country, but is more an indication of the level of general education and wealth. Thus residents of the richer counties near London will often speak with clearer accents, and originally the BBC (British Broadcasting Corporation) conformed to the standard that is often termed 'plummy', as if speaking with a plum in the mouth. Since the 1980s, there has been a sharp revival of interest in local dialects and using regional pronunciation is no longer a social gaffe. In many media, it is positively encouraged, with a few TV sitcoms built entirely around regional tones. Like *Eastenders* that reflect a largely London or Cockney heritage, or *Coronation Street* that projects a more Midlands accent.

The reason for this change is that it is the language of the people. Which perhaps explains why most state schools have not put too much emphasis on Standard English for years. On TV and radio programmes, the norm is to juxtapose the different regional accents—in short it is not de rigueur any more for the announcers to sound uniform.

With so much population diffusion and movement related to work, specific speech patterns tend to be restricted to small groups. Within an office, the managing director could very well have risen from the ranks, to lock his Cockney vowels with the junior executive's public school consonants.

In Victorian times, language separated the classes with a fine divide. The division is less strict today though it still exists. And in these very same great houses that are now bed and breakfast places or divided into birdcage size flats, language is a mash of different accents with the occasional plum. With so much diffusion of working population and migrant second and third generation peoples freed from the need to be within their ethnic enclaves, most major cities in Britain are a veritable jumble of linguaphone tapes gone mad.

Not surprisingly, a few European and Asian children born in Britain retain some of their mother tongue accents. You soon learn to spot the son of a Mauritian-born woman or the daughter of a Gujerati merchant.

The characteristic sing-song lilt of Mauritian English and the 'yindian' accent are unmistakable. This again depends on how much the peer group influence is. Your linguistic hurdle can be sinister or simply quaint, depending on who you meet first. The immigration officer's probing tone is frightening enough without your having to translate his strange vowels into intelligible English. You should simply say, "Would you speak slowly, sir, I cannot understand you," and he will be more helpful. He is highly suspicious of anyone who does not speak English, never mind that you don't understand his.

After getting past this forbidding civil servant, you will be assailed by the more raucous—and initially unintelligible—tones of a Cockney taxi driver. Both speak English but they could be from different planets. Still, the taxi driver would regale you with the story of his life, the current political disorder or the vagaries of British weather. Just emit the occasional 'uh-huh' and he'll thank you profusely when you tip him, as you should, about 10 per cent being the standard practice here.

It has taken me 20 years to distinguish between the soft lilt of the Yorkshireman, the clipped burr of the Scotsman and the strangeness of Liverpudlian which, at first, sounded positively Germanic! English as you have been taught completely disappears. Actors have been known to spend years at speech classes to iron out their tongues, even to bury their oral origins so as to deliver their lines with thespian panache. Or at least clear enough to reach the furthest stall seat. After being orientated, I found it an absolute delight to sit through two hours of pure Cockney in the West End musical *Me and My Girl*.

What, Rather than Where

From banks to beauticians, from schools to supermarkets, your ears will be assailed with what seems like a dozen different tongues. Never mind where they originate, it's what they mean that's important if you are to assimilate into the British life.

The groundswell feeling is that regional accents should not be derided but preserved and perpetuated. Gone is the belief that to get places, you have to speak the Queen's English. That is to quote Eliza Doolittle the erstwhile Fair Lady on her exchange with Professor Higgins : "I have come to learn how to speak proper like." The next time you watch a rerun of this classic movie, pay close attention to the dialogue. The day is yet to come when the national news, that fount of media articulation, goes regional though some weathermen

I wait with bated breath for a forthcoming West End production of George Bernard Shaw's *Pygmalion* (a.k.a *My Fair Lady* on the big screen) that is the quintessential play about this linguistic pastiche. Get hold of a copy of this classic and devour every word and syllable to afford you an in-depth understanding of British accents.

on TV are barely intelligible at first to the foreign ear, and regional news programmes are generally presented with regional accents.

STREET ENGLISH

'Butter' is pronounced with the 't's all but gone, replaced by a glottal stop—'bah-er'. Or if your name is 'Peter', don't be miffed when someone calls you 'Pee-er'. A favourite tag phrase among many is the quaint 'Know wot oy maen?' It seems a polite poser to the recipient of such accented English and so universally known it even comes on TV advertisements. A definite plus for keeping taproot language alive.

A 'nipper' is also a small child and 'tatty' could be a potato rather than your cut-price decor. A 'moggy' is the affectionate name for a cat and many grandmothers are called 'nans'. The epitome of an English parlour scene is someone's 'nan' cradling her 'moggy' on her lap while waiting for her kettle to boil to make a 'cuppa' (tea).

The list is far too long to chronicle here but don't be diffident about asking someone what he means when a word seems alien. Not that explanation will enlighten you any further, but it's the start of better communication when you have to explain your own language peculiarities.

COLLOQUIALISM

The dictionary definition of 'conversational idiom' does little justice to this rich patois of the people. With a definite penchant for oversimplification, they top it with sheer inventiveness. Possibly the Australians fare a close second in the alternative stakes. After all, they inherited most of their speech semantics from the British, giving it a twist only Crocodile Dundee can deliver with stunning panache.

A 'quid' is a pound. Small change is 'coppers' and a 'copper' is a policeman or a bobby. To 'come a cropper' is to fall down or get into trouble, for instance if you've 'nicked' a copper or two from someone's open handbag. To 'nick' is to steal and 'nosh' is food. You can get 'knackered' just thinking about it. Or exhausted if you prefer. If your car or house is 'in good nick', it needs no repair.

'Wonderful, innit?' Isn't it? Or is it not? if you prefer Shakespeare. A 'prezzy' is a present and a 'pratt' is someone who's plain obnoxious. Especially when he lurches at you 'pie-eyed and legless', too drunk to get his knees up or to party.

When someone is 'chuffed', he's happy and pleased. When something is 'naff', it is very unstylish, almost embarrassing to be associated with. This particular word has its salty use when the situation demands. 'Naff off' is a polite euphemism of that favourite Anglo-Saxon dismissive term not generally used in polite company.

Rudeness, it seems, is excusable as long as the rude word or term is masked over with another one usually found in respectable dictionaries. In fact more and more of these words and terms are sneaking into the best of almanacs.

'Bonkers' means mad, but 'bonking' is now acceptable, even on TV, though it is a word that describes the sexual act. It is now so acceptable–perhaps as a valve for verbal frustration–you could use it in front of your nan and she wouldn't ask you to naff off. A 'nerd' is a term of abuse

Comedies & Sitcoms

Be advised to watch as much British comedies and sitcoms, even classic programmes from the 1960s, 1970s and 1980s that are still rerun regularly. Each is a tableau of quintessential British idiosyncrasies, lifestyles and mannerisms.

- *Birds of a Feather*—about two Cockney sisters whose husbands are in jail for armed robbery and their coming to grips with life. Hilarious, and full of Cockney humour and accents.
- *To the Manor Born*—on the other end of the social scale, about one Audrey Hamilton-Fforbes who is lady of the manor and rather grand. And how she copes with her new neighbour Richard Cavendish, a nouveau riche son of Czechoslovakian immigrants who do not quite meet her standards of behaviour. Full of class divide attitudes.
- *Dinner Ladies*—about a group of working class women who run a canteen and indulge in salty humour while buttering endless slices of bread and making bacon 'sarnies'. Very life below stairs type.
- *Upstairs Downstairs*—an eponymous satire about the two levels of Victorian socieçty and the cross purposes therein. Although it is a lifestyle now gone, it provides a rare insight into current attitudes about social types.

really meaning a person who is ungainly, rather fumbling and incompetent. It is more generally used in 'you nerd' if a person does something silly or idiotic. There was recently a whole West End play called *The Nerd* about a man who was a born loser in life.

When someone says he's 'thick as two planks', it's self-deprecatory mocking of his mental capabilities. And to be 'thick and wet'—well, there must be air between the ears. Or an air-head. Or simply plain stupid. Or you've got nothing for a 'noggin' (brains).

And when asked to 'sod off', you can either take offence or not, depending on the tone of voice and who is issuing this dismissal. This is the saltier, less polite dismissive akin to the other word 'naff', as in 'naff off'. Both take their cue from that famous four-letter Anglo-Saxon word. Sod, by the way, is an abbreviation of Sodom and you know what sodomy is. Nuff said.

Back in 1968 when I first arrived in London, I had asked a newspaper seller where a particular place was and he responded with "sod off!" I thought he had meant 'sort of' so I asked again "Sort of where?" and got a real earful of the real meaning; suffice to know his comeback had a lot of 'f's' in it.

There's something to be said for a language that can be used to convey displeasure without ensuing fisticuffs. Not surprisingly, it has given the British a reputation for biting sarcasm, sardonic put downs and other verbal killers. The dreadful alternative employed among the 'yobos'—now there's a descriptive idiom—is the repetitive use of that famous four-letter word.

It appears colloquialism has been invented so that refined society can let off steam without blurring the meaning of their vocal intention. It in fact has laid a fine film over obscenities, allowing even little old ladies to indulge in occasional swearing without turning a blue-rinsed hair.

'Yob' is boy spelt backwards and generally refers to unruly and uncouth males, some of whom make it their sole ambition in life to get as drunk as often as they can afford to while tearing around the country appearing to support their football team but in reality making a right nuisance of themselves. This problem multiplied a thousand fold became a national headache.

The yobo sub-culture is a real social disease, spreading its scruff-bag, pie-eyed philosophy right across to Europe, mainly Spain. Some European authorities have begun to ban those undesirables. And now the females have joined the fray earning themselves the sobriquet of 'ladettes'—like in one of the lads, only with a gender difference. Know wot oi maen!

There was a time when youthful enthusiasm for life and all it had to offer resulted in no more than some hot-in-the-head lad being called 'Jack the lad'. As portrayed by Michael Caine in the classic *Alfie*. Even with the 2004 remake starring Jude Law, this message is quite clear. This term is nonetheless somewhat antiquated and today actually reflects a virtue compared to the mayhem created by the other lot. Alas, choice idiom or epithet cannot stem causeless rebellion and the advice is, when confronted

When you encounter youthful enthusiasm on a tube or train, try to be tolerant of their exuberance as it is merely letting off steam and rarely violent, unless there is one among the group who has had a pint too many and is being belligerent. Avoid any encounter or smile benignly when accosted with verbal assault. You know that one about sticks and stones may break your bones....

with such characters on the street, tube, train or building site, refrain from using any. Just go away or report to the police if you have been physically manhandled.

As well as a wide range of colloquialisms, some of which have been outlined here, you may very occasionally come across the impenetrable Cockney Rhyming Slang in some old TV sitcoms. As a literary heritage, it is deader than a dodo. A couple of examples will show its wry sense of humour: the telephone is the 'dog and bone' ('bone' rhymes with 'phone') and the wife is 'trouble and strife'. It's not just individual words that floor foreigners. Jargon is made even more garbled with terms of reference largely alien to the rest of the English-speaking world. Here is a typical example:

"Ere, what wos you doin, giving that old geezer my bacon sarnie?"

Translation: "Look here, what do you think you were doing, giving my bacon sandwich to that old man?"

TOUCH
On the pleasant side of physical contact, the British are generally free of taboos that beset others, especially Asians who don't like any kind of overt physical gestures.

With a first time acquaintance, a firm handshake is in order whatever your gender, though young people, especially teenagers, would find this too formal. On knowing someone a little better—some may call it affectation but it's regarded as refinement among many British—a peck on the cheek is acceptable. Male and female of course. Many Europeans kiss both cheeks resoundingly and across all gender. The British way is very restrained, more the woman proffering her cheek with a slight tilt of her head so the man may gently touch it with his cheek at the same time making a puckering sound.

PARK BENCH INTRODUCTIONS

This is one of the best ways to communicate with a Briton: he's already in the right and receptive frame of mind basking in the sun. There is no other reason (or time) to sit on a park bench. Talk about the weather is the usual ice breaker but don't ask nosy questions like where he or she works, lives or salary earned. Even among close acquaintances, such topics are deemed too personal. I know many British friends who have never mentioned what they do, and very few would dream of mentioning how much they earn. Money is generally a taboo subject: you should not ask how much people have paid for purchases. Okay in Singapore, Bangkok or Kuala Lumpur but definitely not in Britain.

Interacting with the Brits

I must admit I made a few social gaffes in my early years, once when invited to a private home. Now, the lady of the house happened to be titled (her late husband was Lord something or other) and his son had married a Singapore friend of mine. Spying a beautiful antique chair, I boorishly asked, "Eh, how much ah?" Upon which the titled Lady replied rather frostily, "Well I can't say I remember as my husband's great grandfather bought it 200 years ago." As a polite sidestep, it was classic and I have never made a similar faux pas since then.

Once in a while you will meet a jolly old soul, a bit worse for drink, who'll tell you everything including the size of his belly button. There are thousands of lonely old people in Britain who long for some sort of social contact and, on a nice day, a park bench is the best stage for dispelling woes. I used to be slightly annoyed when someone persisted in making conversation—having learnt to respect the British sense of privacy—amid the waft of alcoholic breath. Humour these people because often a few kind words can give a lift in their otherwise dreary lives.

HELPING THE BLIND

It's an automatic reaction to want to reach out to help a blind person when he or she seems lost, tap-tapping with regulation white stick. The blind in Britain are fiercely independent, having been trained to be so, and have a sixth sense more developed than most of the five in sighted people. They are not as helpless as they seem and if they have a routine of travelling to and from work on public transport, they know exactly where to get on and off. Offer your help verbally by telling them what train is arriving, especially lines with different branches forking off at some point. Blind school instruction teaches them to be wary of strangers offering physical assistance as there are too many cases of the blind being robbed and mugged. So don't be offended if a blind person shrugs off your arm because he'd rather be safe than sorry.

Sign Language

Certain TV programmes and news bulletins have an interpreter using sign language and sub-titles for the benefit of the deaf. Hearing aids are obtainable from the National Health Service and most partially deaf will have had one fitted, so don't shout when talking to someone you know to be hard of hearing.

DOING BUSINESS

CHAPTER 9

'You will be welcomed in your new workplace—
if you do not have a chip on your shoulders so large it
becomes a log. If you want to be somebody and
go somewhere, perceived racism and all other negative
'...isms' will get you precisely nowhere.'
—Terry's journal, September 1984

ASIDE FROM WORKING IN AN INDUSTRY in which you are ensconced among people of your own nationality or at least of the same cultural background, adapting to the British working environment can be a little difficult. Sensitivities can be inadvertently rubbed the wrong way. Whatever the level of insidious racism, imagined or real, degree of acceptance and inter-cultural bonhomie, being one of a few minority can be at first uncomfortable.

Given the general nature of most British, colleagues, while welcoming you to the firm, often still remain fairly aloof. Make the first tentative steps by asking to be guided into the firm's machinations. You probably know what to do already, but the 'foreigner asking for help' bit is an essential exercise in this instance. A simple 'Where is the best place to eat?' will often garner response from those genuinely keen to help you settle in.

In many instances, the cultural differences can be misinterpreted. You may come from a culture that teaches absolute respect for seniors, therefore your behaviour towards them may seem overly servile. Absolute respect for one's senior may appear to be sycophancy. Or the spirit of bonhomie may seem to be cavalier. It's a minefield that you have to tread carefully.

If you start by loping off alone on your tea or lunch break, chances are you will not be welcomed into their bosom for a while. It's making your colleagues feel you have every intention of being one of the team: appealing to their sense of being the national host to your guest status. At least that's what you are technically and hopefully not for too long before cultural differences disappear in an atmosphere of professional brotherhood.

Don't be anti-social even if you are disinclined to have 'one for the road' after work. This latter is a big thing in any sizable office in Britain, where staff wind down for various reasons. One is to avoid the rush hour traffic and the other is simply to enjoy a pint or two outside the workaday pressures. It's a wonderful chance for colleagues to get to know each other on a personal level. No one is saying you should take up drinking if it's against your inclination. It's the inter-relationship possible only outside office hours and that can put you on a firmer path to being accepted, so do make an effort to participate.

Don't forget that there could be some distrust in a few British who themselves may not have been exposed to foreigners before. Don't see it as bloody mindedness—it is probably simply ignorance and lack of exposure to alien mores. The way you speak, what you wear, eat, and how you conduct yourself could be strange to most of your colleagues, and vice versa. Start on this premise and make an effort to explain anything that jars within your adopted environment.

If it is compulsory to wear a suit and tie, do so. Bucking the system on personal grounds, like you hate ties or you never wear suits, isn't being positive. Most establishments, be it a supermarket or bank, have house rules and refusing to comply is being bloody minded. As for office politics, depending on how crucial your position is in the pecking order and whether your survival depends on it, the cardinal rule is never get involved. Unless your job is at stake and there is still the question of personal ethics.

There is no yardstick for this battleground—only one of integrity. If you are falsely accused of being political just because your attitude towards your boss may be different, try and explain it. If everybody addresses the boss by his first name, do likewise, whatever your culture teaches you. Remember, you have to adapt to them, not the other way round.

FORMALITIES

One of the prerequisites of obtaining a berth in Britain is to get a job. Normally, permanent residency is not granted straight off unless you belong to a special category that entitles you to this right. The British immigration people will be able to give you the details.

Technically, if you have a job offer from a British company/employer, they would have had to advertise in at least two national newspapers for the job you are about to fill. It is to prove that no local qualified. Of course there are many avenues to get into Britain on a bona fide permit but this is the most straightforward way.

Once you have the permit, it will normally be granted for four or five years. This does not mean it is an automatic stretch as you still have to have it renewed on a yearly basis. It seems paradoxical but this is the way it works. Once you have passed the fourth year, you may then apply for permanent residency which again is not automatic. It all depends on the points system and how many you have earned to qualify.

During this period, you may change your job but you MAY NOT change your profession. In other words, if you are an engineer, you may switch to another firm or employer. But you may not become a hair dresser on the same permit. Generally, if you have satisfied the four-year period, it is plain sailing. On the fifth year of your stint and after obtaining permanent residency, you may then apply for British citizenship that may take anything up to a year to be awarded.

Permanent residency entitles you to most of the rights a citizen gets but it is not inviolate as it can be revoked, for instance, if you commit a crime or do something that labels you an undesirable resident. Nationality (citizenship) cannot be revoked and there are many requirements like having to sit for an English test etc.

If you are married, your spouse will be allowed to work if you are on a work permit. If you have permanent residency, your spouse and all children under the age of 21 will automatically become permanent of course residents as well. Of course you and your family will have to pass all the requisite medical checkups before your permit is granted. Documents required are a valid passport, work permit, police permit (for certain countries) and heath papers.

SETTING UP A BUSINESS

Your local *Yellow Pages* have a listing of business and management consultants who, even if they cannot help your particular needs, will direct you to the relevant government or local council agencies. Many firms will give you all the help you need in presentations to banks and financial institutions, how to get a government grant, taxation and corporate structures. One of the biggest firms dealing in business and financial advice is Price Waterhouse which has offices all over the country. Other firms deal with the training of staff, market research and analyses.

It would be foolish to set up business in a foreign country without seeking the advice of people who know the rules. If you are applying for residence on the premise of setting up a business, the Home Office will give you the guidelines. Basically, you have to set up a business worth about £ 250,000 and only if the type of business is approved by the Home Office. There are categories of businesses which are saturated and therefore an application will be a waste of time. The Home Office will be able to tell you what these are.

Once approved, you have to give employment to at least two locals and pay wages, taxes and national insurance according to the national minimum guidelines. Should you want to employ someone from overseas who may have a skill you cannot find locally, you have to advertise in a relevant newspaper and prove this fact to the Home Office. He or she will then be given a work permit, renewable every year for four years. After this, your employee may apply for permanent residence subject again to Home Office approval. There is no automatic granting of permanent residence under any category—and there are many. Check with the Home Office.

Be prepared for bureaucracy with the different authorities, especially Health. You have to satisfy many requirements–some of which may seem pointless to you, but the British are sticklers for rules and regulations. For example, if you are setting up a factory for food production, there is a quagmire of regulations. One is that you may not use the same sink for food processing and hand washing. It seems impractical but it is a hard and fast rule. Fire exits in your premises are another sticky area, whatever your business may be. Because of the weather and constant draughts, doors have to be shut all the time. Therefore, in case of fire, there must be adequate exits as specified by the Fire Department.

When it comes to dealing with staff, suppliers, clients and other business contacts, there are a few cardinal rules to remember.

Suppliers

Expect weeks rather than days for things to be done, especially for office fittings and appliances installations. Be precise about what you want. Most fitters and engineers take orders from a central office and will not deviate, should you dither over where you want this or that to be permanently sited. It could cost you a lot in time and money if you don't have a firm plan of action. Always ask for several quotes and look for hidden extras like transport charges, call out fees and overtime. Few British workers are given to flexible give and take. An hour overtime is an hour overtime.

Very often the person who installs your equipment will not be authorised to collect money. You will be invoiced by the firm's head office which can be in a totally different part of the country. If you are dissatisfied with the service, the installation person may not be the person to complain to, like if the equipment sent is incorrect. Always speak to the head office and be prepared to wait days or even weeks before the problem can be rectified. Most big suppliers have specific days on which they deliver and install.

Staff and Wages

Expect to pay a receptionist/stenographer in the region of £ 8,000–£ 10,000 a year gross. The employers pay the tax which is around 25 per cent and national insurance. Most workers are PAYE, or Pay As You Earn, and they take home money generally on a weekly basis after taxes. Every worker is entitled to two weeks' sick pay and an average of two weeks' paid holiday per year. Also, employees are not required to present a medical chit if they are sick for less than two days. If you advertise for staff, you may not stipulate the gender, nationality or age of would-be applicants as it is politically incorrect. Unless you have special circumstances which can overrule this.

National Insurance

Every working person pays NI, whether himself (self-employed) or by the employer as it has direct bearing on your eventual state pension when you are 65 for men or 60 for women. There are different bands of payment, averaging between £ 2 per week to £ 7. If you are an employer, it is an offence if you do not pay NI for your staff. Check with your local DHSS office for regulations.

BRITAIN
AT A GLANCE

CHAPTER 10

'Travel through Britain was an ardent passage
of time, distilling much that was unbeknownst to
me before; from the first perky daffodils and crocuses
that spoke of the joy of spring to the seasonal changes
of a temperate climate, and interacting with English,
Scottish, Welsh and a dozen different nationalities.'
—Terry's journal, November 1984

FAST FACTS
Official Name
Britain

Capital
London

Land
England
Surface area: 130,000 sq km (50,193.3 square miles)

Wales
Principality of Great Britain
Surface area: 2,080 sq km (803.1 square miles)

Scotland
Constitutional monarchy
Surface area: 78,000 sq km (30,116.0 square miles)

Time Zones
From the last Sunday in March until the last Sunday in October, the UK (The United kingdom of Great Britain and Northern Ireland) moves it's clocks forward from Greenwich Mean Time by one hour (GMT + 1). This is known as British Summer Time or BST for short. The time for the rest of the year is Greenwich Mean Time

Telephone Country Code
44

Voltage
The standard electrical voltage in Britain is 240 v AC, 50HZ. A three square pronged adapter plug and/or electric converter for appliances is required

Flag
Blue field with the red cross of Saint George (patron saint of England) edged in white superimposed on the diagonal red cross of Saint Patrick (patron saint of Ireland), which is superimposed on the diagonal white cross of Saint Andrew (patron saint of Scotland); commonly called the Union Jack

Climate
Temperate
- Spring (March–May)
  Cold to cool, around 12°C (53.8°F), showery in April
- Summer (June–August)
  Cool to warm, between 15°C (59°F) and 25°C (77°F)
- Autumn (September–November)
  Cool to cold, between 10°C (50°F) and l5°C (59°F)
- Winter (December–February)
  Cold, between 8°C (46.4°F) and -2°C (28.4°F), snow generally in January and on highlands

History
Archaeological evidence suggests that England has been inhabited since at least the Palaeolithic period. The succeeding Neolithic and Bronze Age cultures left abundant remains throughout the country, the best known being Stonehenge near Salisbury. In the latter part of the Bronze Age, the Goidels, a people of Celtic race, invaded the country and brought with them Celtic civilisation and dialects. Remains of Neolithic implements date back to 4000 BC, but progress came only in 400 BC with the discovery of iron. Julius Caesar claimed it for the Romans in 55 BC. In the 100 years following Caesar's invasion, Roman

Britain prospered, cities built, roads laid down that endure to this day

Population
England & Wales: 52.5 million
Scotland: 5.2 million
By ethnic breakdown: 51.1 million white, 0.2 million other European, 2.3 million Indians (Pakistanis, Gujeratis, Bangladeshi and others from the sub-continent), 1.2 million of African origin, 0.2 million Chinese and 0.5 million other Asian races

Nationalities
There are more than 200 nationalities in the UK speaking more than 300 different languages and dialects. Chances are, whatever your nationality and language, there will be someone of the same ilk and tongue

National Language
English, Welsh, some Gaelic with sprinklings of many European languages, like French, German, and Italian and now increasingly East European tongues

Religion
Some 71.6 % are Christian, 2.7 % Muslim, 1 % Hindu, 0.6 % Sikh, 0.5 % Jewish, 0.3 % Buddhist and 0.3 % others

Currency
British and Scottish pound, interchangeable
£ 1 sterling—100 p (pence). Euros acceptable in some places

Credit Cards
Acceptable widely, even by small local stores and can be used like other debit cards for withdrawing cash from ATMs. Most machines accept all major cards. Some ATMs charge a fee of around £ 3–£ 5 for the service

Cheques
Cheque cards are rapidly replacing cheque books UK wide

Bank Accounts

Foreigners may open any accounts but must have proof of residency for some. Check with the bank of your choice as rules vary

Water

Tap water is safe for drinking but some in London can be hard. Many companies can install water-softening systems

Gross Domestic Product (GDP)

US$ 1.782 trillion (2004 est.)

Industries

Machine tools, electric power equipment, automation equipment, railroad equipment, shipbuilding, aircraft, motor vehicles and parts, electronics and communications equipment, metals, chemicals, coal, petroleum, paper and paper products, food processing, textiles, clothing, and other consumer goods

Exports

Manufactured goods, fuels, chemicals; food, beverages and tobacco

Imports

Manufactured goods, machinery, fuels and foodstuffs

Government

- As a supreme law-making authority, Parliament can legislate for the UK as a whole or for any parts of it separately. (The Channel Islands and Isle of Man are Crown dependencies and not part of the UK.)
- The UK constitution evolved over time, formed partly by status, common law and convention. A Constitutional Monarchy, the UK is governed by Ministers of the Crown in the name of the Sovereign, head of both the state and the government.
- The organs of government are the Legislature (Parliament), the Executive and the Judiciary. The Executive consists of

Her Majesty's Government (Cabinet and other ministers) and local authorities. The Judiciary (independent of both the legislature and the executive) pronounces on law, both written and unwritten, interprets statutes and is responsible for the enforcement of law.

- The Sovereign personifies the state and is, in law, an integral part of the legislature, head of the Executive, Judiciary, Commander-in-Chief of all armed forces and Supreme Governor of the Church of England. In the Channel Islands and the Isle of Man, the Sovereign is represented by a Lieutenant-Governor.

- In practice, the powers of the monarchy are very limited, restricted mainly to the advisory and ceremonial but there are important acts of government which require the Sovereign's participation.

- These include summoning, dissolving parliament, appointing the Prime Minister, giving royal assent to bills passed by Parliament, appointing important office holders, e.g. ministers, judges, bishops and governors, conferring peerages, knighthoods and other honours and granting pardon to a person wrongly convicted of a crime.

Environment, Food and Rural Affairs

The department for Environment, Food and Rural Affairs is responsible for government policies on agriculture, horticulture and fisheries in England and for policies relating to the food chain. In association with the agriculture departments of the Scottish Executive, the National Assembly for Wales and the Northern Ireland Office.

Social Welfare

The National Health Service (NHS) came into being in 1948 covering England and Wales, and under separate legislation, Scotland and Northern Ireland. The function is to provide a comprehensive health service designed to secure improvement in the physical and mental health of the people and to prevent, diagnose and treat illness. It was founded on the principle that treatment should be provided according to clinical need rather than ability to pay, and should be free at the point of delivery.

Acronyms

A1 (2,3,4, etc)	Secondary Motorway
APR	Annual percentage rate, the interest you pay for a loan
BR	British Rail
BT	British Telecom
CH	Central Heating
CoE	Church of England
Co-op	A chain of budget priced supermarkets
DesRes	Desirable residence
DG	Double Glazing
DHSS	Department of Health and Social Services
DVLA	Driver and Vehicle Licencing Agency
ISA	Individual Savings Account—a tax-free way to own shares, cash savings or life insurance
LTV	Loan to Value, the size of your mortgage as a percentage of the value of the property. Eg. A £ 90,000 mortgage on a house valued at £ 100,000 means an LTV of 90 per cent
M1 (2,3,4, etc)	Major motorway
MOT	Ministry of Transport. Checks vehicle for roadworthiness.
NHS	National Health Service
NSPCC	National Society for the Prevention of Cruelty to Children
OAP	Old age pensioner
OSP	Off street parking

FAMOUS PEOPLE
Tony Blair

Prime Minister and wife Cherie Blair, herself a QC and recently in the news for trading in on her husband's status for financial gain.

Jude Law

Oscar-winning actor extraordinaire and now partnered with Sienna Miller, herself a thespian of no mean talent. Scarcely a day passes that the media do not mention the glamorous pair.

Gordon Brown

Chancellor the Exchequeur—love him or hate him, he's up there in the thick of monetary matters, be it tax or GDP.

Anne Robinson

Journalist and presenter of hit show *The Weakest Link*, and reviled by some as the Queen of Mean with her cutting dismissal of television show guests. She made millions from the show that has now crossed the pond to America.

Kelly Holmes

Double Olympic gold medallist, recently made a Dame in the Queen's Honours List.

Alan Titchmarsh

Gardening supremo, best-selling author and television icon dispensing information about every conceivable plant and garden pest.

Jilly Cooper

Best-selling writer of sexy pot-boilers usually set in the world of bespoke sports like polo and horse racing.

JK Rowling

Author and creator of Harry Porter. Rapidly accumulating hundreds of millions of pounds with her blockbuster fantasy books.

Kate Moss

International model and fashion icon as with Naomi Campbell, who's better known for her diva tantrums than fabulous catwalk stride.

Hugh Grant

Actor who became famous not so much for his thespian talents, although considerable, but for his former association with Elizabeth Hurley, actress and Estee Lauder's muse. As well for that one unfortunate episode involving a Los Angeles hooker. Now linked to Jemima Khan, former wife of Imran.

David and Victoria Beckham

He of the football genius and she, formerly of Spice Girls and now desperately trying to re-launch her singing career.

Dawn French

Roly-poly comedienne and much-loved actress who has been a fixture on British television for more than two decades.

Joanna Lumley

Actress, once karate-chopping Purdey of *The Avengers* and later Patsy in *Absolutely Fabulous*, winning her a new legion of fans. Not bad for a near old-age pensioner but still gorgeous.

Bob Geldof

Musician and charity spokesperson who put Live Aid on the map and still an untiring champion of Third World problems.

Charlotte Church

The Voice of an Angel, blessed with a soaring soprano and who became a multi-millionaire at the age of 16. Much in the news as much for her drink-fuelled shenanigans as for her voice.

Andrew Lloyd Webber

Producer, theatre impresario and all-round musician who gave us *Phantom of the Opera* and countless other musicals that have been elevated to the hall of fame.

CULTURE QUIZ

SITUATION 1

You have been working in the London office of your company for some time now. It is Friday evening and your colleagues are about to 'hit' the pubs and wine bars before heading home, as they have been doing all the time you've been here. Having settled in more, you've now become 'one of the lads' and they have asked you to join them. You are generally teetotal and have a long way to travel home. Your reaction is:

A Demur politely saying that you don't drink and want to get home as soon as possible.

B React with annoyance when they persist and firmly refuse, even lecturing them for drinking too much, having heard many 'Monday morning after' stories about hangovers.

C Rationalise with them that even an hour after office closing will still see rush hour traffic, so what's the point?

D Show enthusiasm, even if a little feigned, commenting that you will go along but will only have a small drink.

Comments

This Friday evening ritual is fairly common especially among single men, and increasingly, women who see little reason to rush home from work. It is as much an evasive action to avoid being caught in rush hour traffic as it is a social occasion to spend a few convivial hours with friends and colleagues. With the men, it's a time to commune in a 'matey' way and for the women; it's a time to indulge in girl talk.

Generally, it is not PC to chastise you about being teetotal/anti-social as sensible people today realise it's not a virtue to drink to excess. As for not drinking beer, it will come as mild surprise to most British people as the brew is practically mother's milk to them.

D will not only give you the opportunity to get to know your colleagues better outside the work environment and also give you valuable insights into the British psyche. Do not be surprised at how much beer some people can down in a few hours.

SITUATION 2

You have been asked to join a colleague and his friends for a meal after work. It is a sort of casual 'come along with us' invitation and not a 'be my guest' gesture. You have a good meal and when the bill is presented, your friend takes out his wallet to pay, and perhaps to your surprise, everyone in the group does the same with nonchalance. Your reaction is.

Ⓐ You make no attempt to foot your share, feeling embarrassed about this 'Dutch' treat that you are not accustomed to. You rightly or wrongly assume the 'invitation' was all-embracing and you feel your friend is being tight-fisted.

Ⓑ Feel insulted that you should have to pay as you were invited and cover up by insisting to pay the whole bill. Even throwing in casually that it is not the done thing where you come from.

Ⓒ Do as the others do without any feeling of discomfiture. You do NOT comment that it's not the done thing where you come from.

Comments

Unless it is specifically made clear that you are a special guest, or your host is giving a business lunch or dinner, when you are asked to join in a group for a meal, going Dutch is always the norm in Britain and has no bearing on any attitudes about money.

It is common practice among friends and colleagues to split restaurant bills as the cost of eating out is much higher in Britain than most other countries. Restaurant staff are often piqued when six people present six credit cards to settle one bill. There's nothing to be embarrassed about, no matter how high-powered your dinner group is unless it was a pre-arranged corporate meal. Thus **Ⓒ** is your best option.

SITUATION 3

You have just emerged from a railway or tube station and need directions to get to your destination. You have an address but have no idea of the local layout of side streets and house numbering system which can be confusing in British cities—especially older ones like London. What you do know is that it's quite near to the station you emerged from. Your reaction is to:

Ⓐ Ask the nearest tradesman—usually a newsvendor or greengrocer—expecting him or her to know the local environs.

Ⓑ Catch someone you think seems local, i.e. it's not a bag-laden tourist and appears to work in the area.

Ⓒ Ask the first person who passes near you.

Ⓓ Go the station ticket/information counter.

Comments

Depending on whether it's a city, town or village you are at, the options vary. Tradesmen outside busy metropolitan stations often seem brusque and unhelpful. This is because they are asked by hundreds of visitors and get short-tempered. The 'local' person is likely to be as much a stranger to the area as you are, and is transiting. As for asking the first person you see, the same applies as he/she is likely to be a tourist.

Ⓓ is the ideal as you will get positive help, and if not, will be pointed to the right source i.e. a map of the local area usually posted somewhere in the station.

SITUATION 4

You are sitting on a bench in a public park and someone (British) sits down next to you. He gives you a brief nod and a half-smile but does not open any conversation. He proceeds to read his newspaper. It is a nice day and you feel chatty. You attempt to make conversion, but get monosyllabic answers from the gentleman who does not even lower his newspaper in response. Your reaction is:

Ⓐ Persist in trying to get his attention, even if he does not respond beyond taciturn answers and cryptic replies.

❸ Leave off and let him alone, turning your attention to something else or simply appear to bask in the nice weather.

❸ Get huffy and leave abruptly, your body language and grunts displaying obvious displeasure. You are convinced the British are cold and aloof.

Comments

While is it generally true that the British are reserved and slow to warm up to casual, impersonal conversation in a public place, there is a difference between this attitude and one that is obviously aloofness. Do not persist if you get no response after protracted efforts to talk about inconsequential matters like the weather. If this does not thaw the iciness, nothing will. When you get a smile and a nod, it still does not mean the person is willing to talk. It's the inherent British politeness and no indication of progressive friendliness. It is rare that you will forge a friendship within the time you spend in a public park bench, or any other public place. Thus, **❸** is your best reaction.

SITUATION 5

You are in a designer room in an upmarket department store and you spy a Versace blouse on a mannequin and would like to try it on. However, you see no salesperson around and see that the item is also on a shelf, folded. Your reaction is:

Ⓐ Reach for the item yourself and look for a changing room to try it on.

Ⓑ Barge in while a salesperson is dealing with another customer and expect to be served. Show annoyance when told to wait.

Ⓒ Leave the store in disgust after waiting what seems an eternity for the salesperson to be free.

Ⓓ Browse and wait patiently until a salesperson comes to you.

Comments

Most British stores are not overflowing with staff (unlike some Chinese emporiums in Asia) and unless trade is slow, you will rarely see any salesperson at a loose end. No matter how long it takes for a salesperson to deal with a customer, you have to wait your turn. This one-to-one service is across the board in Britain whether it's at a village newsagent or at Harrods.

Most stores are self-service and if you find the item you want, simply take and find the changing room. If it fits and you want to purchase it, go straight to the checkout to pay without need for sales help. If you cannot find the size or colour you want, you have to wait for a free salesperson. Thus **Ⓐ** or **Ⓓ** is your only bet depending on the circumstance.

SITUATION 6

You live in a house that looks out on a wild nature reserve or protected country patch. You have a large garden and spend much time attending to your plants, pruning and generally maintaining its beauty. You also incur much garden waste and accumulate much in autumn when falling leaves can be a nightmare. Your reaction is:

Ⓐ Collect all the garden waste and simply hurl them over your back fence into the nature reserve, believing it will all mulch down in time.

Ⓑ You place all garden waste in a bin and when it is full, you burn it during the day.

Ⓒ You wait for after dark to burn it.

Ⓓ You telephone the local council and ask if they can supply you with a Green Recycle Bin for garden waste.

Comments

Nature reserves, however small or wild, are protected places and it is illegal, not to mention unhealthy to throw garden waste onto it. There is usually a good reason for a certain area to be deemed a nature reserve, like the protection of wildlife species. You can collect garden waste in your bin; you may only burn it after dark and away from your neighbour's drying laundry. You may not burn rubbish during daylight hours. The government's latest green move is to provide a green recycle bin for those households who want them; these will be collected weekly for recycling. Caring for the environment is top priority in this country. You may choose **Ⓒ**, or if the garden waste is substantial, go for **Ⓓ**.

DO'S AND DON'TS

DO'S

- Shake hands when greeting someone, male or female. Among the more genteel and upper classes, people of opposite sex and female to female greet each other with a peck on the cheek; continental kiss on both cheeks. This is optional and generally observed if you know the person you are greeting.

- Use the appropriate honorific when addressing someone older and those whose position demand respect.

- Talk about things in general, like the weather, as this is a great icebreaker among the more conservative British.

- Give way to older people and pregnant women when boarding public transport or offer your seat. For the more infirm or handicapped, offer your assistance after asking if they would like to be helped. Do not assume that they will accept help without being asked.

- Take off your hat when entering a church and observe all traditions when entering other places of worship like mosques and temples. In all these places, there are usually signs telling you what to do but do ask if you are not sure.

- Telephone or write in advance should you want to visit someone, especially if you do not know them well.

- Make telephone calls before 10:00 pm—it is considered impolite and intrusive to do so after this watershed time.

- Learn to be patient and join the queue for all services, even if it's a corner shop. Trades people will only serve customers one at a time, no matter how small the transaction.

- Offer a little something extra if the service is above par, although this is generally included in taxi fares and gratuities are included in restaurant bills.

- Check if smoking is allowed in any shopping centres, concourses and other public areas that are enclosed.

- Be considerate about noise on weekends—like using a lawn mower in the early hours of the morning, or playing music very loud at any time.

- Inform your immediate neighbours if you are going to have a party with dance or disco music.
- Hold a teacup by the handle and not cup it when drinking at a friend's house.
- Place your fork and knife down side by side on your plate when you have finished eating in someone else's home.
- Try to have exact change when travelling on buses, especially in those that do not have conductors.
- Press the stop buzzer on buses before your destination, and then only once.
- Offer thanks when helped with directions by strangers. Most British people are extremely helpful when asked for help, especially in provincial areas. City folk are invariably in a rush and do not always have time to help.
- Hire a skip, a council facility of a large, metal container for containing debris when refurbishing your house. This will be collected by a forklift truck on the appointed day.

DON'TS

- Ask personal questions when meeting someone for the first time. Such as reference to one's marital status, income and even a person's residential whereabouts. This is considered very rude and intrusive.
- Blunder into the private areas of a home you are visiting without first asking. Like asking to use a toilet.
- Ask to use a personal telephone, even at a friend's house, unless it is an emergency. If at all you need to do so, assure your friend it is a local call and make it brief.
- Barge into a restaurant without being ushered in. Even in smaller places, there will invariably be some waiter to seat you.
- Shy away if a hostess wants to greet you with a peck on the cheek. Gently tilt your face forward to make it smooth and comfortable.
- Spit out bones at a meal when invited out or to a home, but unobtrusively remove it and place on a side plate provided or by the side of your dinner plate.
- Belch or make unpleasant noises after a meal whether in a restaurant or someone else's home.

- Pick at your teeth after a meal. Ask to be excused and do it privately out of view. Or pick up food with your fingers unless it is a cocktail or snack item proffered to you without cutlery.
- Smoke in someone else's home without first asking if it's okay. And never stub out cigarettes in any but a provided ashtray.
- Swear in front of ladies or any other guests. It is very bad form.
- Ask the price of any item in someone else's home. Paying a compliment is much more polite and accepted.
- Stare at strangers in public or in public transport. This is considered very rude.
- Engage bus drivers in conversation as it is deemed distracting and can be dangerous.
- Use a mobile while driving unless it is a hands-free model, or in theatres, cinemas and other places that have signs requesting you not to do so.
- Speak loudly on your mobile, especially on trains and buses, public places or confined offices.
- Cross roads except at designated zebra crossings. Jaywalking is illegal.
- Overtake while driving without the proper signals. This can be extremely dangerous on motorways.
- Flash your headlights for any reason other than when it is extremely necessary, like warning another driver in heavy fog or bad weather.
- Blare your care horn unnecessarily, especially in built-up areas and near schools and hospitals.
- Throw sweet wrappers or any other debris, or spit on the street. Britain's city centres already have a problem with littering so don't aggravate the problem.
- Remain stationary on the left side of a moving escalator; do so on the right or you are likely to be shoved aside during peak travelling hours.
- Let your pet dog foul sidewalks if you keep one. It is allowed in small parks but not where there are flowers.
- Step out of your house in pyjamas or any other nightwear. This is considered very vulgar. Street wear in Britain does

not generally stretch to flip flips and shorts, except during the warmest summer months.

- Burn garden rubbish before 7:00 pm or better yet, when it is dark, which comes as late as 10:00 pm during summer.
- Use a hose to water your garden if there is a hose ban during dry summer months.
- Have your mobile switched on in a concert hall or auditorium, or eat potato chips as the sound of crackling paper can be irritating in an acoustically controlled hall.
- Be late for any theatre performance as in some cases, the management will not allow you in until the first interval.

GLOSSARY

English is the official or primary language of 60 countries and it is estimated that nearly 400 million people speak it as a first language and a further 600 million speak it as a second language. For first-time visitors to Britain, fathoming the regional accents is a linguistic quagmire in itself. Then there are those oft-used words and phrases that punctuate the language to a remarkable degree. Here are some notable examples:

A bun in the oven	Pregnant
A copper's nark	Cockney slang for an informer, a grass
A load of cobblers	Alluding to someone talking rubbish
A load of codswallop	As above, but even more pungent
A lot of bottle	Daring, courage, bravery
A lot of malarkey	A load of nonsense
A toff	An upper class gentleman
An It Girl	Someone who's always in the news for outrageous behaviour
An old geezer	A grubby old man
Bad hair day	Someone who has a bad hair day is in a depressing or lousy frame of mind. How the hair bit came about is anybody's guess
Bet you a penny to a pound	An absolute sure thing
Brekkie	Breakfast

Capped Rate	Mortgage arranged for a set period of months or years can go up or down with the variable rate but there is a maximum (capped) rate which it cannot go above
Cashback	A cash payment you receive when you complete your mortgage—may be a fixed amount or a percentage of the amount of the mortgage
Champagne taste with beer money	Having desires beyond one's monetary means
Doing porridge	A jail sentence, reflecting the food in prison
Don't get sarkie with me	Cease the sarcasm
Don't get shirtie with me	Don't be pushy, unreasonable, irritable, or annoyed
Don't give monkey's	Don't care, indifference
Don't give a toss	As above, but more pungent
Endowment	A life insurance policy that is designed to produce a lump sum to pay of an interest-only mortgage
Ernie	Income bonds
Get a life	A barbed retort to anyone not seeming to do anything worthwhile
Get off your high horse	Come down to earth and don't be snooty
Get up one's nose	Irritating to the nth degree
Get your leg over	An euphemism for having sex

Give me a bell	Phone me
Guest cloakroom	Downstairs toilet
Hang about	Meaning 'hold on, just a minute, what do you mean?'
Have a fry up	A typical British breakfast of sausages, bacon and eggs
Have a swig	Have a drink, usually alcohol
Having a knee up	Enjoying a great party
He cannot organise a piss-up in a brewery	Someone who's absolutely hopeless at organising anything
He's on the bender	He's participating in a drinking orgy
Hosepipe ban	In times of drought, watering with a hosepipe is forbidden
I'm really chuffed	Extremely pleased
In for a penny, in for a pound	Go the whole hog
Know wot I mean	A favourite latch-on phrase to mean, 'get the drift'
Laddish	One of the boys, rather gung ho in essence
Lager Lout	One of the bad boys, inclined to swearing and loutish behaviour
Like the dog's dinner	Something awful, usually expressing disapproval of something
Looking like the cat's whiskers	Someone who's self-important

Lord love a duck	Cockney exclamation, like 'good grief'
Lots of dosh	Very rich
Luvvies	Precious people, inclined to be theatrical
Not on your nelly	To mean 'not by a long shot, don't be ridiculous'
Off the back of a lorry	Alluding to stolen goods
OTT	Over the top, in bad taste
Prezzie	A present
Pull a bird	To seduce a woman
Pull us a pint	An order to fill up with beer
Reception rooms	Reference to the sitting/living room of a house
Road rage	Anger aroused when someone overtakes you on the road
Sally Army	Members of the Salvation Army
Separate the wheat from the chaff	Separating the good from the bad
Stop mucking/messing about	Admonishment to stop behaving foolishly
The bee's knees	Just about the best there is
The Bill	The police force
The cat that stole the cream	Someone who's smug about some secret knowledge
Toffee-nosed	A snob, usually referring to someone pretentious
Treading the boards	The acting profession, 'boards' here meaning the stage

Trouble and strife	Wife in Cockney slang, less often used these days
Up the creek	In a difficult or bad situation
Winding one up	Deliberately saying or doing something to annoy someone
Wot a Plonker	Cockney slang for what an idiot

RESOURCE GUIDE

EMERGENCIES AND HEALTH
Emergency Numbers

- **Fire, Police or Ambulance and Coastguard**
  Tel: 999/112
- **Electricity** (24-hour emergencies)
  Tel: 0800-783-8866 or 0208-247770-880
- **Transco Gas**
  Tel: 0800-111-999
- **Thames Water**
  Tel: 0845-9200-800
- **Malicious Phone Calls** (advice line)
  Tel: 0800-666-700
- **Specialist Bureau** (trained investigators)
  Tel: 0800-661-441
- **24-hour Emergencies**
  Tel: 01707-081152
  Email: emergency@heatcomplete.co.uk
- **Hospitals**
  Tel: 0845-4647
- **NHS Direct**
  Tel: 0845-4647
  Website: http://www.nhsdirect.nhs.uk
  Telephone service staffed by trained nurses to give patients advice on self-help as well as to direct them to the appropriate medical service)
- **Animal Welfare RSPCA**
  Tel: 0870-555-5999
- **Crimestoppers**
  Tel: 0800-555-111

Websites:

- http://www.police.uk
  For reporting minor and specific crimes
- http://www.localhomewatch.co.uk
  Neighbourhood watch schemes

- http://www. victimsupport.com
  An independent charity that supports crime victims
  throughout the UK

LOST AND FOUND

Enquire at tube or train stations, as each will have an office
dealing with lost articles. For items lost in taxis and the
underground, contact:

Metropolitan Police Lost Property Office
200 Baker Street, London NW1 5 RZ
Tel: (020) 7486-2496; fax: (020) 7918-1028.
Allow three full days (excluding day of loss) before making
a report.

Passports

As of January 1983, under the British Nationality Act of 1981,
UK passports are issued to British citizens, subjects, Dependent
Territories citizens, overseas citizens, protected persons and
nationals (overseas). You are eligible for a UK passport by
birth in the UK or British Colony, naturalisation in the UK or a
British Colony, registration as a citizen of the UK and Colonies
or legitimate descent from a father to whom one of the
above applies.

HEALTH

For details of hospitals contact the following NHS
Regional Offices:

- **Eastern Region**,
  Victoria House, 2 Capital Park, Fulbourn, Cambridge
  CB1 5 XB
  Tel: (0190) 884-4400
- **London and South-east regions**
  40, Eastbourne Terrace, London W2 3 QR
  Tel: (020) 7725-5300
- **Northern and Yorkshire regions**
  John Snow House, Durham University Science Park,
  Durham DH1 3YG
  Tel: (0191) 301-1300

- **North-west region**
  930-932, Birchwood Boulevard, Millennium Park, Birchwood, Warrington WA3 7QN
  Tel: (0192) 570-4000
- **South-west region**
  Westward House, Lime Kiln Close, Stoke Gifford, Bristol BS34 8SR
  Tel: (0117) 984-1750
- **Trent**
  Fulwood House, Old Fulwood Road, Sheffield S10 3TH
  Tel: (0114) 263-0300
- **West Midlands**
  Bartholomew House, 142 Hagley Road, Birmingham B16 9PA
  Tel: (0121) 224-4600

Websites:

- http://www.nhsdirect.nhs.uk
  A telephone advice service with information on home-treatment.
- http://www.bupa.co.uk
  Health fact sheets, special offers on health and insurance covers, health tips and competitions. Find your nearest BUPA hospital and instructions on referral.
- http://www.drugnet.co.uk, http://www.alcoholics-anonymous.org
- http://www.tht.org.uk, http://www.lovelife.hea.org.uk
  The two sites deal with AIDS and HIV.
- http://www.cancerbacup.org, http://www.crc.org.uk
  The two sites deal with cancer.
- http://www.bcc-uk.org (Breast Cancer Campaign)
- http://www.allergy-info.com
- http://www.alzheimers.org.uk
- http://www.patient.co.uk
  A collection of links to other health sites, from where you can find web sites on health-related topics with a UK bias.
- http://www.embarassingproblems.co.uk
  An award-winning and highly recommended site that helps you deal with health problems that are difficult to discuss with anyone.

- http://www.quackwatch.com
  Exposes fraudulent cures and old wives' tales, and provides information on where to get the right treatment.
- http://www.medicalanswer.com
  A search engine with some 800 medical and health sites listed. See also http://www.medisearch.co.uk
- http://www.disability.gov.uk, http://www.radar.org.uk
  Websites for handicapped facilities.

Dental Clinics

There are an estimated 17,000 dentists in England that provide NHS dental services. Patients pay 80 per cent of the cost and the maximum charge for any treatment is £ 348. The following qualify for free treatment: people under 18, full-time students, pregnant women. women who have had a child in the last 12 months, people on income support, fully disabled people on tax credit by up to £ 70, people named on a HC2 Certificate issued by the Health Benefits Division.

A booklet on HC2 is available from all main post offices and local social security offices. For a list of family dental clinics, telephone: (01642) 320-000.

HOME AND FAMILY
Accommodation and Housing

Every estate agent worth its salt will have a website. The following will help you find your ideal home:

- http://www.upmystreet.com
  Every postal code and statistic you need. A good guide providing house prices, schools, local authority information, crime and links to services.
- http://www.propertyfinder.co.uk
  UK's biggest property database with more than 20,000 properties available, with detailed information about each property and links to estate agents.
- http://www.conveyancing-cm.co.uk
  A minefield and this site helps with advice and competitive quotes.

- http://www.reallymoving.com
  Take the pain out of moving house with advice from the National Association of Estate Agents, lists of properties and a quick search facility.
- http://www.homelet.co.uk
  Claims to take the risk out of renting with sound advice and insurances for both tenants and landlords.

Budget Hotels

- London Tourist Board
  Tel: (0207) 2345-8000
  Website: http://www.touristinfohub.com
- http://www.hotelguide.com
  With services available in eight languages and a listing of some 85,000 hotels and budget establishments.
- http://www.from-a-z.com
  A UK site with more than 20,000 hotels in Britain, Ireland and France and 40,000 world-wide with online booking.
- http://www.best-inn.co.uk
  60,000 hotels listed and focus on London.

Building Societies & Banks

- http://www.fsa.gov.uk
- http://www.oft.gov.uk
- http://www.abbeynational.co.uk
- http://www.alliance-leicester.co.uk
- http://www.barclays.co.uk
- http://www.halifax.co.uk
- http://www.banking.hsbc.co.uk
- http://www.nationwide.co.uk
  (with hyperlink to http://www.yourmortgage.co.uk)
- http://www.natwest.com
- http://www.lloydstsp.co.uk
- http://www.northernrock.co.uk
- http://www.bankofscotland.co.uk
- http://www.scottishwidows.co.uk

Child Care

- **Essex Children's Information Service**

  Offers information for parents on looking for childcare with registered child minders, pre-schools, day nurseries, playgroups, working families tax credit, holiday schemes, signposting local early years and childcare services, crèches, breakfast and after school clubs

  Tel: (01245) 440-400

  Email: cis@essexcc.gov.uk;

  Website: http://www.childcarelink.gov.uk

- **Home-Start**

  The leading family support charity in the UK. Home-Start volunteers offer friendship, support and practical help to families with at least one child under five years old. There are many reasons why parents and families go to Home-Start. These include bereavement, children's behavioural problems, disability, relationship difficulties, single parenthood and postnatal depression. For further information contact

  Home-Start UK Office

  2 Salisbury Road, Leicester LE1 7QR

  Tel: (0116) 233-9955; fax: (0116) 233-0232

  Email: info@home-start.org.uk;

  Website: http://www.home-start.org.uk

- **Citizens Advice Bureau**

  An independent general advice service offering free and confidential advice on a wide range of subjects. These include general information on benefits and welfare rights, help with appeals and tribunals, help with form filling, guidance on qualification for Disability Living Allowance as well as advice on debt, employment, personal and family problems. Home visits are often available for clients unable to call in at the Bureau.

  Website: http://www.nacab.org.uk and
  http://www.adviceguide.org.uk

Other Relevant Websites:

- http://www.webbaby.co.uk
- http://www.ukparents.co.uk
  Covers all aspects of parenthood from conception to birth and beyond.
- http://www.babydirectory.co.uk
  Lists local facilities and amenities to care and occupy your child.
- http://www.teenadviceonline.com
  Good track record with adult and teenage counsellors.
- http://www.mamamedia.com
  A selection of interactive games, puzzles and quizzes designed to encourage children to communicate by submitting messages and voting on what's important to them.
- http://www.bbc.co.uk/ccbc
  Catch up on the latest news, play games and find out about other recommended sites for children.

BANKING, FINANCE AND SHARES

The Internet is proving to be a real winner when it comes to personal finance and share dealing. Some useful sites:

- http://www.fsa.gov.uk
  Financial services authority that you can go to for help with your rights, or to find out about financial products. It also verifies if the financial institution you're dealing with is legitimate.
- http://www.financial-ombudsman.org.uk
  When you have a complaint about a financial service, this is a good point of call.
- http://www.find.co.uk
  Internet directory for financial services with hundreds of links split into eight sections: investing, insurance, information, share dealing, banking and savings, mortgages and loans, business services and a centre for independent advisers.
- http://www.unbiased.co.uk
  Good, independent financial adviser, provides a list of specialists for every need.

- www.ftmoney.com
  Offers up-to-the-minute news and information, based towards personal finance.

Insurance

- http://www.insurancewide.com
  Home of insurance on the Internet, one of the fastest ways to get insurance cover with a wide range of policies including life, travel, transport, home and business.
- http://www.easycover.com
  UK's biggest independent insurance web site.
- http://www.elephant.co.uk
  A high-profile site with instant quotes on a wide selection of policies. However, they specialise in car insurance.

Mortgage Specialists

- http://www.charcoalonline.co.uk
  An established mortgage adviser offering more than 500 mortgages from over 45 lenders
- http://www.mortgagepoint.co.uk
  Geared towards first-time buyers and those with less than perfect credit history.

FOOD AND DRINKS

The top supermarket chains in Britain are massive, with hundreds of outlets in every town, city and even village. They are Sainsbury's, Tesco, Marks & Spencer, Asda, Waitrose, Somerfield, Iceland and Safeway. All are generally open seven days a week, most until 10:00 pm and a few for 24 hours from Monday to Saturday. Sunday opening hours are fixed between 10:00 am–4:00 pm according to trading laws.

There is also a chain of Chinese supermarkets including cash and carry departments under the name of Wing Yip with centres in London, Manchester and Birmingham. They stock a large range of Chinese, Thai, South-east Asian and Japanese products.

- **Wing Yip** (main London store)
  395 Edgware Road, London NW2
  Tel: (020) 8450-0422
  Opening hours: seven days a week from 9:30 am–
  7:00 pm and from 11:30 am–5:00 pm on Sundays.
- **Oriental City**
  399 Edgware Road, London NW9
  Tel: (020) 8200-0009
  Open seven days a week from 10:00 am–9:00 pm
  (Monday to Saturday) and noon–6:00 pm (Sundays).
  Stocks an extensive range of South-east Asian, Thai and
  Japanese products. The centre also features a food court
  with some dozen or so food stalls selling dishes covering
  most of China, Japan and South-east Asia.
- http://www.icelandfreeshop.com
  One of the best online services with nearly all of the UK
  covered. Orders for £ 40 or more.
- http://www.waitrose.comi
  A good comprehensive and well-designed site for grocery
  shopping online.
- http://www.tesco.co.uk
  For food and other household goods online.
- http://www.orientalfood.com
  Tons of information on all forms of Asian cuisine including
  a Chinese recipe archive, nutritional information and
  food culture.
- http://www.straitscafe.com
  Interesting site with lots of recipes from South-east Asia.
- http://www.hwatson.force9.co.uk
  Online champion of British cookery, Helen Watson.
  Check out also http://www.greatbritishkitchen.co.uk and
  http://www.recipes4us.co.uk with some 2,000 recipes.

RESTAURANTS AND CAFÉS
Indian
- **Porte des Indes**
  32 Bryanston Street, London W1H 7EG
  Tel: (020) 7224-0055
  Tube: Marble Arch

Opening hours:
- For lunch: noon–2:30 pm (Monday–Friday); noon–3:00 pm (Sunday)
- For dinner: 7:00–11:30 pm (Monday–Saturday); 6:00–10:30 pm (Sunday)

Average cost per head: £ 35

Lavish, palatial Franco-Indian cuisine and frequent Indian festivals featuring regional cuisines.

Italian

- **Emporio Armani Café**
  191 Bromptom Road, London SW3 1NE
  Tel: (020) 7823-8818
  Tube: Knightsbridge
  Open: 10:00 am–6:00 pm, Mondays to Saturdays
  Average cost per head: £ 25

Japanese

- **Nobu Metropolitan Hotel**
  19 Old Park Lane, London W1Y 4LB
  Tel: (020) 7447-4747
  Tube: Hyde Park Corner
  Opening hours:
  - For lunch: noon–2:15 pm (Monday–Friday)
  - For dinner: 6:00–10:15 pm (Monday–Thursday); 6:00–11:00 pm (Friday & Saturday); 6:00–9:30 pm (Sunday)

  Expensive, average cost per head: £ 60. The biggest name in Japanese cuisine in the UK.

- **Budget Japanese Donzoko**
  15 Kingley Street, London W1B 5PS
  Tel: (020) 7734-1974
  Tube: Oxford Circus
  Opening hours:
  - For lunch: noon–2:30 pm (Monday–Friday)
  - For dinner: 6:00–10:30 pm (Monday–Saturday)

  Average cost per head: £ 15

Malaysian/Indonesian/Singaporean

- **Nusa Dua**
  11-12 Dean Street, London W1 3RP
  Tel: (020) 7437-3559
  Tube: Tottenham Court Road
  Opening hours: noon–midnight (Monday–Saturday);
  4:00–10:30 pm (Sunday)
  Average cost per head: £ 21
  Small, intimate family-run with genuine dishes like *gado gado*, *rojak* and *nasi goreng*.

- **Singapore Garden**
  83 Fairfax Road, London NW6 4 DY
  Tel: (020) 7624-8223
  Tube: Swiss Cottage
  Opening hours: noon–2:30 pm and 6:00–11:00 pm daily
  Average cost per head: £ 20
  Well-established Singaporean restaurant with consistently good standard. Features Singapore favourites like *Or Luak*, *Laksa* and *Kueh Pietee*.

LEISURE AND ENTERTAINMENT
Theatres

There are some 40 shows in London's West End theatreland six days and nights each week. Check the local papers for shows. The best booking agency online is:

- **Ticketmaster**
  Tel: (020) 7734-9037
  Website: http://www.ticketmaster.co.uk.

Websites

- http://www.whatsonstage.com
  Home of British theatre, with masses of news and reviews, search facility and booking service.
- http://www.aloud.com
  Search by venue, location or by artist. Mainly music and festivals and also comedy.
- http://www.rsc.org.uk
  The Royal Shakespeare Company with news and information on performances and tours. Book online.

- http://www.nt.online.org
  Details of the National Theatre's shows and forthcoming productions. No booking online but you can fax or email.

Nightspots

- **Jongleurs Camden Lock**
  Middle Yard. Camden Lock, Chalk Farm Road, London NW1
  Tel: (020) 7564-2500
  Opening hours: 7:00 pm–2:30 am on Friday, 10:30 pm–3:00 am on Saturday
  Shows at 8:15–11:00 pm on Friday, 7:15 pm–9:45 pm, 11:15 pm–1:45 am on Saturday. Top-rated floor shows.

- **Football Football**
  57–60 Haymarket, London SW1
  Tel: (020) 7930-9970
  Opening hours:12:00 noon–midnight.
  Eat and drink while ogling memorabilia of football greats. Get to rub shoulders with some world cup players. Diverse menu from pie and mash to chicken piri.

- **Jazz After Dark**
  9 Greek Street, London W1D, 4 DQ.
  Tel: (020) 7734-0545
  Website: www.jazzafterdark.co.uk
  Tube: Leicester Square.
  Opening hours: 2:00 pm–2:00 am (Monday–Thursday); 2:00 pm–3:00 am (Friday–Saturday)
  For funk, soul, jazz.

Shopping (London)

Major department and chain stores can be found along both Oxford Street and Regent Street. Big names abound like Selfridges, Marks and Spencer, British Home Stores (BHS), Debenhams, Dickens & Jones, Liberty's, John Lewis and dozens of other smaller independent shops selling everything under the sun. Bond Street is where you get the designer labels like YSL, Burberry and other haute couture. Upmarket jewellers like Tiffany and Asprey are on Old Bond Street.

Lilywhites on Piccadilly Circus is a sprawling one-stop store devoted to sporting goods. Knightsbridge is where THE store, Harrods, holds court to customers from around the world. There are 300 departments within the store; you need a whole week and a lot of plastic money to get through it. Don't miss the food hall.

Most West End stores open from 9:00 am–6:00 pm on Monday to Saturday, with some opening on Sunday from noon to 6:00 pm. Late-night shopping varies. Oxford and Regent Streets open until 10:00 pm on Thursdays. For a full list of London shops, buy the *Time Out Shopping and Services Guide* at all bookstores and newsagents. For locations, check your *A-Z of London* that is every visitor's bible. Some useful websites are:

- http://www.marks-and-spencer.co.uk
  Good selection of products from clothes to food and gifts, fashion advice and a quick order facility.
- http://www.argos.co.uk
  An excellent range of products.
- http://www.wellbeing.com
  A clinical site that offers advice as well as shopping for a whole range of health, beauty and alternative products.
- http://www.virgin.net/shopping
  A comprehensive site covering all major categories of leisure and entertainment.
- http://www. Shop-London.net

Cinemas

- http://www.virgin.net/cinema
  With links to what's on guides.
- http://www.odeon.co.uk
  Book online.
- http://www.uci-cinemas.co.uk
  Comprehensive information on films and previews.
- http://www.warnervillage.co.uk
  Excellent source for online booking at all Warner Village cinemas.

Bookshops

Britain is the land of books, especially London with thousands of stores and chain shops scattered throughout the country. Charing Cross Road in Central London, smack in the heart of Chinatown is a dream world of specialist bookstores. Foyles is reputedly the world's largest bookshop with some cutting edge innovations. It is home to Silver Moon women's Bookshop and also the unusual Ray's Jazz Shop.

In the past ten years many more specialist shops have sprung up in London, like Books etc in Sheperd's Bush, Forbidden Planet in new Oxford Street, Hatchard's in Piccadilly and Waterstone's in Gower Street. W.H. Smith remains the most high profile chain store with outlets in every major city.

- http://www.bol.com
  German media giant where you can get access to books in seven European countries.
- http://www.bookshop.co.uk
  Owned by W.H.Smith, also sells videos, cds and games with links to other magazines and stationery.
- http://www.bookbrain.co.uk
  All you do is type in title of book and this site will search out the online store that is offering the cheapest.
- http://www.achuka.co.uk
  Specialists in children's books with a comprehensive listing of what's available.
- http://www.audiobooks.co.uk
  Books on tape, with around 6,000 titles in stock and access to a further 10,000.

LIBRARIES

The British Library was established in 1973 with a collection of more than 18 million volumes, 1 million CDs and 55,000 hours of tape recordings. The library is based at two sites—London St Pancras and Colindale, and Boston Spa, West Yorkshire.

- **British Library, Boston Spa**
  Wetherby, W. Yorkshire LS23 7BQ
  Tel: (01937) 546-000.
- **British Library, St Pancras**
  96 Euston Road, London NW12DB
  Tel: (020) 7412-7332
  Education and Visitor Services Tel: (020) 7412-7797.
- **Bodleian Library**
  University of Oxford, Broad Street, Oxford OX1 3BG
  Tel: (01865) 277-000 for enquiries or (01865) 277-182 for administration
  Website: http://www.bodley.ox.ac.uk.
- **University Library**
  University of Cambridge, West Road, Cambridge CB3 9DR;
  Tel: (01223) 333-000; fax: (01223) 333-160.
- **Newspaper Library**
  Colindale Avenue, London NW95HE
  Tel: (020) 7412-7353.
- **National Library of Scotland**
  George IV Bridge, Edinburgh EH11EW
  Tel: (0131) 226-4531; fax: (0131) 622-4803.

HEALTH CLUB CHAINS

- **Cannons** (UK-wide with 16 centres in London)
  Tel: (08707) 808-182/8336
  Website: http://www.cannons.co.uk
  Memberships: £ 55–£ 75 per month
  Joining fee: £ 100–£ 295
  Full facilities: café/bar, exercise studio, gym, pool, sauna, splash pool, squash court and therapy rooms.
- **Curzons** (UK-wide with 12 centres in London)
  Tel: (020) 7387-9674.
  Website: http://www.curzons.com
  Membership: £ 42–£ 45 per month
  Joining fee: £ 50–£ 100
  Aimed at city executives with fully equipped gyms, but generally no-frills approach and no sauna and spas.

- **David Lloyd** (seven centres in London)
  Tel: (08708) 883-015
  Website: http://www.davidlloydleisure.co.uk
  Membership: £ 45–£ 95 per month
  Joining fee: £ 50–£ 100
  Holistic and highly specialised approach with state-of-the-art equipment, pools, spas, resident threapists, GPs and dentists.
- **Fitness First** (UK wide with 25 centres in London)
  Tel: (01292) 845-222
  Membership: £ 33–£ 42 per month
  Joining fee: £ 100
  A user-friendly centre with fully equipped gym, exercise room, therapy rooms, spas and free video rental.

MUSEUMS

- http://www.nationalgallery.org.uk
  A comprehensive site for information on collections, events, search facility and news.
- http://www.thebritishmuseum.ac.uk
  World cultures, shopping and tours.
- http://www.royalacademy.org.uk
  A modern site with all relevant information on the Royal Academy, tickets, support for schools, colleges and exhibitions.

ALTERNATIVE LIFESTYLES
Gay and Lesbian

- http://www.rainbownetwork.com
  Magazine style site catering to all aspects of gay and lesbian lifestyles. News, fashion, entertainment, health and travel. Forums and chat shows, classified ads and profiles on well-known personalities.
- http://www.blackberricafe.com
  Sisterhood chat site.

Karma and Zen Lifestyles

- **Ark Health & Beauty**
  111 Wandsworth Bridge Road, London SW6
  Tel: (020) 7731-8890
  Tube: Fulham Broadway
  A holistic approach to health and beauty with an extensive range of services that also cater to pregnant women.
- **Bharti Vyas Holistic Therapy & Beauty Centre**
  24 Chiltern Street, London W1
  Tel: (020) 7935-5312
  Website: http://www.bharti-vyas.com
  Tube: Bond Street
  Offers Ayuverdic treatments, reflexology and other holistic treatments.
- **Calmia**
  52-54 Marylebone High Street, London W1
  Tel: (020) 7224-3585
  Website: http://www.calmia.com
  Treatments for Naturopathica Aromatic Herbal Message and Balinese Blossom Ritual.
- **Urban Retreat**
  5th floor, Harrods, Knightsbridge, London SW1.
  Tel: (020) 7893-8333
  Website: http://www.harrods.com.
  A whole host of treatments for cellulite, electrolysis, Aveda spa and 5,000 sq ft Russian spa.

Websites

- http://www.thinknatural.com
  A mass of information on every aspect of natural health and a wide range of products online.
- http://www.alt-med.co.uk
  A directory of alternative medicine aimed at people looking for complementary and alternative therapies.

TRANSPORT AND COMMUNICATIONS
Useful Numbers

- **National Rail Enquiries**
  Tel: 0845-7484-950
  Website: http://www.nationalrail.co.uk
- **Rail Europe**
  Tel: 08705-848-848
- **Transport for London**
  Tel: (020) 7941-4500
- **Eurostar Enquiries**
  Tel: 08705-186-186
  Website: http://www.eurostar.com
- **Eurotunnel Car Passenger Service**
  Tel: 08705-353-535
- **JourneyCall UK** (trains, buses, cars)
  Tel: 0906-550-0000
  Website: http://www.ferrybooker.com
  The best site for information on crossing times with help on planning, special offers and ticket booking.

Buses, Trains & Taxis

- **London Underground**
  Tel: (020) 7222-1234
- **Talking Pages** (general taxi services)
  Tel: 0800-600-900
- **Central London Black Cab Services**
  Tel: (020) 7402-2424 or (020) 7373-577

The black cab is Britain's most familiar taxi with a passenger capacity of a maximum of four. Black cabs are expensive; the flag down fee can be anything between £ 1 and £ 1.50 depending on the area. A typical journey from Heathrow airport to Central London averages £ 45. Generally very difficult to find outside city areas.

There are many licensed minicab companies operating in every major town centre and prices average half that of black cabs. Negotiate price before boarding. A typical one way journey from Central London to Heathrow Airport is £ 20.

Websites

- http://www.pti.org.uk
  Offers information on public transport, time tables and maps.
- http://www.thetube.com
  Lots of features, articles on visiting London, journey planner and tube maps. See also http://www.tubeplanner.com
- http://www.gobycoach.com
  Get tickets from National Express and other information on Britain's coach services.

General Enquiries and Information (24 hrs)
01304 225 222

Airports UK and Eire

- **Aberdeen**
  Tel: (01224) 722-331
- **Belfast International**
  Tel: (02890) 448-4848
- **Dublin**
  Tel: (003531) 814-1111
- **Jersey**
  Tel: (01524) 492-000
- **London-Gatwick**
  Tel: (0870) 000-2468
- **London-Heathrow**
  Tel: (020) 7228-0181
- **London-Luton**
  Tel: (01582) 405-100
- **London-Stansted**
  Tel: (0870) 0000-303
- **Newcastle International**
  Tel: (0191) 286-0966
- **Southampton International**
  Tel: (01851) 702-256

Useful Websites

- http://www.lastminute.com
  Excellent reputation as a travel agent, shopping guide, hotel reservations, holidays and flights. Including a superb London restaurant guide and entertainment section.
- http://www.motortrak.com
  Find the right used car.
- http://www.baa.co.uk
  Details on all the major UK airports run by BAA - British Airport Authority - all the essential information, flight data, weather and shopping information.
- http://www.worldairportguide.com
  This guide has details on every airport – how to get there, where to park, facilities, key phone numbers and a map. Also guides on cities, resorts and world weather.

COMMUNICATIONS
Telephone IDD Codes

International dialling codes are composed of four elements which are dialled in sequence:

- The international dialling code (to UK 00 44)
- The country code (example Singapore 00 65)
- The area code (example outer London 0208)
- The customer's number

A typical Singapore–outer London call: 00 44 208 999 9999
All London numbers are now eight digits beginning with a 7 or 8. All regional numbers vary between six and eight digits with different area codes of 3, 4 or 5 digits.

Telephone Services

- **BT (British Telecom)**
  81 Newgate Street, London EC1A 7A
  Tel: (020) 7326-5000; fax: (020) 7356-5520
  Website: http://www.bt.com
- **BT Cellnet**
  260 Bath Road, Slough, Berks SL 1 4DX
  Tel: (017) 5356-5000; fax (017) 5356-5010
  Website: http://www.o2.com

- **Cable & Wireless Communications**
  26 Red Lion Square, London WC1R 4HQ
  Tel: (020) 7528-2000; fax (020) 7528-2181
  Website: http://www.cw.com.
- **One2One**
  Imperial Place, Maxwell Road, Borehamwood WD6 1EA
  Tel: (020) 8214-212; fax: (020) 8214-360
  Website: http://www.T-mobile.co.uk
- **Orange Plc**
  St. James Court, Great Park Road, Almondsbury Park, Bradley Stooke, Bristol BS324QJ
  Tel: (01454) 624-600; fax (01454) 618-501
  Website: http://www. orange. co.uk
- **Vodaphone Group**
  The Courtyard, 2-4 London Road, Newbury, Berks RG14 1JX
  Tel: (016) 3533-251; fax: (016) 3654-5713.

Internet Facilities

There are so many Internet Service providers that it would be impossible to list them all. The following are some of the sites that will help you choose the right one.

- http://www.net4nowt.com
  A directory of Internet Service providers with news and advice on the best ones. Also a good summary table featuring all the ISPs.
- http://www.ispreview.co.uk
  Plenty of news, offers and a top 10 ISP list.

Postal Services

On 26 March 2001 the Post Office became a public limited company expanding into the global market and domestic services including Royal Mail, Parcelforce and local branches of the Post Office. There are post offices in every city, town and village with many functioning as general stores offering a whole range of services from licence renewal, dole collection, lottery, sweets, stamps, stationery, cigarettes —in fact they operate like mini supermarkets. Most are open Mon–Saturday between 9:00 am and 5:00 pm, with some closing half days once a week.

Export Matters:

- **Export Data Branch**
  Overseas Trade Division, Department of Trade and Industry
  1 Victoria Street, London SW110ET
  Tel: (020) 7215-5000
- **Royal Mail** (for letters and small packets)
  Tel: 0845-795-0950
- **Parcelforce** (for parcels)
  Tel: 0800-224-466

RELIGION
Christian Churches

- **Catholic Media Office** (Bishop's Conference Secretariat)
  England and Wales
  39 Eccleston Square, London SW1V 1PD
  Tel: (020) 7630-8220; fax: (020) 7630-5166
  Website: http://www.catholic-ew-org.uk
  Email: secretariat@cbcew.org.uk
- **Action of Churches together in Scotland**
  Scottish Churches House, Kirk Street, Dunblance,
  Perthshire FK15OAJ
  Tel: (01786) 823-588; fax: (01786) 825-844
  Website: http://www.acts-scotland.org
  Email: acts.ecum@dial.pipex.com
- **Churches together in Wales**
  Cytun Ty John Penri, 11 St Helen's Road, Swansea
  SA14AL
  Tel: (01792) 460-876.
- **Church of England and Archbishop's Council**
  Church House, Great Smith Street, London SW1P 3NZ
  Tel: (020) 7898-100; fax: (020) 7898-1369
  Website: http://www.bishopthorpalace.co.uk.
- **Churches Together in Britain and Ireland**
  Interchurch House, 35-41 Lower Marsh, London SE1 7SA.
  Tel: (020) 7523-2121; fax: (020) 7928-0010
  Website: http://www.ctbi.org.uk
  Email: gensec@ctbi.org.uk

- **Irish Council of Churches**
  Inter-Church Centre
  48 Elmwood Avenue, Belfast BT96AZ
  Tel: (02890) 663-145.
- **Interfaith Network for the UK**
  5-7 Tavistock Place, London WC1H 9SN
  Tel: (020) 7388-00080; fax (020) 7387-7968
  Website: http://www.interfaith.org.uk
  Email: ifnet.uk@interfaith.org.uk

African & Afro-Caribbean Churches

There are an estimated 70,000 adherents in the UK. The Afro-West Indian United Council of Churches has about 30,000 members and 65 places of worship. The Council of Afro-Caribbean Churches UK has about 17,000 members and 125 congregations.

- **Afro-West Indian United Council of Churches**
  c/o New Testament Church of God
  Arcadian Gardens, High Road, London N22 5AA
  Tel: (020) 8888-9427.
- **Council of African and Afro-Caribbean Churches UK**
  31 Norton House, Sidney Road, London SW9 0UJ
  Tel: (020) 7274-5589.

Baha'i Faith

- **The Baha'i Information Office**
  27 Rutland Gate, London SW7 1 PD
  Tel: (020) 7584-2566; fax: (020) 7584-9402
  Website: http://www.bahai.org.uk
  Email: nsa@bahai.org.uk

Buddhism

There are an estimated 25,000 Buddhist adherents, 500 groups and centres and 20 Buddhist temples and monasteries in the UK.

- **British Buddhist Association**
  1 Bidulph Road, London W9
  Tel: (020) 7286-5575.

- **The Buddhist Society**
  58 Eccleston Square, London SW1V 1 PH
  Tel: (020) 7834-5858; fax: (020) 7976-5238
  Website: http://www.thebuddhistsociety.org.uk
  Email: info@thebuddhistsociety.org.uk
- **Friends of the Western Buddhist Order**
  London Buddhist Centre, 51 Roman Road, E20HU
  Tel: (020) 8901-12253.

Hinduism

There are an estimated 380,000 Hindu adherents and 150
temples in the UK.

- **Bharatiya Vidya Bhavan**
  Institute of Indian Art and Culture 4a Castledown Road,
  London W14 9HQ
  Tel: (020) 7381-4608.
- **National Council of Hindu Temples (UK)**
  Bhaktivedana Manor, Dharam Marg, International
  Society of Khrisna Consciousness (ISKCon), Hilfield Lane,
  Aldenham, Watford WD2 8EZ
  Tel: (0192) 385-6269
  Email: bimal.krsna.bcs@pamho.net
- **Swaminarayan Hindu Mission**
  105–119 Brentfield Road, London NW10 8JP
  Tel: (020) 8965-2651
  Website: http://www.swaminarayan-baps.org.uk
  Email: shm@swaminarayan-baps.org.uk
- **Vishwa Hindu Parishad (UK)**
  48 Wharfedale Gardens, Thornton Heath, Surrey,
  CR7 6LB
  Tel: (020) 8684-9716.

Islam

There are an estimated 2 million Muslims and about 1,200
mosques in the UK.

- **Imams & Mosques Council**
  20-22 Creffield Road, London W5 3RP
  Tel: (020) 8992-6636.

- **Islamic Cultural Centre**
  146 Park Road, London NW8 7RG
  Tel: (020) 7724-3363.
- **Muslim Council of Britain**
  P.O. Box 52, Wembley, Middlesex HA9 7AL
  Tel: (020) 8903-9024; fax: (020) 8903-99026
  Website: http://www.mcb.org.uk
  Email: admin@meb.org.uk
- **Union of Muslim Organisations of the UK and Eire**
  109 Campden Hill Road, London W8 7TL
  Tel: (020) 7229-0538.

Judaism

There are an estimated 285,000 Jewish adherents and 365 synagogues in the Britain and Ireland.

- **Chief Rabbinate Adler House**
  735 High Road, London N12 0US
  Tel: (020) 8343-6301.

Sikhism

There are an estimated 400,000 Sikh adherents and 250 Gurdwaras in the UK. Every Gurdwara manages its own affairs, so there is no central body.

- **The Sikh Missionary Society UK**
  10 Featherstone Road, Southall, Middlesex UB2 5AA
  Tel: (020) 8574-1902.
- **World Sikh Foundation** (The Sikh Courier International)
  33 Wargrave Road, South Harrow, Middlesex HA2 HLL
  Tel: (020) 8864-9228.

Zoarastrianism

- **World Zoarastrian Organisation**
  135 Tennison, London SE 25 5NFWuiauXZo.

GENERAL COUNTRY INFORMATION
Times and Calendars
GMT

Greenwich Mean Time is the local time on the zero of longitude (the Greenwich or prime meridian) which passes through the Old Royal Conservatory at Greenwich, London. GMT has been replaced by International Atomic Time (TAI) for scientific purposes and the term GMT is generally used to mean co-ordinated universal time.

Summer Time

Summer time or daylight saving is an adjustment of regional standard time that was adopted to conserve fuel by reducing the need for artificial light in the evening. It is ordained that legal time should be an hour in advance of GMT.

Weights and Measures

Metrication is becoming the most common measure, although a wide range is still used. Imperial measures are used for the following:

- Pint for draught beer and cider
- Milk sold in reusable containers
- Troy ounce for transactions of precious metals
- Inch, foot, yard and mile for road signs
- Acre for land registration

Websites

- http://www.ex.ac.uk/cimt/dictunit/dictunit/htm
  Summary of units of measurements around the world.
- http://www.bipm.fr/enus
  Official site of the body set up in Paris in 1875 that co-ordinates world standards for mass, time, length, electric current and other quantities.

Immigration, Residency and Nationality Issues

For detailed information about immigration rules contact:

- **Immigration and Nationality Directorate**
  Block C, Whitlift Centre, Wellesley Road, Croydon, CR9 1 AT
  Tel: (0870) 606-7766 (general enquires)
  Tel: (0870) 241-0645 (application forms).
  Website: http://www.home office.gov.uk/ind/hpg.htm.

Goods brought into the UK
From EU
800 cigarettes, 200 cigars, 1 kg smoking tobacco, 10 litres of spirits, 20 litres of fortified wines, 90 litres of wine, of which no more than 60 litres can be sparkling wine, 110 litres of beer.

Outside the EU
200 cigarettes or 250 g of tobacco or 100 cigarettes and 50 cigars, 2 litres of table wine, 1 litre of spirits or strong liqueurs or 2 litres of fortified wine, 60 ml of perfume, 250 ml of toilet water, £ 145 worth of other goods including souvenirs and gifts.

Complaints
- **The Adjudicator's Office Haymarket House**
  28 Haymarket, London SW1Y 4SP
  Tel: (020) 7930-2292; fax: (020) 7930-2298.

GOVERNMENT DEPARTMENTS
- **Cabinet Office** (Office of Public Service)
  70 Whitehall, London SW1A 2 AS
  Tel: (020) 7270-3000; fax: (020) 7270-0196.
  Website: http://www.cabinet-office.gov.uk.
- **Culture, Media and Sport**
  Trafalgar Place 2-4, Cockspur Street, London SW1Y 5DH
  Tel: (020) 7211-6000; fax: (020) 7211-6210.
  Website: http://www.culture.gov.uk.
  Email: enquiries@culture.gov.uk,
- **Department for Education and Skills**
  Sanctuary Building, Great Smith Street, London SW1P 3BT
  Tel: 0870-001-2345; fax: (020) 7925-6000
  Website: http://www.dfes.gov.uk
  Email: info@dfes.gov.uk
- **Foreign and Commonwealth Office**
  King Charles Street, London SW1A2AH
  Tel: (020) 7270-1500; fax: (020) 7211-8800
  Website: http://www.feo.gov.uk

- **Department of Health Richmond House**
  79 Whitehall, London SW12NL
  Tel: (020) 7210-3000; fax: (020) 7210-5523
  Website: http://www.open.gov.uk/doho/dhhome.htm
  Email: dhmail@doh.gsi.gov.uk
- **Board of Inland Revenue**
  Somerset House, London WC2R 1LB
  Tel: (020) 7743-86622
  Website: http://www.inlandrevenue.gov.uk.
- **Serious Fraud Office Elm House**
  10-16 Elm Street, London WC1X OBJ
  Tel: (020) 7239-7272; fax: (020) 7837-1698
  Website: http://www.sfo.gov.uk.
- **Home Office**
  50 Queen Anne's Gate, London SW1H 9AT
  Tel: (020) 7273-4000; fax (020) 7273-2065
  Website: http://www.homeoffice.gov.uk
  Email: gen.ho@gtnet.gov.uk
- **Northern Ireland Office**
  11 Millbank, London SW1P4PN
  Tel: (020) 7210-3000
  Castle Buildings, Stormont Castle, Belfast BT4 3SG
  Tel: (01232) 520-700; fax: (01232) 528-195
  Website: http://www.nio.gov.uk.
- **Scotland Office Dover House**
  Whitehall, London SW1A 2 AU
  Tel: (020) 7270-6754; fax: (020) 7270-6812
  Website: http://www.scottishsecretary.gov.uk.
- **Wales Office Gwydyr House**
  Whitehall, London SW1A 2AU
  Tel: (020) 7270-3000
  Website: http://www.ossw.wales.gov.uk.
- **Malaysian High Commission**
  45, Belgrave Square, London SW1X 8 QT
  Tel: (020) 7235-8033
  Email: mwlondon@btinternet.com
- **Singapore High Commission**
  64-65 Vincent Square, London W!P 2 RX
  Tel: (020) 7235-8033

Website: http://www.mfa.gov.sg
Email: information@singaporehc.org.uk

BOARD OF CUSTOMS AND EXCISE
London Offices

- **Thomas Paine House**
  Angel Square, Torrens Street, London EC1V1TA
  Tel: (020) 7865-3000/0845-010-9000 (general inquiries)
- **Dorset House**
  Stamford Street, London SE19PY
  Tel: (020) 7928-3344
  Website: http://www.hmce.gov.uk
- **Cardiff Portcullis House**
  21 Cowbridge Road East, Cardiff CF1 9SS
  Tel: (02920) 386-000.
- **Glasgow Portcullis House**
  21 India Street, Glasgow G2 4PZ
  Tel: (0141) 221-3828
  Website: http://www.hmce.gov.uk
- **Newcastle upon Tyne Dobson House**
  Regent Centre, Gosforth NE3 3 PF
  Tel: (0191) 201-1700; fax: (0191) 201-1594.
- http://www.ukonline.gov.uk
  A massive website devoted to the workings of the British government, a superb source for anything official at national and local levels.
- http://www.europarl.eu.int
  How the European Parliament works.
- http://www.parliament.uk/commons/hsecom.htm
  What's on in the House of Commons.

BUSINESS INFORMATION
Business Organisations

- http://www.economist.com
  The Economist magazine covering business and politics worldwide. Useful for business people.
- http://www.asiannet.com
  Business information on Asia, market information, news, services and links all geared to the main Asian markets.

- http://www.nacab.org.uk
  Citizens' Advice Bureau, often the first port of call for people with debt issues.
- http://www.adviceguide.org.uk
  Which contains basic advice and information on your rights.

Legal Aid Services

- http://www.compactlaw.co.uk
  Legal information for England and Wales, an informative site that covers many aspects of the law. Download, some free, case histories, news, tips and fact sheets.
- http://www.legalservices.gov.uk
  An official line on legal matters with guidance on how to access legal assistance and the latest changes to the Community Legal Service and Criminal Defence Service.

Career Services

- http://www.careerguide.net
  Career advice resource, with sections on job hunting, vacancies, CVs, and professional institutions that offer help.
- http://www.careers-gateway.co.uk
  Great advice on how to evaluate your options to decide on a career of your own.
- http://www.icg-uk.org
  Institute of Career Guidance for basic advice and resource information on furthering your career.
- http://www.transdata-inter.co.uk/jobs-agencies
  Directory of job sites, an excellent place to start your search. Lists major online employment agencies, the regions they cover and what industries they represent.
- http://www.freelancecentre.com
  A great site for the self-employed, with plenty of (mostly free) advice.

MEDIA

Newspapers and Magazines

There are more than 120 local and national newspapers in the UK and one is spoilt for choice. The main broadsheets are *the Times*, *Independent*, *Guardian*, *Telegraph* and *Business Times* with their Sunday editions. The more popular tabloid publications that easily outsell their broadsheet cousins are *Daily Express*, *Daily Mail*, *Evening Standard*, *The Sun*, *People* and *News of the World*. Do not be surprised by some of the contents in the tabloids as they tend to veer towards sensationalism and sex.

- http://www.dailymail.co.uk
- http://www.guardian.co.uk
- http://www.telegraph.co.uk
- http://www.thesun.co.uk

Television

There are four main national stations: BBC1, 2, 3 and Channel 4. Channel 5, a more recent entry is a little left centre and telecasts more controversial programmes. If you subscribe to SKY or Cable, you have a choice of some 50 channels for an average cost of £ 25 per month.

- http://www.bbc.co.uk
  The UK's most popular website, a huge site with some 300 sections covering everything from business to the weather.
- http://www.itv.co.uk
  Includes links to all the major programmes, topics and categories.
- http://www.citv.co.uk
  Children's ITV, a bright and breezy site aimed at educating and informing children.
- http://www.channel4.co.uk
  Includes links to specific web pages and a learning programme.
- http://www.sky.com
  Includes links to sports, news and topical events.
- http://www.itn.co.uk
  Independent television news.

Radio

With literally hundreds of stations from local to national and independent stations, it is a minefield of choice.

- http://www.mediauk.com/directory
  Directory of radio stations, search facility by station, presenter or type, background on the history of radio and articles on topical events.
- http://www.radioacademy.org
  A charity that covers all things to do with radio, including news, events and education. Includes a list of all UK stations.
- http://www.bbc.co.uk/radio
  For news and the latest hits, information on each major station, with some interactive facilities.

FURTHER READING

GENERAL

Dickie Bird's Britain. Dickie Bird. UK: Hodder and Stoughton, 2002.
- A fully illustrated and sometimes quirky look at many aspects of British life, especially in the cricketing world in which Bird is a past master.

Collins Complete DIY Manual. Albert Jackson and David Day. UK: HarperCollins, 2004.
- In a country where service can be enormously expensive, having basic knowledge for repair and maintenance around the house can be a godsend. This manual is a must-have , detailing such as how replace tiles, change a faucet washer and much much more.

The Property Book. Anne Maurice. UK: HarperCollins, 2004
- An inside guide to buying, selling, moving and letting property in the UK.

The Book of Lists. David Wallechinsky and Amy Wallace. UK: Cannongate Books, 2004.
- A compulsive reference book packed with many fascinating facts

Watching the English. Kate Fox. UK: Hodder & Stoughton, 2004.
- The hidden rules of English behaviour—a brilliantly observed study of what it is to be English by social anthropologist Kate Fox. She dissects and explains the quirks and habits of the English.

I Never Knew That About Britain. Christopher Winn. UK: Ebury Press, 2005.
- A compendium of facts, anecdotes and other snippets of useful information about Britain.

Whitakers Almanac 2005. Joseph Whitaker. UK: A & C Black, 2004.
- The ultimate single volume reference source packed with thousands of facts and figures, overviews and statistics relating to Britain and the world.

Check your tax and money facts. Graham Kitchen MCA. UK: Foulsham, 2005.
- Money matters and tax liability can be a minefield in Britain. This is a very clear and readable book for first time tax payers and pensioners alike.

The Complete Guide to Antiques. Martin Miller. UK: Carlton Books, 2003
- This is the ultimate coffee table tome, a lavishly illustrated encyclopaedia of some 6000 items including retail prices, dates and origins. A very handy book for serious collectors and antique lovers.

GARDENING

The Complete How to be Gardener. Alan Titchmarsh. UK: BBC Books, 2002.
- By Britain's doyen of gardening and TV personality, Alan Titchmarsh.

A-Z Encyclopaedia of Garden Plants. UK: Dorling Kindersley, 1996
- A publication by The RHS (Royal Horticultural Society), Britain's premier horticultural organisation. A magnificent book with information on 15,000 plants and 6,000 photographs. Edited by Christopher Brickell, chairman, International Commission for the Nomenclature of Cultivated Plants.

HISTORY

Empire—How Britain made the modern world. Niall Ferguson. UK: Penguin, 2003.
- A remarkably readable précis of the whole British imperial story.

A People's History of Britain. Rebecca Fraser. UK: Random House, 2004

ROYALTY

Philip and Elizabeth. Gyles Brandreth. UK: Century Random House, 2004
- A fascinating biography of the reigning Queen Elizabeth II and her husband Prince Philip

PETS

Choosing the Right Dog for You. Gwen Bailey. UK: Hamlyn, 2004
- Profiles of more than 200 breeds and pertinent facts about pet ownership. Like which dog would suit your family? What sort of dog will you puppy become?

POLITICS

Brown's Britain. Robert Preston. UK: Short Books, 2005
- The biggest story in British politics today by Robert Preston who draws back the veil on the man who is Britain's longest serving Chancellor of the Exchequer, Gordon Brown.

- *Contemporary British Politics*. Bill Coxall, Lynton Robins & Robert Leach. UK: Palgrave Macmillan, 2003

OUT AND ABOUT

- *London, the Biography*. Peter Ackroyd. UK: Vintage, 2001.
  A magnificent vocation of all the London has meant down the centuries. Ackroyd also penned the biographies of T.S. Eliot, Charles Dickens, Thomas More and Oscar Wilde.

AA Exploring Britain. UK: AA Publishing, 2005.
- A fully mapped guide with comprehensive information on car drives, walks and cycling

Rough Guide to Great Britain. Lonely Planet.
- A definitive handbook to England, Wales and Scotland with lots of background information on British culture, history, festivals etc.

1001 Days Out. UK: Paragon Books, 2005.
- A comprehensive guide to the castles, museums, stately homes and gardens in Britain's historic towns and villages.

1001 Days Out with Your Kids. UK; Paragon, 2004
- A must-have for families who love to explore the country. It lists castles, museums, theme parks and zoos among other interesting places for children and adults alike.

1001 Walks in Britain. UK: AA Publications, 2003
- A comprehensive guide to Britain's walkways, in each city, town, village and county; a veritable bible for people who love the art of ambulating.

BRITISH HOTELS, INNS & OTHER PLACES
Special Places to Stay British Hotels, Inns and Other Places. Ed. Nicola Cross. UK: Alastair Sawday Publishing, 2005 (6th ed)
- A nostalgic trip through English counties, special places to stay with all the character of the country revealed in these irresistible places.

FOOD
Delia's How to Cook Books 1 & 2. Delia Smith. UK: BBC Books. 1999.
- Britain's best-selling cookbook by the doyenne of British cookery. Reprinted more than seven times since its publication in 1998.

Asian Cook. Terry Tan. UK: Aurum Press, 2003
- More than 200 Asian cooking tools and equipment plus more than 100 recipes. Awarded the Best Asian Cookbook (published outside Asia).

Tools for cooks. Christine McFadden. UK: Aurum Press, 2000
- Comprehensive cookbook with masses of information on culinary tools and equipment for the modern kitchen.

EDUCATION

Student Book 2006. UK: Macmillan Press, 2005
- An essential guide for applicants to UK universities and colleges

The Virgin Alternative Guide to British Universities. Piers Dudgeon. UK: Virgin Books, 2004.

English Idiom Use. UK: Cambridge University Press, 2003
- A useful and fascinating guide to the use of English idiom across every conceivable situation.

An Independent Schools Guide 2005-2006. UK: Kogan Page, 2005
- A complete guide by Gabbitas Educational Consultants

Schools for Special Needs 2005-2006. UK: Kogan Page, 2005
- A complete guide by Gabbitas Educational Consultants.

ABOUT THE AUTHOR

Born in Singapore, Terry Tan first trained as a broadcaster and worked as a radio producer for ten years. He also did some television presenting for news and other entertainment programmes. He later switched to advertising as a copywriter and then as a feature/food writer for the now defunct Sunday Nation. His first cookbook was published in 1979 and he has written 16 to date, the last of which *Asian Cook* (Aurum Press London) won the award for the Best Asian Cookbook in the World 2004.

In 1983, Terry moved to England as a restaurant consultant and a freelance culinary writer for several British magazines and other publishing groups, writing on food and other topical subjects. He also worked as Chief Editor for the Singapore-based *Wine & Dine* magazine for 11 years, in that time travelling to Israel, Rumania, Canada, Iceland, Chile, China, Korea, Japan and most of Western Europe among other countries. He is currently a food development consultant for UK food companies and teaches at several colleges. Terry has also presented many food programmes over the BBC, Carlton Food Network and Satellite TV.

INDEX

Titles in the CULTURE**SHOCK**! series:

Argentina	Hong Kong	Paris
Australia	Hungary	Philippines
Austria	India	Portugal
Bahrain	Indonesia	San Francisco
Barcelona	Iran	Saudi Arabia
Beijing	Ireland	Scotland
Belgium	Israel	Sri Lanka
Bolivia	Italy	Shanghai
Borneo	Jakarta	Singapore
Brazil	Japan	South Africa
Britain	Korea	Spain
Cambodia	Laos	Sweden
Canada	London	Switzerland
Chicago	Malaysia	Syria
Chile	Mauritius	Taiwan
China	Mexico	Thailand
Costa Rica	Morocco	Tokyo
Cuba	Moscow	Turkey
Czech Republic	Munich	Ukraine
Denmark	Myanmar	United Arab
Ecuador	Nepal	Emirates
Egypt	Netherlands	USA
Finland	New York	Vancouver
France	New Zealand	Venezuela
Germany	Norway	Vietnam
Greece	Pakistan	

For more information about any of these titles, please contact any of our Marshall Cavendish offices around the world (listed on page ii) or visit our website at:

www.marshallcavendish.com/genref